AMERICA IN THE TWENTIES

AMERICA IN THE TWENTIETH CENTURY
John Robert Greene, *Series Editor*

AMERICA IN THE TWENTIES

Ronald Allen Goldberg

With a Foreword by *John Robert Greene*

E784.G656 2003
Goldberg, Ronald Allen.
America in the twenties
Syracuse, N.Y. : Syracuse
University Press, 2003.

SYRACUSE UNIVERSITY PRESS

Library of Congress Cataloging-in-Publication Data
Goldberg, Robert Allen
America in the twenties / Ronald Allen Goldberg ; with a foreword by
John Robert Greene.—1st ed.
p. cm. — (America in the twentieth century)
Includes bibliographical references and index.
ISBN 0–8156–3008–5 (alk. paper) — ISBN 0-8156-3033-6 (pb. : alk. paper)
1. United States—History—1919–1933. 2. Nineteen
twenties. I. Title. II. Series.
E784.G656 2003
973.91'5—dc22   2003015312

Manufactured in the United States of America

For Kathy and Jeffrey

Ronald Allen Goldberg is professor of history at Thomas Nelson Community College in Hampton, Virginia, and also serves as chair of the History Department. He previously published a study of the perspective of former Senator A. Willis Robertson (Democrat of Virginia) on the Vietnam War.

Contents

Foreword

John Robert Greene

THERE JUST NEVER SEEMS to be enough time"—"The textbook is so bland, the students won't read it"—"Don't *teachers* ever write?"—"If I could only find more than one book that I feel good about assigning . . ."

These are several of the complaints endemic to those of us who teach survey American history courses. The book series America in the Twentieth Century was designed to address these issues in a novel fashion that attempts to meet the needs of both students and instructors. Using decades for its organizational schema (admittedly a debatable choice, but it is our experience that chronology, not theme, makes for a better survey course), each book tackles the main issues of its time in a fashion at once readable and scholarly in nature. Authors are chosen by the editors of this series primarily for their teaching skills—indeed, each book proposal was accompanied by syllabi that showed the prospective author's course pedagogy. In fact, contributors have been urged to write these books from their lecture notes and to limit footnote references, which can often distract the student-reader. In a departure from virtually every textbook series of note, one member of our editorial board is a presently sitting college student, whose comments on the manuscript may well be the most helpful of all. Each volume ends with a bibliographical list representing the author's favorite books, as they would recommend them to their students. It is, admittedly, not an exhaustive list, but no list of our favorite works is.

The result is a readable, concise, and scholarly series of books from master teachers who know what works in the classroom. We offer it to instructors and their students in the hope that they will, in the words of the Latin maxim, do the one thing that we all hope in the academy that professor and student will do together: *Tolle et Lege*—"Take and Read."

Preface

THE DECADE OF THE 1920s was a period of extraordinary change and great turbulence in the United States. The traditional image of an era marked by frivolity and good times was only partly true. Only certain segments of the economy enjoyed the prosperity of the period, with the preponderant share of the wealth going to the urban-based business community. The new social standards were also winning greater acceptance in the urban areas. In contrast, in rural America economic hardship existed alongside a strong determination to retain old-fashioned morals and values.

The best way to understand the decade is to see a number of critical developments all converging on the nation at the same time. American industry was experiencing a production revolution and was turning out seemingly endless quantities of products for the public. The traditional noninvolvement in foreign affairs was being reexamined. The rural way of life was being replaced by a more urban lifestyle. There were early stirrings for greater freedom for both women and the black community. A deluge of new immigrants threatened to significantly change the traditional ethnic makeup of the American people. The turmoil engendered by World War I and the Bolshevik Revolution was disrupting American society. Science and technology were revealing new truths about people and nature, as well as making available to the average person some of the most wonderful "gadgets" of the twentieth century, including the automobile, the radio, and motion pictures.

These modern marvels in transportation and communication were bringing change to all parts of the nation. Defenders of the older values, particularly in rural areas, attempted to slow these revolutionary changes through a variety of means including immigration restrictions, Prohibition, censorship of movies, the Ku Klux Klan, and restrictions on what could be taught in the public schools. This conflict between the champions of the older America and those who welcomed the newly emerging society led to a "cultural war" that lasted throughout the decade.

In analyzing this period, I have deliberately avoided looking for heroes and villains. Rather than searching for greedy businessmen, incompetent and corrupt political leaders, or narrow-minded bigots, I have tried to examine the interplay of the important new forces that were converging upon the nation and causing so much pain and disruption. Ultimately, older ideas in religion, politics, and social values gave way to the forces of change. Putting aside the occasional violence of the Klan, labor disturbances, race riots, and antiradical clashes that marked the decade, this transition into the modern age was accomplished with a minimum of violence—especially when compared to more violent forms of change that were attempted in Russia, Germany, Italy, and other less democratic societies.

The three Republican presidents of the 1920s traditionally have been judged by historians as disappointments. In an era of exciting changes, these presidents' general philosophy of limited government with a bias toward the business community usually has been seen as being inadequate to solve the problems of post–World War I America. Were they merely "hollow" political figures, unfit for the position they held? Looking only for a long list of presidential achievements gives a mistaken impression of these administrations. In actuality, Warren G. Harding, Calvin Coolidge, and Herbert Hoover each brought a well-defined political philosophy to the White House, reflecting their small-town, rural upbringings in late-nineteenth-century America. During the generally prosperous times of the 1920s, their theories of limited government centering around a healthy business community were extremely popular with the voters. As the economy expanded, the public continued to reaffirm its support for these policies by giving landslide victories to the Republican Party.

The famous phrase from Charles Dickens's *A Tale of Two Cities,* "It was the best of times. It was the worst of times," aptly applies to the 1920s. This was a period of winners and losers in the United States, with the business community entering a "golden age" and the small farmer and certain segments of the labor market beginning a long cycle of decline. Unfortunately, when this decade of such important changes ended, an even more challenging period awaited the nation when it grappled with the worst economic depression in American history.

This study is an examination of the major trends and forces of change of the 1920s. I have relied mainly upon secondary sources, an appropriate strategy for this type of study. It is hoped that the reader will be inspired to do further research on the period, which is now seen by historians as one of the most misunderstood periods in American history.

Acknowledgments

MANY PEOPLE HELPED in the preparation of this manuscript. Bob Greene and his associates at Syracuse University Press were supportive as the work progressed. My colleague Dr. Vic Thompson served as critic and made many helpful suggestions. Bobbi and Ed Rudzinski were invaluable in lending timely reassurance. Above all, I would like to express my appreciation to my wife, Kathy, and son, Jeffrey, who made many important contributions and never lost confidence in the ultimate success of the project.

AMERICA IN THE TWENTIES

1

Prelude to the Twenties

AFTER THE INITIAL EUPHORIA of victory in 1918, the United States found itself embroiled in a wave of controversies as the nation adjusted to the postwar world. "World War I . . . was for the United States the beginning of the 20th century, the era . . . of the global economy, the Leviathan state, the mass society, and the age of anxiety."[1] The period of transition from the Armistice to the inauguration of President Warren G. Harding was both painful and tumultuous and set a pattern for much of the decade to follow. In 1921, the Republican governor of Illinois, Frank Lowden, commented upon the turbulence that followed the Armistice in 1918: "I felt that when peace came we'd all be so joyful that nothing would weigh upon us again. I find, however, the problems of reconstruction loom so large that we are as much occupied with them as we have been with the problems of war."[2]

Many of these postwar difficulties can be attributed to President Woodrow Wilson, whose last two years in office marked the low point of his administration. By the end of his presidency, Woodrow Wilson was in poor health and was unable to check the many problems that had emerged in foreign affairs, the economy, race relations, and prohibition, as well as the rise of the Ku Klux Klan and anti-immigrant feeling. Wilson played almost no role in resolving these postwar domestic problems. Preoccupied with the coming peace conference, he provided no domestic program and his administration seemed to lacked direction. Even before his illness in late 1919, he was not an effective president, as "the government drifted aimlessly before the sea of post-war problems."[3] A prominent journal, the *Nation,* stated in February 1921, "President Wilson's legacy to Mr. Harding will be one of debts rather than assets. With the single exception of Lincoln, probably no President in

1

our national history has taken office with as pressing a burden of unsolved problems as will fall to the lot of our next Executive."[4]

Worsening this situation were several extremely important changes that put American society under great stress at the end of the war. For the first time in history, the mass of Americans had been brought into contact with events abroad and the previous nineteenth-century insular American view of the world was under serious challenge. The theories of Sigmund Freud were causing Americans to reexamine traditional social and moral values. A torrent of immigrants threatened to destabilize even further a society already in flux. Reeling from so many changes, by 1918 the American mood was characterized by "confusion, fear and despair."[5]

Complicating the post-World War I situation were the November 1918 elections, which changed the political scene dramatically. The Republicans won control over both houses of Congress and soon engaged in a struggle with President Wilson over the League of Nations to the exclusion of virtually all other issues. "A dozen urgent problems involving foreign trade, tariffs, taxes, veterans' welfare, appropriations, and immigration begged for solution while Wilson and [Massachusetts Senator Henry Cabot] Lodge engaged in their dance of death over the League."[6]

This period of turmoil from the Armistice through November 1920 paved the way for Harding's victory and helped shape the decade to come. For two years, such unresolved problems as demobilization, reconversion, race riots, and an extreme fear of Communism at home and abroad disrupted American society and ultimately moved the nation in a more conservative direction. Rather than initiating great changes, Harding, Calvin Coolidge, and Herbert Hoover took control of a country already predisposed to moving in the direction they chose to go. "Wilson was largely responsible for the form of the country by March 1921, and he helped set the decade in a path he probably would not have approved of."[7]

After the Armistice, one of the first problems that plagued Wilson was the transition to the peacetime economy. The Wilson administration was woefully unprepared to handle the usual stresses of demobilization and the conversion to peacetime conditions at the end of the war. As early as October 1917, Wilson was urged to create a reconstruction commission to study postwar problems but he considered this action premature. Although resolutions to create postwar study commissions were introduced in Congress in September 1918, none were passed because of wrangling between Democrats and Republicans. By December 1918, on the eve of his departure for the peace conference, Wilson once again rejected an active role by government for reconstruction at home. He chose instead to become more involved in reconstructing the world through the post-World War I peace process and in the creation of the League of Nations. When the suggestion was raised to use the wartime agencies (such as the Food Administration) to solve domestic problems, Wilson rejected the notion. Newton Baker, Wilson's secretary of war, echoed his superior's lack of concern on the transition problem. On Armistice Day, 1918, Baker stated, "There is work enough in the United States for all the laborers in the country."[8] Like the president, Baker seemed oblivious to the economic dislocation about to erupt. Its government having made no meaningful plans to deal with the war's aftermath, "the United States was as unready for peace in 1918 as it had been unready for war in 1917."[9]

Wilson was similarly unprepared to deal with the most immediate transition problem, demobilization of the army and bringing the troops home. At war's end, the army contained about two million men and every day's delay in demobilizing them added to the burden of taxation required to help maintain that army. Family pressures also added incentive to bring the soldiers home as soon as possible. When General Pershing cited a need for only two hundred thousand soldiers for occupation duty in Germany, his remarks made possible the sending home of most of the soldiers within a few months.

The end of the war and the release of the servicemen left open the problem of government contracts and possible unemployment for the former soldiers. The sudden liquidation of war contracts whose long-term commitments had reached $35 billion represented a staggering blow to the industrial community, most of which was left to shift for itself. The United States Employment Service initially tried to find jobs for released soldiers but its effectiveness was destroyed when, with little protest from Wilson, Congress slashed the Employment Service's appropriation by four-fifths in January 1919. The postwar layoffs and contract cancellations caused an immediate economic decline. After a temporary upsurge in midsummer 1919, the economy collapsed again in the spring of 1920. Wilson, who was preoccupied with negotiating the post-World War I peace treaty, generally ignored the deteriorating economic situation. Instead of taking an aggressive approach, such as backing a federal public works program that might ease the economic transi-

tion into peacetime and employ returning servicemen, Wilson called a conference of governors and mayors and urged *them* to undertake more public
works. This action had little impact.[10]

The American farmer was particularly hard hit when the economy sank
into depression in 1920. The great prosperity of American agriculture during
the war and the hope that it would continue partially explain Wilson's seeming indifference to the agricultural crisis that followed the Armistice. The
problem of the farmer after the war exemplified the cyclical, often uncontrol-
lable, aspects of agricultural life. American agriculture had prospered as never
before during World War I and expanded greatly to meet the enormous demand created by that conflict. The United States government had encouraged
this expansion by providing price supports that, coupled with the devastation
in Europe and the cutting off of exports from Australia and Argentina, caused
American farm prices to rise and created a "golden age" for American agriculture.[11] But both the farmer and the government failed to anticipate how difficult things would become in the few months after the war. Just before the
Armistice, the Department of Agriculture concluded that "post-war agriculture would not be very different from [the good times that existed even be-
fore] the war,"[12] a judgment that proved to be as incorrect as Secretary of War
Baker's predication on postwar employment.

Unfortunately, agriculture experienced a serious decline in 1919, when a
number of new developments quickly eroded the farmer's position. The
United States ended price supports, European agriculture began to recover,
and exports from Australia and Argentina were once again available. As a consequence, by 1921 farm income had dropped more than 50 percent from its
1919 level and land values began to collapse, leading to the failure of many
rural banks that had used the land as collateral.[13] The failure of these banks became progressively troubling over the ensuing decade and helped lead to the
devastating banking collapse in 1929.

One of the other casualties of the postwar economy was labor. The war
had been a great boon to organized labor and the bulk of American labor had
flourished, gaining such benefits as union recognition, shorter hours, higher
wages, and federal mediation and conciliation services. During the war, good
relations existed between the federal government and unions and the president of the American Federation of Labor, Samuel Gompers, strongly supported the war effort. After the war, however, the government showed little
support for labor's efforts to keep these advantages while management talked

about taking them away. Labor's prospects worsened as government contracts were canceled and many people were thrown out of work. Adding to the problem were the millions of war veterans returning home only to face a declining labor market. In 1920, the economy fell into a depression, leading to levels of unemployment that were not again reached until 1931–32, the depths of the Great Depression.[14]

Given the severity of these crises, Wilson's inactive response was uncharacteristic of a "progressive" president who previously had taken an activist approach in solving economic problems. By 1920, a clear outline of the government's transition policy had emerged, with the government withdrawing from its wartime functions on terms that were not generous toward agriculture or labor. The Wilson administration retreated from its strong support for unions and failed to back labor in several important strikes. President Wilson largely ignored the declining economic situation, and his few suggestions were rejected by a hostile Republican Congress.[15]

In addition to unemployment, labor faced a host of other serious problems in the next two years. Determined to protect their wartime gains, labor fought back in 1919 with a number of strikes, nearly all of them ending in defeat for labor. Union membership declined because of these strikes as well as from a vigorous counterattack by a more assertive business community. Labor's problems were compounded by increasing hostility from both the courts and the more conservative Congress, which had been elected in 1918. Their former ally President Wilson, who was weakened by the elections of 1918 and then almost totally preoccupied with foreign affairs, suffered a stroke in 1919. In addition, the steady stream of low-wage immigrants pouring into the country was keeping wage levels depressed. Labor, which had cooperated with business during the war with the encouragement of a friendly Wilson administration, found itself in a desperate fight to hold on to its gains in the coming decade.

Faced with all these difficulties, organized labor presented the government with a comprehensive set of demands, most of which would go unheeded. Labor wanted immigration restrictions and the retention of excess profit and inheritance taxes. It requested a forty-hour workweek and transition aid for displaced workers. It sought municipal control of public utilities and continued government control of the railroads. Except for immigration restriction, labor experienced one disappointment after another in the postwar period. Its political support eroded first as its former ally President Wilson "deserted" them and later from strong opposition by several unsympathetic Republican administrations.

Labor's adversary, the business community, similarly presented a set of demands to the government but found a much greater degree of success. Business wanted the return of the railroads to their private owners. It requested the immediate abolition of excess profits and wartime taxes. It demanded the protection of American industry through a high tariff and the elimination of all wartime controls. In the conservative, pro-business climate that emerged after the war, the business community's most important demands were all implemented. The latter years of the Wilson administration and the three Republican administrations of the 1920s proved to be far more accommodating to business than to organized labor.

Weakening political support helped lead to disasters for labor when it began to confront its main protagonist, the business community. In the turbulent year of 1919, more than four million workers went on strike. Labor lost its 1919 struggles with only a few exceptions and the new hostility of the Wilson administration was an important factor in these defeats.[16] Also important was the general hysteria of the period concerning the possibility of revolution in America. Employers were quick to capitalize on fears of a possible link between labor and revolutionary activities, using them to successfully outmaneuver labor in the contest for public opinion.[17]

As the tension with labor steadily escalated in 1919, business resorted to other weapons in its arsenal. The companies hired private detectives to spy on the workers and extended the use of "yellow-dog" contracts (a pledge by an employee not to join a union). After the war, more than a million workers were forced to sign these contracts, the legality of which was upheld by the United States Supreme Court. When labor decided to use the strike to defend itself against these attacks by business, the action was labeled by the press as a Communist conspiracy.[18]

In this highly charged atmosphere, an unprecedented general strike broke out in February 1919 in Seattle, Washington, paralyzing a major city for the first time in American history. Although it lasted only briefly, the failed strike proved to be a catastrophe for both the workers and the city. The strikers failed to gain any wage increases, and those associated with the Industrial Workers of the World (IWW)—the radical union linked to the strike—were rounded up. Sensing a hostile environment, industry began to avoid the city and industrial growth in Seattle lagged for more than twenty years.[19]

Equally upsetting to public order was a police strike that broke out in Boston in September 1919 over the issues of higher wages and union recognition. This strike lasted only two days and ended in defeat for the police: all those who had taken part were fired. Governor Calvin Coolidge thundered, "There can be no right to strike against the public safety by anybody, anywhere, anytime," a denunciation that turned him into a national celebrity and a prospective presidential candidate for 1920.[20]

That same month a steel strike began, lasting 109 days but ultimately resulting in defeat for the workers. The dispute was over the steelworkers' low wages, lack of union recognition, and extremely long hours. Their average workload was 68.5 hours, with more than one-third actually working in twelve-hour shifts seven days a week. Elbert H. Gary, the head of United States Steel Corporation and a bitter opponent of organized labor, stated that what the workers really wanted was "the closed shop [jobs for union members only], Soviets [workers councils similar to those in the Soviet Union], and the forcible distribution of property."[21] Wilson, who also opposed the strike, sent in federal troops to protect the strikebreakers and in January 1920 the strike was lost.[22]

The coal strike of that year followed a similar pattern, with the actions of the Wilson administration once again crucial in the defeat of the strikers. Wilson directed Attorney General A. Mitchell Palmer to get a sweeping injunction to end the strike. John L. Lewis, the head of the miners, called off the strike, saying "We cannot fight the government."[23] Wilson's actions in the strikes of 1919 indicated an economic conservatism in the last two years of his administration that was in stark contrast to his first term.

The turbulent year of 1919 proved to be disastrous for organized labor. In this most strike-filled year in United States history, there were an estimated three thousand strikes, which ultimately involved about four million workers. Although nearly all of these strikes were lost by the workers, the strikes had an upsetting effect and raised in the United States the fear of class warfare that was to torment organized labor throughout the decade. Employers seized upon this public fear and antilabor sentiment to resist such traditional labor demands as higher wages, shorter hours, and union recognition.[24] After the lost strikes and the ensuing business counterattack, labor's position worsened even further when the depression of 1920–21 began. At a time when business profits had fallen from $8 billion in 1919 to $1 billion in 1920, wages had fallen by 10 to 20 percent in most industries, unemployment had risen to approximately 20 percent, and labor was reeling from other problems, the economic environment did not favor advances for organized labor.[25]

The proper relationship between the government and certain key industries also became a major source of controversy after the war. To promote greater efficiency, the railroads, telegraph and telephone industry, and oceanic shipping industries had been taken over by the government during World War I. In August 1919, the government returned the telegraph and telephone industry to private control. However, in both the railroad and the shipping industries, serious political controversy ensued about the future government role.

The railroad debate was a particularly contentious one, involving a possible permanent government takeover. Eight months after American entry into the war, the government had taken control of the railroads, claiming the industry could not operate efficiently enough to meet wartime needs. The government then spent $500 million on capital improvements, vastly improving operating efficiency. After the war, Treasury Secretary William McAdoo recommended that the government run the railroads for another five years, while an alternative Plumb Plan advocated that the United States nationalize the railroads. Although backed by the railroad union, the plan was opposed by Wilson, the Congress, and the private investment sector and was rejected. Ultimately, the United States adopted the Esch-Cummins Transportation Act of 1920, which returned the railroads to private management but kept them under the jurisdiction of the Interstate Commerce Commission.

Paralleling its involvement with the railroads, the federal government had also become heavily involved in the shipping industry during the war, building and operating a fleet of about two thousand ships. However, these were not competitive without a subsidy. After the war, the government debated whether to operate private shipping in the interest of national defense or to disengage. President Wilson and Congress decided to withdraw the federal government from operation of the merchant marine and instead to subsidize privately owned companies. In 1920, the Jones Merchant Marine Act was passed, under which the government sold its ships at bargain prices and provided a $25 million loan fund to private shippers. The government further agreed to provide private shipping with generous mail contracts and to exempt them from corporate income taxes if this money were used for new ship construction. Eventually, when even these concessions failed to foster a healthy merchant marine, the shippers asked Congress for more aid, engendering a debate that continued into the Harding administration.[26]

Alongside the problems of the economy, the United States faced the destabilizing effects of the Red Scare, one of the major developments after the war that helped shape attitudes and policies throughout the 1920s. Prophetically, Wilson had stated earlier that war "required illiberalism at home to reinforce the men at the front" and that a "spirit of ruthless brutality" would enter American life.[27] When the war ended, the United States transferred its fear of the "Hun" to the Bolsheviks, unleashing a wave of hatreds and hysteria unmatched in modern American history.[28] The Communist revolution in Russia led to fear of similar revolutions in Europe and the United States. All of the Western countries had seen the creation of Communist parties, ostensibly loyal to and subservient to the Communist leaders in Russia. In the wake of the first general strike in American history (in Seattle) and terrorist bombs being sent to such prominent people as J. P. Morgan, John D. Rockefeller, and Seattle's mayor, Ole Hanson, many Americans concluded that the nation faced an impending revolution.

The crusade against the "Communist menace," which lasted from the Armistice through the presidential election in November 1920, had many far-reaching effects. It fostered the decimation of radical organizations (such as the IWW), the creation of patriotic clubs, continuous imprisonment for political crimes, and the arrest and deportation of aliens. It led to "Americanization" drives, the outlawing of the Communist Party (driving it underground), and the nativist laws of 1921 and 1924. This anti-Communist hysteria also weakened unions, strengthened business, increased hostility toward the Soviet Union, and generally shaped the society over which Harding and Coolidge presided. So strong was the fear and resentment toward the Left at this time that no position seemed too extreme to express. General Leonard Wood, a leading contender for the Republican nomination in 1920, suggested a means of dealing with the Communists: "SOS—ship or shoot. I believe we should place them all in ships of stone, with sails of lead and that their first stopping place should be hell. We must advocate radical laws to deal with radical people."[29]

The hysteria from the Red Scare led to a major setback in civil liberties. Much of this uneasiness resulted from the unsettling effects of World War I. Wartime passions had made dissent dangerous; the federal government had jailed those who openly opposed the war even if they had committed no overt acts. The government also had checked the mail of suspected citizens and denied the use of the mail to left-wing publications. These passions once unleashed could not easily be defused and after the Armistice led to erosion of some of the basic freedoms guaranteed by the Constitution.

With President Wilson both suffering from a major health crisis and being preoccupied with foreign affairs, leadership in the antiradical campaign was assumed by Attorney General Palmer. The attorney general, like the president himself, formerly had been a strong progressive and seemed an unlikely champion to lead the crusade against the Left. Previously he had favored many progressive policies including support for organized labor, votes for women, and the abolition of child labor. He had secured presidential clemency for nearly one-half the people still in prison under the Espionage Act (a restrictive act passed during World War I to crush dissent) and had opposed efforts to round up aliens and radicals. He had dropped scores of pending Espionage Act cases from prosecution. However, Palmer's response to escalating violence in the nation dramatically changed his reputation. On 2 June 1919, after a wave of bombings in various cities that targeted business leaders and government officials (including Palmer himself), he launched his raids on the Left. The culprits were never found, but the public blamed the IWW and the Bolsheviks.[30]

At the time of the Red Scare, the number of radicals was small but they aroused much fear in the United States. Although total membership of all the Marxist parties in 1919 constituted only one-fifth of 1 percent of the population—and fell dramatically in the following years—many people believed the United States was on the verge of violent revolution. Fear of the Left was exacerbated by the Seattle general strike, although there was no evidence it was led by radicals. The public also came to believe that radicals were the instigators of the many strikes of 1919.[31]

Attributing most of the domestic troubles to the call for world revolution by Communist leader Leon Trotsky and to its dissemination in the United States by the swarm of immigrants fleeing from a war-torn Europe,[32] Attorney General Palmer led a national drive to wipe out radicalism by the wholesale deportation of aliens. In early January 1920, the Justice Department rounded up thousands of known radicals. Of the more than five thousand people arrested, more than five hundred were deported and the state governments prosecuted about one-third of the others. Palmer described the radical threat by stating, "Like a prairie fire, the blaze of revolution was sweeping over every

American institution of law and order." He added, "the Reds were criminal aliens and . . . the American government must prevent crime." [33] Palmer expressed special concern toward the Communists in America, whom he labeled "direct allies of Trotsky." [34]

In this highly charged atmosphere, Palmer launched his crusade against any potential enemies of the republic. The government adopted the policy of deportation through a series of laws passed during World War I. In 1917, Congress had passed the Espionage Act, a broad-based law that gave the secretary of labor great latitude to arrest and deport any alien advocating lawless activities or the overthrow of the government. The following year, Congress gave the government power to exclude radicals from entry into the country and indicated that membership in a radical organization was grounds for deportation. Two of the major targets were the IWW and the Communist Party, groups favoring the overthrow of the capitalist system.

Palmer feared that a Communist revolution in the United States was about to break out and launched major raids in late 1919. On 7 November 1919, many aliens were arrested across the country and in December, 249 aliens suspected of radical activities were put on the *Buford* (nicknamed the "Soviet Ark") and deported. In January, 2,000 people were arrested in a series of government raids. Palmer, who had originally predicted a revolution on the previous 4 July, now believed the attempted overthrow of the government would occur on May Day (1 May) 1920. When this day passed without incident, Palmer's stature began to decline. He had developed presidential ambitions as his celebrity grew with the raids and now saw his presidential hopes disappear.[35]

The Wilson administration did nothing to restrain these raids on aliens and radicals, often based on flimsy evidence. As the domestic crackdown on possible subversives intensified, Wilson remained uninvolved despite his reputation as a progressive and civil libertarian. He deferred in leadership at home after the war, concentrating instead on world affairs. Wilson was actually out of the country while many of these assaults on the Left occurred. Between December 1918 and July 1919, he spent only ten days in the United States, so preoccupied was he with the Paris peace conference. He came home for good in July 1919 but suffered a stroke in September, leaving him partly paralyzed, bedridden, and unable to exert leadership during this turbulent period. Regarding Wilson's inaction after 1918 as the nation drifted farther to the right, "Harding might as well have been in the White House from 1918 onward." [36]

Some of the more celebrated government actions after the war actually involved punishing those who had opposed American entry into the war—not those that had fomented a revolution afterward. The Espionage Act of 1917 allowed the government to prosecute anyone who opposed the war effort and was the main weapon during the war against internal dissenters. The government especially targeted the Socialists, who had opposed World War I as a "capitalists' " war. Bill Heywood (leader of the IWW), Eugene Debs (leader of the Socialist Party), and Victor Berger (Socialist congressmen from Milwaukee) were the best-known members of the Left to be convicted and sentenced to lengthy prison terms. Both Debs, who ran for president on the Socialist Party ticket in 1920, and Victor Berger, who was elected and re-elected to Congress by his constituents in Milwaukee, were candidates while still in prison. The Left challenged the legality of the broad-based Espionage Act without success. In the famous Schenck case of 1919, the Supreme Court ruled that the Espionage Act was constitutional under the "clear and present danger" thesis.[37] (Essentially the court ruled that the United States government's powers expanded considerably in the case of "a clear and present danger" such as a wartime crisis.)

The attack on dissenters also occurred at the state level. Thirty-two states passed laws forbidding membership in organizations dedicated to revolution (used mainly against the IWW), while twenty-eight states even passed laws forbidding the display of red flags. New York was one of the states most active in vigorously attacking the Left. Its legislature expelled five members who were Socialists, required loyalty oaths of teachers, and outlawed the Socialist Party. A May Day parade in New York in 1919 was broken up by a mob and vigilante groups took action against people who seemed to be less than 100 percent patriotic.[38]

Both the government and the private sector intensified their pressure on the Left in 1919 and 1920. Even former progressive Wilson joined in the crusade, giving wide latitude to his attorney general and showing little sympathy for those caught up in the Red Scare. Fearing a Communist revolution in America, the president became inflexible on pardoning radicals imprisoned under the Espionage Act. He refused to pardon Eugene Debs, stating, "This man was a traitor to the country and he will never be pardoned during my administration."[39] In 1919, the American Legion was founded, which would soon become the most important and durable organization dedicated to the cause of "100 percent Americanism." Returning veterans joined this organization en masse, transferring their wartime patriotism to the civilian scene. In November 1919, this newly formed and ultra-patriotic organization engaged in a violent confrontation with members of the IWW and one Wobbly (as the IWW's members were called) was lynched. In the spring of 1920, fourteen IWW members were shot in a riot that also involved the American Legion.[40]

The antiradical movement was further aroused when two Italian immigrant radicals were arrested in 1920 on suspicion of robbery and murder. The case of Nicolo Sacco and Bartolomeo Vanzetti, who were ultimately convicted and executed, proved to be a rallying point for liberals throughout the decade, involving as it did the two controversial issues of antiradicalism and nativism. So intense were the passions aroused by the case that, only five days after their indictment on 16 September 1920, a bomb exploded near the headquarters of J. P. Morgan and Company (generally attributed to the Bolsheviks), leaving thirty-four people dead and more than two hundred injured and inspiring the government to step up its antiterrorist campaign.[41]

Much of the feeling behind the Red Scare actually resulted from underlying tensions in American society after World War I rather than from overt acts committed by the radicals. By 1919, the rapid changes in American life—brought about first by industrialization and urbanization and then by World War I—created much anxiety, which weakened America's self-confidence. "The anti-Red hysteria may have been an attempt to reaffirm traditional beliefs and customs and to enforce conformity by eradicating the aliens and those with different ideas who appeared to be wrecking the traditional society."[42]

By the end of 1920, the Red Scare had abated and the Left appeared to be in retreat nearly everywhere. Many radicals had been deported and the great labor conflicts of 1919 had ended, usually in defeat for the workers. If the strikes of 1919 had led to a fear of social revolution, labor's retreat into quiescence now created a reassuring calm as American labor entered the "lean years" of the 1920s.[43] Abroad, Communist revolutions in Germany and Hungary had failed. Palmer's prediction of May Day riots in 1920 failed to materialize and indicated to many that the crisis was ending. By late 1920, the hysterical phase of the Red Scare was over, although it had a lingering effect in America throughout the decade. "The United States in 1920 had not recovered from the distempers of 1915–1919. The fervor of war and the panic over revolution had passed but a healthy virus was still at work."[44] So extensive were its effects that "the whole pattern of thought and action common to the 1920s was in part traceable to the Red Scare."[45]

In reaction to this tense atmosphere, a conservative mood settled over America's political and social environment. The continuing effects of the Red Scare, emphasizing fear of any semblance of radicalism, led to both economic and social innovators being viewed with suspicion. The union movement was seriously weakened while the influence of the businessman was on the rise. A movement known as "100 percent Americanism," stressing patriotism and conformity, developed in reaction to the Red Scare and had a major effect upon American institutions. There was an emphasis on loyalty oaths, textbook censorship, and an "American Plan" for labor unions (essentially an anti-union drive). One of the most visible targets to emerge in this patriotic fervor was the immigrant, a development that led to a clamor for tighter immigration controls. In foreign affairs, the antiradical crusade led to hostility toward the Soviet Union, the lynchpin of world communism.

This public mood of uneasiness and fear, which inspired the growth of the American Legion, also made possible the rise of the Ku Klux Klan. Originally formed during the Reconstruction period following the Civil War, the Klan had been reborn on Thanksgiving Day, 1915, on the initiative of a former Methodist minister, William Simmons. During World War I, the Klan had become a vigilante organization stressing traditional morality and patriotism and attacking draft dodgers, prostitutes, idlers, IWW sympathizers, and those of "impure background." By 1920, the Klan had recruited only about five thousand members and appeared to be a permanently weak organization; over the decade ahead, however, it became a major force. Clearly appealing to the downtrodden and to those who felt unimportant, the Klan functioned like a fraternal organization, attracting those at the bottom of the economic ladder and of old-stock American heritage. It offered status and a sense of belonging to those who felt dispossessed by the vast changes in society, with the result that "a nobody in the world became a somebody in the Klan."[46]

The Klan of the 1920s had no direct connection with the earlier Klan of Reconstruction days, differing widely from it in philosophy. The original Klan had been a white supremacy group that targeted only blacks; the newer Klan also targeted Jews, Catholics, radicals, and foreigners as objects of its intolerance. So broad-based were its prejudices that "the Klan almost ran the gamut of modern bigotry."[47] The reborn Klan also had a much wider geographic support area than had the post-Civil War Klan, extending far beyond its original southern base and reaching into many parts of the nation. Rather than focusing only upon race, the organization was essentially a countermovement against the new urban multicultural civilization. Nostalgic for an older America, it claimed to represent only Americans of the old pioneer stock who had dominated the America existing before World War I.

Alongside these ever-mounting domestic problems of intolerance and economic disarray, Wilson faced a host of foreign problems, especially those relating to the end of World War I. Defaulting on leadership at home after the war, Wilson instead gave his primary attention to international problems as he attempted to reform Europe's political system. His most immediate problem was helping arrange a peace settlement and create the League of Nations. In December 1918, Wilson sailed for Europe, where he was hailed as Europe's savior and the greatest man in the world.[48] With only a brief interruption, Wilson spent the next several months in Europe negotiating a treaty that even he recognized as flawed. Whatever the faults of the peace treaty, Wilson believed the proposed League of Nations would provide a suitable remedy.

Having negotiated the Treaty of Versailles, Wilson now faced the problem of securing Senate approval. He had taken no leading senators with him to Paris, and upon his return he exhibited a lofty and even scornful attitude toward that body. When the Senate proved recalcitrant, Wilson decided to take his case to the people and embarked on an exhausting speaking tour in spite of the recommendations of his personal physicians. Giving several speeches a day to large audiences, Wilson suffered a stroke in the middle of the speaking tour that left him paralyzed and near death. Between his stroke in September 1919 and March 1921, the nation was without effective leadership, and the fight to approve the Treaty of Versailles was severely limited.

Wilson's continuing health crisis not only impeded passage of the treaty but also limited his overall effectiveness as president. In October 1919, Wilson suffered another, more serious, stroke. His left side was now permanently paralyzed, and for weeks he was in critical condition and unable to carry out the functions of his office. During this time, Wilson was kept in nearly complete isolation by his physician and Mrs. Wilson. During President Wilson's last seventeen months in office, Mrs. Wilson served as a sort of stand-in president, screening all presidential visitors and even messages. In late December 1919, the well-known journalist Ray Stannard Baker noted that it appears "as though our government has gone out of business."[49] A political foe, Senator Albert Fall of New Mexico, complained, "We have petticoat government. Mrs. Wilson is President."[50] When Fall visited Wilson to see if impeachment was warranted on grounds of health, he declared, "Mr. President, I'm praying for you," and Wilson immediately replied, "Which way, Senator?"[51]

While still quite sick, Wilson urged Senate Democrats to reject a compromise version of the League of Nations. This step ultimately proved fatal to his hopes for the League. In the absence of a mutually suitable arrangement, the Senate totally rejected United States membership in that body. Wilson's refusal to accept a compromise was called the "the Supreme Infanticide" and opened him to criticism that "with his own sickly hands, [he] slew his own brain child."[52]

For many years afterward, scholars would question the president's motives on the League question. Was Wilson's stubbornness actually a desire to justify the American role in World War I? Because of the treaty's imperfections, did Wilson need the League to forestall the wars that the treaty's terms might engender? Without a lasting peace, Wilson probably lacked justification for having taken the United States into World War I and a "sense of guilt hung over him like a cloud."[53]

Wilson faced a number of other seemingly insoluble foreign-policy problems after the war—involving Mexico, Russia, and Japan—which he ultimately passed on to his successors. Mexico's government had been friendly to Germany during World War I and was threatening to seize foreign-owned oil concessions. Wilson came under pressure to intervene (as he had previously done in 1914 and 1916) but refused. Wilson also declined to act with regard to Russia; instead of opposing the Bolsheviks, he chose to withdraw the American troops then stationed in that country. He did, however, strongly condemn the immorality of the Communist ideology and began a strong anti-Bolshevik tradition that lasted for many years. As for Japan, Wilson identified that nation as a threat to United States interests in the Far East and encouraged England to break its alliance with Japan, a move that would pull the United States and England closer together. When Wilson left office in 1921, the groundwork was already being laid for the Harding administration's Washington Conference of 1921–22, out of which would come a series of treaties and naval agreements designed to protect United States and British interests in the Far East from a possible Japanese threat. Wilson's post-World War I policy of avoiding military interventions, coupled with the Republicans' later policy of opposing any collective security agreement that might lead to military action, became the basis of United States foreign policy during the 1920s.

One problem that reflected the public's uneasiness about radicalism and wariness of foreign nations after World War I was the growing opposition toward the immigrant and an increasing desire to end the country's historic open-door policy. Beginning in the 1890s, a major shift in immigration patterns had occurred in the United States. The so-called New Immigrants from Southern and Eastern Europe, consisting mainly of Catholics and Jews, became the majority (nearly 80 percent by 1914) in the annual immigration of approximately one million people into the United States. Not only the religion and culture but also the sheer numbers of immigrants entering the United States aroused concern. By 1920, there were 105 million people in the country, of whom fourteen million were foreign-born. Also by this time little more than one-half of the white population were the offspring of American-born parents. Old-stock Americans became deeply troubled and some began to ask whether "it was possible to contemplate a United States that is neither Protestant nor Anglo-Saxon?" [54]

Apart from the enormous number of New Immigrants, Americans raised questions about the incomers' cultural heritage and intelligence, even asking whether these people could ever be assimilated. On the IQ tests widely used for the first time during and after World War I, old-stock Americans did better than the New Immigrants. Two noted psychologists reported afterward that "the intellectual superiority of our Nordic group over the Alpine, Mediterranean and Negro groups has been demonstrated." [55] Some wondered whether the New Immigrants brought dangerous ideas like socialism into the country. Were they more likely to become paupers or to go insane? Such fears concerning the New Immigrants led initially to a movement to Americanize them and later to efforts to restrict their entry into the United States. When the 1920 immigration total reached the prewar level of one million people, pressures rose in Congress to pass restrictive legislation. Although President Wilson vetoed the restrictive Immigration Act of 1921, a new phase of immigration was about to begin for the United States.

Like the immigrants, the black community also experienced much hostility in the changing social environment after World War I. Although black-white tensions predated World War I, tensions escalated in its aftermath in response to major new population patterns within the black community. Before 1910, 90 percent of the black population lived in the South (one-third of that region's population). Between 1910 and 1920, however, the number of blacks living outside the South doubled. In Detroit, the number of black people increased from 5,700 to 41,500 in that decade. Similarly, some 50,000 black people moved to Chicago during an eighteen-month period in 1917–18.[56]

These changing demographic patterns provoked serious race riots for the first time in American history. In 1917, tensions over black employment in a defense plant set off a riot in East St. Louis, Illinois, in which forty-nine people (nine whites and forty blacks) lost their lives. When the war ended, troubles soon arose over jobs and over the expanding black neighborhoods, which were evolving into "ghettoes." Previously black neighborhoods had been scattered, connected in loose networks but not bunched together. In 1919, race riots broke out in at least twenty northern towns and cities, the most serious being the Chicago race riot that summer. When these riots finally subsided, 120 black people were dead, of whom 78 had been lynched. The riots were generally attributed to competition for jobs, the expansion of black neighborhoods into areas previously inhabited by whites, and greater assertiveness by blacks—partly as a result of their wartime service. (Several hundred thousand black servicemen served in World War I, although fewer than fifty thousand were combat troops.) The 1919 race riots also reflected a nostalgic desire by whites to put blacks "in their place," where they had been before World War I.[57]

The black community attempted to strengthen itself by aligning with the Republican Party in 1920. Wilson's administration had been seen as antiblack, causing that voter group to solidly back the Republican Harding in 1920. A black publication wrote in 1921, "the outgoing [Wilson] administration was a failure. . . . Negro leaders worked hard to elect [Harding]. The race was almost solid for the Grand Old Party and now more than ever before, the colored brother [expects] a benefit for his race."[58] By the end of the 1920s, black hopes were again dashed as the Republican leaders offered little more than token gestures.

Another response by the black community to these new pressures in society was the strengthening of racial consciousness, best exemplified by the rise of the Marcus Garvey black nationalism movement. Having come from Jamaica during World War I, Garvey began to create an organization dedicated to black pride, black capitalism, and black separatism. By 1919, through his United Negro Improvement Association (UNIA), which emphasized "black pride," he became the first black to win a mass following (later estimated in the millions during the 1920s). The Garvey movement exemplified the dissatisfaction in the black community that would face Wilson's successors in the coming decade.

By the census of 1920, several other important demographic and social changes were evident and would have marked implications for the new decade. For the first time, more than one-half the population lived in urban areas, identified as incorporated communities of 2,500 people or more. In 1920, the United States population was 106 million, of whom 54,318,000 lived in urban areas and 51,390,000 in rural areas. Urbanization was a central factor in American life after World War I. (Not to exaggerate the idea of the "big city," of the nation's overall population, 59,400,000 people lived in places with a population of fewer than 8,000.) This increased growth rate in urban areas continued throughout the 1920s.[59]

Perhaps because of these demographic trends, nostalgia for small-town America was widespread at the beginning of the new decade. In 1920, the nation's mind-set hovered closer to the small town than the big city, fostering broad concern over the loss of "community" and small-town values. By 1920, the style and pace of city life had already begun to intrude on the countryside, and many Americans struggled with the problem of creating the city while retaining the old sense of community and individual autonomy. This conflict between rural and urban cultures would permeate American life in the decade ahead.[60]

The significance of a rural mind-set for the United States after World War I can not be overstated. Despite its industrial power, innovative technology, and commercial drive, America essentially preserved a nineteenth-century rural outlook. In most areas of the country, especially in the South, the Midwest, and the Southwest, the old rural folkways remained, existing alongside an antagonism toward city values. "The conservatism of these predominantly rural areas would give way only gradually before the on-slaught of cars, paved highways, radios, and movies. and the process would be painful."[61]

Another important social change during the period was the emergence of the "new woman" in society as the 1920s began. By this time, the "Flapper" had replaced the "Gibson Girl" as the ideal of American womanhood. World War I had strengthened the women's movement, which led to such important social developments as passage of the Eighteenth Amendment(Prohibition) and the Nineteenth Amendment (women's suffrage), the ban on child labor by Congress, and the rising numbers of women working outside the home or attending college. By 1920 the cultural status of women was also changing dramatically, manifested by a radical change in manners and morals.

One of the most important goals championed by women (as well as by other interested groups) was reached in 1919 with the ratification of the Eighteenth Amendment imposing Prohibition, an event that led to profound cultural conflict during the decade. Prohibition, like teaching the theory of evolution, ending the open-door immigration policy, and challenging the newer attitudes on sex and morality, was to become a battleground between the defenders of the older morality and advocates of the newer values coming from the urban areas. Support for Prohibition was highest where the population was Protestant, rural, and nativist; passage of the Eighteenth Amendment in 1920 reflected the temporary victory of Protestant rural morality.[62] The Protestant clergy expected profound social change to follow the enactment of Prohibition. A leading preacher of the day, Billy Sunday, stated, "Slums will soon be a memory. We will turn our prisons into factories and our jails into store houses and corncribs. Men will walk upright now, women will smile, and the children will laugh. Hell will be forever for rent."[63] Unfortunately, Prohibition proved more disruptive rather than healing, adding more controversy to a society already filled with turmoil.

Other, more peaceful, cultural changes occurred in America's recreational habits after World War I. The changing leisure patterns reflected a decline in the normal work week (reduced by up to twenty hours since 1870) in some industries and more personal vacation time. Recreation was becoming more "democratic." By 1920, sports such as golf and tennis, once enjoyed only by the privileged few, were within reach of urban workers, reflecting shorter work schedules and higher incomes. The increased standard of living also supported the new automobile culture: by 1919, with five million cars for twenty-five million families, the United States had more cars than the rest of the world put together.

Alongside these recreational outlets, other venues for leisure were becoming more popular, especially spectator sports, movies, and the newborn radio industry. Perhaps the most important of the new leisure industries by 1920 was the motion picture, already the fifth largest industry in America. Important, too, was the great interest in spectator sports, of which baseball was the most popular. Professional sports heroes such as Babe Ruth were already attracting much public acclaim, a trend that would continue throughout the 1920s.

In 1919, in a preview of what was to happen in the ensuing decade, a spectacular combination of technology and personal courage resulted in the earliest flights across the Atlantic Ocean. Two British pilots flew a plane from Newfoundland, Canada, to Ireland, while a dirigible crossed the ocean with thirty-three passengers aboard. These flights inspired an American businessman to offer a $25,000 prize to the first person to fly solo from New York to Paris, thus setting the stage for one of the heroic events of the coming decade.

One reaction to the new values and interests springing up by 1920 was the determination of religious fundamentalists to preserve the older, more conservative, religious values. The long, slow emergence of an urban, non-Protestant, non-Puritan, secularized American population, which had been causing increasing alarm among Protestant leaders since the Civil War, had become a clear pattern after World War I.[64] The war had deeply influenced the fundamentalists, especially by intensifying their anxiety over the sinfulness of man. In 1920, they were ready to defend the old values, especially by opposing the teaching of Darwin's theory of evolution in the public schools. The fundamentalists, based in rural America, would lead the counterattack on the newly emerging modern America in the 1920s.

World War I had spawned a troubled society, a change that led a large majority of Americans in 1920 to vote for a change of political parties in Washington. The elections of 1920 reflected a society that had moved from the exhilaration of the Armistice through the final two tumultuous, problem-filled years of the Wilson administration. In addition to problems overseas and the lingering effects of the Red Scare, Wilson left a host of other unsolved domestic problems to his successor. By the time of Warren G. Harding's inauguration in March 1921, the new president faced demands from the business community for high protective tariffs, subsidies for American shipping and commercial aviation, guaranteed profits to the railroads, and help in disciplining labor. Unions were trying to defend themselves from suspicions emanating from the Red Scare and an increasingly hostile relationship with business. In Congress, a rebellious Farm Bloc was anxious to pull the farmer out of the agricultural depression with assistance from government programs. The problems that broke out after World War I remained unresolved when the Wilson administration ended, and a difficult period of adjustment awaited the three Republican presidents who followed him. Wilson was totally discredited by the election of 1920, and his successors would have to deal with the problems he left behind if they wanted to avoid a similar fate.

2

The Travails of
Warren G. Harding

A HARMONIZER BY NATURE and possessed of a genial manner in dealing
with people, Warren G. Harding was ironically destined to experience a troubled presidency. He came into office amid a host of serious domestic and foreign crises while the nation was readjusting to peacetime after the World War
I crisis. His problems included the postwar depression, a devastating collapse
in agricultural prices, domestic turmoil from the Red Scare, and the very tense
racial situation immediately following the war. Harding's presidency came at a
time of transition, with the nation shifting from an agricultural base to an industrial one at the same time the economy was shifting from wartime to
peaceful conditions. One of Harding's most important challenges as president
was to pull together the nation and restore its economic health after the dis-
sension in the final two years of the Wilson administration.

By the last year of his presidency, Harding had achieved immense popularity while the nation basked in the prosperity of the 1920s. His pro-business
philosophy and his assembling of the "best minds" for his cabinet apparently
had solved many of the nation's problems. The depression had finally ended
by 1923 and the acrimonious labor climate had been replaced by industrial
peace. But there were some notable exceptions to this return of good times.
The farm problem continued to plague the nation and several industries such
as coal and textiles failed to recover. For most Americans, however, conditions
had improved and Harding reaped the credit.

Unexpectedly, after little more than two years in office, Harding suddenly
died from problems following a stroke. The president's condition was probably brought on partly by his final crisis, a betrayal by some of his leading sub-

ordinates. Quite trusting of his associates, Harding ironically would ultimately have his reputation destroyed because of a wave of scandals that
plagued the latter part of his presidency. He began his administration amidst a
number of major political and social crises in the United States and, tragically,
once these situations returned to normal Harding was stricken by the betrayal
of those around him.

Although Harding served as president for little more than two years, both
he and his administration would be enshrouded in myths for many years afterward. In polls, historians have consistently rated the Harding administration
as an abysmal failure, usually ranking him as the worst president ever.[1] Attempts to understand how he became president usually have involved notions
of conspiracy or public misjudgments. These myths distort the picture of
Harding and his presidency, creating a caricature of a helpless, pliant figure in
thrall to the forces of greed.[2] However, a close examination of Harding's story
reveals a far different picture.

Harding was born in 1865 in Ohio and nothing unusual occurred in his
early years to indicate he would someday attain the presidency. He graduated
from Ohio Central College in 1882, one of only three in the graduating class.
His early attempts at a teaching career and in the insurance industry failed. He
ultimately found success when he and his partners purchased for $300 the
Marion *Star,* a struggling, five-sheet local newspaper in the small Ohio town
that he considered home for most of his life. His entry into the newspaper
business paved the way for his career in politics, gaining him many valuable
contacts. It also provided him with personal wealth; the newspaper was later
sold for several hundred thousand dollars.

Harding's political views were enormously influenced by his forty years as
a resident of Marion, an agricultural community that was just beginning to in-
dustrialize. He totally accepted its small-town values and learned to believe in
the Republican Party and "old-fashioned politics" that were unfettered by reformers. He strongly supported late nineteenth-century capitalism, unshack-
led by government regulations, and believed in industrial achievement
unaided by government programs. In this setting, people would rise or fall on
their own merits. These became his core values as his political career moved
him steadily toward the White House. Fortunately for Harding as he reached
the presidency, even by the 1920s the nation still retained the old rural mind-
set, and visions of activist government were not those of the majority.

Harding's small-town background proved to be a major asset in his political career. Big cities, linked to the recent wave of New Immigrants, were re-garded as sinful, while small towns were seen as good. Picking candidates from the small towns such as Marion was the general rule in politics through the 1920s. Harding's humble background also served as an asset because, when he was starting his political career, most people were poor and identified with candidates from similar backgrounds.[3] In contrast to the big cities, small towns represented sharing, good morals, and no great disparities in wealth. Harding also represented the sentimental feelings of most Americans, who had been raised in the country and remained attached to the small town. It was easy for them to identify with Harding, who had lived in a town of a few thousand residents for most of his life.

Harding's role as a small-town businessman also helped him evolve his generally favorable views on the role of business in America. He saw no inher-ent conflict between business and labor and held that the government should not try to run any business because private enterprise was the "regular order of things" and would save America from decay. American business was not a monster but the expression of a God-given power to create. His background as a businessman from a small town not only shaped his political views but also gave him the important political advantage of seeming to representing both big business and the rural past.[4]

Harding's rise in the political system occurred rapidly, beginning with his election as Ohio state senator in 1899. In this position he began to employ the basic strategy of conciliator and harmonizer that he practiced throughout his political career. He rose to lieutenant governor in 1903 but resigned a few years later to concentrate on his personal business affairs. In 1910, Harding came out of "retirement" and ran unsuccessfully for governor of Ohio, the only important defeat of his career. By now, Harding had become a well-known figure in both state and national politics, a fact indicated by his nomi-nating President Taft at the Republican National Convention in 1912. Two years later, his career was immensely bolstered when he won a seat in the U.S. Senate.

Harding's victory in his Senate race demonstrated the political skills and style of the rising young politician. Personally, he had many assets to offer the voters. He had good looks, a warm personal manner, a knack for remember-ing names, a habit of using reassuring phrases, and—most importantly—a de-termination to succeed. He usually took sound and popular positions on the issues. Although not as brilliant as many of his Senate colleagues, Harding had become a skillful politician through his lengthy political experience; he was not a political "innocent."

A clear outline of Harding's political views became apparent during his years in the Senate; with few exceptions he would pursue these same policies as president. Harding identified with President McKinley and he endorsed the former president's emphasis on nationalism, support for big business and the high tariff, and abiding faith in the Republican Party. A defining influence on Harding after World War I, which permanently affected his political views, was the Red Scare.[5] Like many Americans, Harding had backed reform and internationalism at one time but now reverted to conservatism and nationalism because of the fear of revolution at home. After the success of the Bolshevik Revolution in Russia and the attempted Communist uprisings in Hungary and Germany in 1919, a Communist revolution seemed possible. By 1920, Harding's basic political views were set for the rest of his career.

Oddly, the death of the internationalist Theodore Roosevelt in 1919 opened the door for the nationalist senator from Ohio to enter the presidential race the following year. The widespread assumption that the colorful Roosevelt would be the Republican nominee in 1920 was shattered by his untimely death. In the political void suddenly created, many lesser Republicans stepped forward as possible standard bearers for the GOP. Harding's capture of the Republican nomination that year became both a great personal triumph for the Ohioan and the source of many myths in American political history.

Contrary to traditional belief, Harding was not the "reluctant" candidate of 1920, urged on by a domineering wife and a clever adviser, Harry Daugherty. Harding was an ambitious politician of great skill. He deliberately chose to soft-pedal his presidential drive because of his limited popular appeal outside his home state.[6] His genial manner had earned him much support within the party, as well as with delegates to the national convention and among the Senate bosses. Within Ohio, his position was strong. He was the state's "favorite son" candidate because all his in-state political rivals had been defeated in earlier elections, a sharp contrast to his election to the U.S. Senate in 1914 by 100,000 votes. He became the only available candidate from a state that had already sent six men to the White House since the Civil War. (In fact, every Republican president since Grant had either been born or lived in Ohio.)[7]

One of the most enduring myths in American political history is the "smoke-filled room" of political bosses at the 1920 Republican convention that nominated a somewhat reluctant Senator Harding. According to this legendary account, the bosses called in Harding to ask whether he had any problems in his background that might disqualify him from the presidency and, after a brief period of reflection, he declared there were none. The bosses then passed on the word to the delegates that Harding should be the party nominee.[8] More recent scholarship has clearly shown that Harding was the key to his own nomination and that the bosses even tried to block Harding's nomination but failed because of his popularity with the delegates.[9] Harding designed his own "second-choice" strategy, wherein he hoped the delegates would turn to him as a backup choice when the front-runners deadlocked. He was clearly not a pawn of his adviser, Harry Daugherty, or of the Senate bosses; Harding's own political skills were the key to his nomination.[10] His cause was helped immensely by the absence of boss control over the convention, a situation that created an opportunity for anyone who could exploit it. Harding was able to move into this void partly because of his great popularity with the delegates, who felt that Harding, like themselves, represented an "older" America and business.

The 1920 election, usually seen as a dramatic rejection of President Wilson and the League of Nations rather than a show of support for Harding, is another persistent myth of that era. Harding shrewdly observed that in 1920 the nation yearned for stability and a respite from both domestic and international turmoil. He cleverly offered the nation a return to "normalcy," to the more tranquil atmosphere of pre-World War I America. Harding defined "normalcy" not as a retreat into the past but as an orderly system for progress, without the rancor of the Wilson years.[11] Running a masterful "front porch" campaign, Harding *deliberately* equivocated on the League of Nations question and gained votes from both the pro-League and the anti-League forces. On the other issues of the day, he took positions that were popular with the voters and in fact prevailed throughout the 1920s. He favored immigration restriction, pro-business policies, tax cuts, and a general pulling together of the nation rocked by crises after World War I. His personal charm and amiable personality made him appear as a healing force to the nation. His Democratic opponent, Governor James Cox of Ohio, was less well known than Harding, lacked his strong personal qualities, and was linked to an outgoing administration that symbolized turmoil to many Americans.[12] So strong was the

Harding appeal in 1920 that he captured 60.2 percent of the vote, a feat un-matched until Lyndon Johnson's landslide victory in 1964.

Harding's victory reflected his shrewdness in turning the campaign into a referendum on his appeal for "normalcy" and nostalgia for a less turbulent era. He directed his campaign at the majority of Americans, those who had once lived in small towns and on farms, even if they were now living in the city.[13] It also aimed at attracting the votes of recent immigrants who were dis-appointed with the results of the war and wished to cast a vote against Wilson and American involvement in World War I. These immigrants were attached to a different kind of "normalcy," hoping to see their former homeland in Eu-rope restored to normal conditions and uncomplicated by the bitterness com-ing out of the war.[14]

Ultimately, Harding's greatest assets were his attractive personal qualities and his successful appeal to a rural past. The League issue was diffused by Harding's shading of his position and the bitter divisions within both parties on this explosive question. In a time of strikes, inflation, and postwar discon-tent, Harding skillfully exploited a longing for the stability of the recent past. With his successful campaign theme based on nostalgia, the election was a vote for Harding even more than a protest against Wilson.[15]

But the unpopularity of the Wilson administration undoubtedly helped in the Harding landslide. Even among the "progressives," President Wilson was not always synonymous with reform. In 1920, it was difficult to cast a pro-gressive vote for the Democratic Party. Wilson had antagonized progressives by his suppression of civil liberties during the war, he had alienated the Ger-man element by the war itself, and he had distanced middle-class liberals by the Red Scare policies of Attorney General A. Mitchell Palmer. Many progres-sives voted against the Democratic Party because they were sated with *false* prophets of the progressive creed, not with idealism and reform itself.[16]

The political skill and determination that enabled Harding to win both the nomination and the election in 1920 were put to use in the selection of his cabinet. Recent scholarship has debunked the earlier myth of a weak Harding forced by party leaders to accept an inferior cabinet. Harding himself played the key role in choosing his cabinet, a group that was highly praised at the time. The three leading members of the cabinet were Charles Evans Hughes at the State Department, Andrew Mellon at the Treasury Department, and Commerce Secretary Herbert Hoover. Hughes, the brilliant former governor of New York and the party nominee in 1916, was a logical choice for the cabinet. Andrew Mellon was an extremely wealthy businessman and a favorite of the conservative business wing of the party. Already sixty-five years old when he was appointed treasury secretary, Mellon was one of the three richest men in the country, with vast interests in Alcoa Aluminum, Gulf Oil, and banking. His appointment symbolized a closer relationship between business and government and raised spirits in the business community at a time of economic depression.[17] Herbert Hoover as commerce secretary was the most difficult choice for Harding to get approved by the Senate. An independent-minded Republican who had worked under Woodrow Wilson during World War I, Hoover was viewed with suspicion by some Republican leaders and Harding had to fight for his accession to the cabinet. With the exception of Attorney General Harry Daugherty, a political crony from Ohio, Harding's cabinet was praised as "one of the strongest groups of presidential choices and department heads in a generation." [18] Unfortunately, some of his other appointments were less capable and principled, and a group of lower-level appointees referred to as the "Ohio Gang" later became known for their greed and dishonesty.

Harding's method of conducting his presidency—as much as his actual record on the major issues of the day—often led to serious misjudgements of his performance in office and became "evidence" for additional myths about his presidency. His presidential style opened him up to criticism of being weak and ineffective. Harding deliberately fostered the myth of the casual and lazy president to disarm his opponents. In reality he was one of the hardest-working presidents, his normal working day being from 8:00 A.M. to midnight. There was little truth to the image of golf three times a week, continuous poker parties, and endless social gatherings.[19] Furthermore, the myth of a kind and generous but hopelessly meek Harding also belies the facts. Although he pardoned Eugene Debs, the most famous World War I dissenter, Harding refused to declare a general amnesty for all wartime dissenters. When he died, twenty-one "political prisoners," mainly IWW stalwarts, were still in jail.[20]

Although Harding entered the White House with a "McKinley" view of the presidency—a belief in the strict separation of powers between Congress and the president—he became more assertive once in office. A harmonizer on most political matters, Harding demonstrated that he was not subservient to Congress. Building upon the precedent set earlier by Woodrow Wilson, he made periodic addresses before Congress on specific issues. In 1921, Harding personally addressed a special session of Congress to strongly oppose the veterans' bonus. Before his death, he addressed Congress five more times to support or oppose key measures and was even charged with "executive tyranny." [21]

While in office, Harding also strengthened himself politically by cultivating excellent relations with the press, which he used as a public-relations tool. He restored the previous tradition of regularly scheduled press conferences. A former newspaperman himself, Harding was able to persuade the press that he was doing a good job and it only turned against him after his death and the disclosure of the scandals. As president, Harding's skill in dealing with the press and the public was even regarded as "genius" [22] and contributed to his extremely favorable image with the public.

With his team in place, Harding faced a host of problems after his election. He wanted to create a more favorable economic atmosphere and to reduce the cost of operating the government. He was confronted by the depression of 1920 and the especially serious problems of the farmer. He had to deal with the legacy of the Red Scare, particularly the case of political prisoners. He also faced the challenge of implementing the newly created policy of Prohibition. Beyond these serious policy matters, Harding inherited a difficult political climate from the Wilson administration. He faced a rebellious Congress, a society filled with hatred and turmoil, and a chaotic situation in foreign affairs.

On 12 April 1921, Harding addressed a special session of Congress to outline his agenda, which ultimately became the Republican agenda for the next eight years. He gave his highest priority to a pro-business strategy, aimed at restoring health to the economy. Harding called for the gradual liquidation of the war debt, slashes in government spending, and tax reduction. He wanted a high tariff passed to protect American industries and agriculture and to provide additional revenue. To cut government spending, he urged the creation of a national budget system. He supported a larger merchant marine and more highways (but mainly paid for by the states). He encouraged the development of the aviation and radio industries. Regarding some of the more sensitive issues, he called for strict limits on immigration and a rejection of the League of Nations. (He did express continued support for some kind of an "association of nations.") This overall pro-business leaning of the Harding administration was in line with public opinion, which would have regarded an anti-business administration as being dangerous to the country's welfare, especially in view of the Red Scare and the 1920–21 depression.[23] By the end of his short presidency, nearly all of these goals had been achieved.

Harding's first great challenge was to cope with the depression of 1920–21, inherited from the Wilson administration. Rather than supporting an activist approach, he backed the ideas of Mellon and budget director Charles Dawes, who applied traditional conservative economic remedies to the downturn. Harding stressed cuts in government spending and reductions in taxes, as well as waiting for the business cycle to reverse. Harding supported Mellon's efforts to repeal the wartime excess-profits tax and to cut the surtax for the rich from 65 percent to 50 percent. He stood behind Dawes's efforts to reduce government spending and opposed a bonus for veterans as something that would unbalance the budget. He even urged unions to accept a "necessary" reduction in wages to let business revive.[24]

Cutting government spending became an important tool to end the depression as well as the catalyst for a major change in the executive branch of the government. Conditions were favorable for a major economy drive by the federal government when Harding began his presidency. During the war years, there had been a substantial increase in both government spending and hiring. Federal spending had risen from less than $1 billion in 1914 to $6,139,000 in 1920, even though the World War I crisis was over. The number of federal employees had risen from 435,000 in 1914 to 691,000 in 1921. The national debt had risen from $1,188,000,000 in 1914 ($12 per capita) to $25,484,000,000 in 1919 ($242 per capita).[25]

To bring down the cost of running the federal government, Harding urged the creation of a national budget system. Previously the president and the Treasury Department had played only a passive role in the budgetary process and exercised little oversight in the submission of departmental budget requests to Congress. By creating the Budget Bureau, Harding gained a major increase in authority over all budgetary matters. The Budget Act of 1921 required the president, with the aid of the Budget Bureau, to prepare an annual budget, giving to Congress complete information regarding revenues, expenditures, the condition of the Treasury, and a forecast of administration plans for the future. The Treasury Department would become more of a watchdog over federal spending rather than an agent of transmitting bills to Congress. The president also no longer acted as merely a "rubber stamp," not really knowing if the departmental requests were valid. He now had complete authority over the budget process when requests were sent to Congress. To serve as the first budget director, Harding named Charles G. Dawes, a wealthy Chicago banker who later served as vice president under Calvin Coolidge. Upon taking the job, Dawes told Harding, "You must realize that you are the first President to tackle the job of a coordinated business control over the departments. I doubt if you realize the strength of the 150 years of archaisms which you must fight." [26]

The combative Dawes was a success as budget director. Inclined to argue with department heads about keeping their budgets down, Dawes put together a federal budget for fiscal 1923 that was $1.5 billion less than the budget for fiscal 1921. The *Commercial and Financial Chronicle* commented upon Dawes's budget efforts: "The government is now on the way to an orderly and healthy system of business management, thanks to the courage and ability of . . . Dawes, and the prompt and unqualified cooperation of the President." [27] In the year ending in June 1922, the federal budget was $1.4 billion less than the previous year. By June 1923, the federal budget was $2 billion under the final Wilson year of 1921. Part of the success stemmed from the efforts of Harding himself. He was firm and unyielding even with his friends on the matter of cost reductions. He turned down pleas for money from dissatisfied cabinet offices and held the line on pork barrel requests from Congress. [28]

The appointment of financial tycoon Andrew Mellon was also part of an effort by Harding to put the government on a greater business footing. Mellon's most important goal as treasury secretary was to cut taxes, especially on those who earned the highest incomes. This was not only a Republican idea; the Wilson administration had proposed the same idea shortly after the war ended. [29] Mellon argued that the high World War I tax rates had shifted the burden to the upper middle class and the wealthy, even though these were the two groups that usually supplied most of the risk capital for economic expansion. He also wished to reexamine the higher tax burden for corporations, which had been hit with excess-profits taxes and higher corporate income taxes. Mellon believed that if economic prosperity were to return, quick relief had to be given to these groups. [30]

The treasury secretary (with Harding's concurrence) believed that tax cuts, along with decreasing the national debt and keeping a tight control on government spending, were the best means to restore prosperity and enhance growth. [31] The key to a healthy economy was to lower taxes, which then permitted the other major economic goals to be reached. By decreasing taxes on the upper class, Mellon said the government had a better chance not only to collect more taxes but also to spur the expansion of business and industry. By paying off the national debt, more funds would ultimately be invested in the economy (and result in higher tax revenue being collected) instead of being allocated for the "useless expenditures" of debt repayment. Rather than being merely a bonus to the wealthy, Mellon envisaged his tax cuts as leading to economic prosperity for all.

To implement this economic strategy, the Tax Bill of 1921 was passed in November of that year. The surtax on the very rich was lowered from 65 percent to 50 percent. The excess-profits tax on business was repealed. (To help make up this lost revenue, the corporate tax rate was raised from 10 percent to 12.5 percent.) The bill also included more tax exemptions and tax allowances for low-income families. The Tax Bill had a significant impact immediately, lowering taxes by $800 million the first year. Along with lower government spending made possible by the Budget Act, the new lower taxes aided business and encouraged economic recovery.

Beyond these efforts, Harding believed that the downturn was part of the natural business cycle and that no drastic government action would be required. He called a conference on unemployment in 1921 but was not prepared to take bold action. He advised the meeting not to seek unemployment subsidies from the federal government as a solution and, in fact, opposed any relief activities by the federal government. "I would have little enthusiasm for any proposed relief which seeks either palliation or tonic from the public Treasury," he bluntly declared.[32] Harding regarded unemployment as "normal" and preferred personal charity as a substitute for government welfare.[33] He followed a strategy of fighting the depression by trying to help business and increasing the number of available jobs. "The best social welfare worker in the world," he declared, "is a man or woman who does an honest day's labor."[34]

The depression of 1920 caught not only the factory worker but also the farmer in its wake. In Secretary of Agriculture Henry Wallace, the farmer had a forceful advocate who was more willing than the president to take bold action on this problem. The secretary believed that, because the agricultural segment of the economy contained approximately 25 percent of the nation's population, government aid was essential. "If we are to have a prosperous nation, we must have a profitable and satisfying agriculture," he declared.[35] Both Wallace and Harding agreed upon several ideas to help the farmer, including promotion of farm exports, national laws protecting farm cooperatives, improvements in the federal farm loan system, increased farm representation on federal boards and commissions, aids to make the farmer more efficient in the business operation of his farm, and greater tariff protection for agricultural commodities. However, on the most controversial aid suggestion of federal subsidies to the farmer, Harding's strong opposition put him at odds with his agriculture secretary.

However limited his efforts, Harding had several reasons to help the downtrodden farmer. The farmer still represented many voters in the 1920s. Harding personally had lived most of his life in a rural atmosphere and identified with the farmer. Yet because of his deeply ingrained conservative views, he was reluctant to support innovative new ideas such as farm subsidies. His failure to act boldly on the agricultural problem did not go unchallenged. The president was increasingly pressed by a group of Republicans in Congress known as the Farm Bloc, which feared that Harding would ignore farmers and concentrate only on business. Their policy was to hold the administration's "feet to the fire" if they felt ignored, which they proved by delaying the Mellon tax bill until the tariff containing farm protection was passed.[36]

The Tariff of 1921 was the most important legislation to aid the farmer in the early 1920s. In the closing days of the Wilson administration, Congress had passed an emergency high tariff bill, which included protection for farm commodities. Wilson, more of a free-trade advocate than Harding, vetoed the bill, declaring, "If we wish to have Europe settle her war debts, governmental or commercial, we must be prepared to buy from her, and if we wish to assist Europe and ourselves by the export of either food, raw materials, or finished products, we must be prepared to welcome commodities which we need and which Europe will be prepared . . . to send us. Clearly this is no time for the creation of high trade barriers."[37] Harding, who favored protection for both business and agriculture, disagreed. He was a lifelong supporter of high tariffs and had earlier pledged to back this idea in the 1920 Republican Party platform. When Congress again passed the same emergency tariff that Wilson had vetoed, Harding signed the bill.

To further aid the farmer, the administration called an agricultural conference in January 1922. Harding opened the conference by declaring agriculture to be the "most elemental of industries," claiming that no part of the nation's economy could be healthy while agriculture was sick. Yet Harding preferred only modest efforts to aid the farmer. Emphasizing that he was not prepared to spend government money to help the farmer, he stated "it cannot be too strongly urged that the farmer must be ready to help himself."[38] In opposing subsidies, he warned, "Government paternalism whether applied to agriculture or to any other of our great national industries, would stifle ambition, impair efficiency, lessen protection and make us a nation of dependent incompetents." Declaring that "the farmer requires no special favors at the hands of the government," Harding concluded that all the farmer really needed was "a fair chance." [39]

Because of Harding's faith in the law of supply and demand, he believed there was little the government could actually do for the farmer. The economic laws must prevail and if there would not be a need for as many farmers as before, he believed many of them would move to the city and replace the immigrants in the factory.[40] In line with Harding's support for only a *limited* government role in aiding the farmer, a number of acts were passed by Congress early in his administration. The Fordney-McCumber Tariff Act, replacing the Emergency Tariff Act of 1921, protected many farm commodities from foreign competition. An Emergency Agricultural Credits Act was passed, extending more credit to rural banks and farm corporations. The Capper-Volstead Act was passed, exempting farm cooperatives from the antitrust laws. However, none of these laws significantly eased the farmer's plight, which continued through the remainder of Harding's tenure.

As he had sometimes done while in the Senate, Harding occasionally deviated from his "regular" pro-business policies to support a "progressive" measure. At a time when Congress did not favor more government social welfare policies, Harding supported (successfully) the Shepard-Towner Act of 1921, which encouraged joint state-federal action in reducing the high death rate of infants and increasing sound hygiene among women and children. This measure, Harding hoped, would also help him capture the women's vote. Criticized by conservatives and seemingly an anomaly in such a conservative period, the measure eventually was struck down by Congress later in the decade. However limited its effects, it was the last important grant-in-aid program before the Great Depression and provided a notable precedent for the social welfare programs of the New Deal.[41]

Besides a host of economic and social problems, Harding also inherited from the Wilson administration a difficult racial situation. The race riots that followed World War I, along with the massive black exodus to the North, had led to a highly charged racial atmosphere. Harding took a more enlightened position on the racial question than had his predecessor, albeit with little success. On 26 October 1921, Harding gave a notable speech on race relations in

Birmingham, Alabama, similar in theme to the famous speech of Booker T. Washington in 1896. In his speech, Harding called for more legal protection of black Americans while at the same time defending segregation and opposing social equality. He requested a more evenhanded literacy test for voting, which would be applied to both whites and blacks, stating, "let the black man vote when he is fit to vote, [and] prohibit the white man's voting when he is unfit to vote." The South should take the lead in solving racial problems so that there might be at last an end of prejudice.[42] He urged political, educational, and economic opportunities for black people—but in the context of segregation. In order to attain greater national progress and unity, Harding concluded, "We cannot go on, as we have for more than half a century, with one great section of our population . . . cut off from real contributions to solving national issues because of a division on racial issues."[43]

Harding's Birmingham speech, called "the most important presidential utterance on the race question since Reconstruction,"[44] was soon followed with a specific legislative proposal urging passage of a law giving federal courts jurisdiction over the crime of lynching. This measure was bitterly opposed by the South and, although passed by the House of Representatives, was ultimately killed in the Senate.[45] Harding then gave up on the issue, which would not be raised by another president until the Truman administration of the late 1940s. His other proposal for an interracial commission to improve race relations was similarly defeated in Congress.

Harding's goals were both practical and enlightened. He was attempting to build up a southern Republican Party, to bind northern black voters more firmly to the Republicans, and to promote racial harmony.[46] All of these efforts ultimately failed. The black community, which had been disappointed by the segregationist policies of the Wilson administration and had expected more from Harding, whom it had supported so strongly in 1920, was disappointed again. Despite his important rhetoric, Harding's record was weak in both patronage and in legislation to help black citizens; there was no significant change in race relations for many years.

A less serious and far more publicized problem confronting the president was the newly enacted ban on alcohol. Harding inherited from his predecessor the difficult problem of enforcing the Prohibition policy. Operating with a thin staff based in the Treasury Department, effective enforcement of Prohibition had obviously failed by the end of the Harding administration. He personally had little enthusiasm for this policy, evidenced by his own drinking in the White House.[47] As would his successors, Harding publicly supported the Eighteenth Amendment but was unwilling to commit vast resources toward enforcing the ban on drinking.

Harding was more inclined to intervene favorably on matters of business than on problems relating to other segments of the economy. His policy toward privatizing businesses and government regulation of the economy demonstrates Harding's pro-business philosophy. He returned the railroads to private control after World War I, and he appointed conservative regulators to the Interstate Commerce Commission, which oversaw the railroad industry. Similarly, he appointed conservatives to the Federal Trade Commission and Federal Reserve Board, essentially converting the regulatory commissions to pro-business agencies.

Harding was less successful in his attempt to sell the government-owned Muscle Shoals project to private interests. During World War I, the government had built nitrogen plants and dams at Muscle Shoals, Alabama, in the Tennessee Valley to manufacture cheap explosives for military purposes. Harding's desire to sell the development elicited an offer to buy from the auto tycoon Henry Ford, who promised to make cheap nitrates for American farmers and continue supplying explosives to the American government. Although the sale was backed by farmers in the Tennessee Valley, by the president and his cabinet, and by a majority in Congress, it was successfully blocked by powerful Senator George Norris of Idaho.[48] When the issue arose during the Coolidge administration, Norris again blocked the sale. The senator hoped for a government operation to produce cheap electricity for the poor people of the region and later saw his wishes fulfilled with the building of the Tennessee Valley Authority during the New Deal.

Not surprising in a pro-business administration, the laborer was the Harding era's "forgotten man," with no real defender in the cabinet. Harding believed more in the benevolent paternalism of employers than in the activities of labor unions. He had treated his own employees at the Marion *Star* in a benevolent fashion and was much admired by them. Harding believed in the right of workers to join a union and to bargain collectively, although he opposed the use of the strike. He felt that union leaders were sometimes unrealistic about the economy, and he periodically complained to AFL president Samuel Gompers about their unwillingness "to accept necessary reductions in wages and give an opportunity for a revival of industry."[49]

Labor relations became one of the most serious problems faced by the administration. The uneasy wartime truce between capital and labor broke down after the Armistice, and the concluding years of the Wilson administration were riddled with labor-management conflicts. Strikes for the eight-hour day, higher wages, union recognition, and a shorter workweek punctuated the postwar scene. The pro-business Harding administration sought some sort of middle ground between the dissatisfied workers and the antilabor atmosphere fostered by the Red Scare. In dealing with this turmoil, the administration ostensibly remained uncommitted and worked behind the scenes for reconciliation. (In labor disputes as in politics, Harding always tended to be a harmonizer.) Harding believed that the primary function of government was to exhibit a spirit of reasonableness and create an atmosphere in which strikes might be prevented and the return of prosperity achieved that much sooner.[50] In the difficult labor situation inherited from the Wilson administration, Harding's policy of conciliation and moderation failed to provide labor peace. He ultimately turned to a totally pro-business policy, leading to a permanent split between his administration and organized labor.

Although willing to concede a raison d'étre to unions, Harding nevertheless regarded them as a conspiracy against business.[51] When serious strikes broke out in the railroad and coal industries in 1922, he at first tried to be conciliatory and refused to intervene. But as the strikes continued and public hostility toward the strikers increased, Harding turned against the unions and permitted his attorney general to obtain a sweeping federal injunction, which effectively halted the railroad strike. The injunction resolved some of Harding's short-term problems but created more lasting problems for the Republican Party. The railroad union lost the strike and soon after the coal strike was settled, with that union feeling the pressure of a possible federal injunction. But Harding's labor reputation was tarnished by the railroad injunction and he and organized labor were irreconcilably at odds after the 1922 strikes.[52] A bitter feud developed between Harding and Samuel Gompers, who was said to be one of the few men Harding ever really disliked.[53]

Harding's intervention in the railroad strike also canceled any good will he might have earned from his persistent efforts to shorten the steel industry work week, which averaged nearly seventy hours when he took office. After about a year of constant pressure on the industry, Harding successfully pressured Elbert Gary, the head of United States Steel Corporation, to agree to the forty eight-hour, six-day workweek, but this failed to overcome the Republicans' difficulties with organized labor. Except for his benevolent intervention in the United States Steel dispute, Harding had little to offer industrial workers. He was against unemployment subsidies from the government, preferring instead a mix of voluntary and local action. He had tried unsuccessfully to achieve industrial peace by expanding the government's role as a nonpartisan mediator (although there was an obvious tilt toward the business side). Not surprisingly, labor relations remained a problem throughout the Harding presidency.

Beyond the particular problems of labor, agriculture, and business, Harding adopted a broad strategy of "America First" to promote the nation's economic interests at home and abroad. A key element in this economic outlook was strong support for a high tariff, regardless of its effect on international trade. The tariff laws of 1921 and 1922 enacted this aspect of the administration's economic game plan. Harding always took a nationalist position when it came to aiding the American economy through a protective tariff. He was unmoved by charges that he was hurting European trade, declaring that America's own interests came first. Europe should take care of its own problems, although if needed he was willing to send charity to Europe, even to starving Communist Russia.[54]

Harding's "America First" philosophy also led to a major shift in American immigration policy, which included both tighter controls on admission of immigrants and greater efforts at assimilation. The Immigration Act of 1921 fitted into the president's nationalist focus. A combination of factors, including the prewar sentiment against aliens and Catholics, the postwar economic depression, and the new wave of aliens entering the country after 1919, led Congress to impose the first substantial curbs on European immigration to the United States. The new policy was backed by organized labor, parts of the business community, and the administration. With much public support, the United States instituted a plan of immigration restriction that limited the annual number of immigrants to 3 percent of the number from that particular country living in the United States in the base year of 1910. For those immigrants already here, the administration urged greater efforts at "Americanization," which included more classes in American citizenship and in learning the English language.

Alongside the new immigration and high tariff laws was Harding's (abortive) fight for a stronger American merchant marine, another aspect of his policy of economic nationalism. Harding supported the sale of the fleet of government-owned supply ships built during World War I to private interests at very low prices. He also backed government subsidies to encourage the private building of a merchant marine fleet. Despite an energetic effort by the president, including a personal address before Congress, lack of support for the project in that body led Harding to abandon the fight in early 1923.

On another front, the administration was more successful in sticking to its economic strategy with its opposition to federal veterans' bonuses. Harding took a major political risk in 1922 when he vetoed the Soldiers' Bonus Bill, a measure that had overwhelming support within the Congress and from the public. Stressing the need for government thrift, Harding was opposed to the bonus unless Congress found the funds to pay for it. The bill would give veterans $1 for each day of home service and $1.25 for each day of overseas duty (after the first sixty days) and would ultimately cost approximately $4 billion by 1942. When the plan was originally proposed in 1921 at the time of the debate over the Tax Bill, Harding and Mellon had expressed strong opposition, claiming that such an expensive bonus program would make tax cuts and lower government spending impossible.[55] Harding's opposition to veterans' bonuses was also designed to prevent other economic problems from occurring. "This effort to expend billions in gratuities," he stated, "would imperil the restoration of normalcy. Tax reduction to revive business, the refunding of the war debt, and a settlement of foreign loans—these were necessary. . . . A modest offering to the millions of servicemen was a poor palliative to more millions who may be out of employment."[56] The bill for a veterans' bonus passed Congress in 1922 and Harding's veto of it was narrowly sustained.

By the middle of the Harding presidency, the administration had earned a mixed record of notable successes and failures. In foreign affairs, the Washington Conference appeared to be successful. The Mellon program for lower taxes had been passed, and a new budgeting system had been successfully implemented. Both business and farmers ostensibly would benefit from the new higher tariff. A limited program to directly aid the farmer had been passed. For the first time in American history, a major curtailing of European immigration had been implemented. With the return of prosperity by 1923, most of the dissatisfaction and confusion that had marked the first two years of the Harding presidency disappeared.

Alongside these achievements, the Harding administration also suffered various political setbacks. The agricultural depression stubbornly persisted in spite of the limited aid offered by the administration. Organized labor was alienated by the pro-business tilt, especially the government's intervention in the railroad strike of 1922. Many veterans were disappointed by Harding's veto of the Soldiers' Bonus Bill of 1922. Even if these problems cost him support with the farm and labor vote, Harding refused to alter his basic pro-business philosophy. He stated that satisfying the farmers would require "some artificial process which violates all economic laws" and satisfying the laborer would mean "maintaining [artificially high] war levels of wages," both courses of action being harmful to the economy.[57]

As the agricultural crisis persisted, the Harding administration continued to insist on only limited measures to help the farmer. With administration support, Congress in 1923 passed the Agricultural Marketing Act, which increased credit to cooperatives, rural banks, and livestock associations. It soon became obvious, however, that the mere expansion of farm credit was not going to solve the farm problem and there was growing interest in farm subsidies, an idea the administration continued to oppose. But Harding died before any action could be taken on farm subsidies, leaving behind an agricultural depression and a growing demand for stronger governmental action in agricultural affairs.

With the exception of the lingering agricultural crisis, the depression of 1920–21 was finally over by 1923. Administration policies, new breakthroughs in the private sector, and the evolution of the business cycle accounted for the return of prosperity. By reducing the national debt and government spending and putting the full support of the Commerce Department behind policies to encourage business recovery, the Harding administration created an environment that helped end the depression of 1920–21. The economy was also helped immensely by the rising new industries in electrical appliances, automobiles, motion pictures, and the radio, as well as from Frederick Taylor's scientific management theories, which increased production and efficiency in industry. But the return of prosperity was not universally shared, with certain industries as well as labor itself continuing to struggle.

With the return of prosperity and a strong business mind-set in place, Harding's vision of the economy won wide acceptance. To solidify in government his conservative, pro-business philosophy, Harding nominated four conservative Supreme Court justices, including the Chief Justice William Howard Taft. The previous Wilson Supreme Court had contained an anti-business bias, generally emphasizing the rights of the worker and the public. Conservatives had argued that these rulings violated property rights and specifically "freedom of contract." The new Harding court attacked the stronger role of the government, arguing in favor of more economic freedom. With a stronger bias toward business than its predecessor, it struck down federal and state minimum-wage laws and the right to interfere too deeply in the free-market economy. It limited labor's right to strike and struck down Congress's attempt to regulate child labor. The four judges named by Harding set a conservative business-minded course for the Supreme Court, enabling the president to affect the direction of the economy throughout the 1920s.[58]

Immensely popular while in office during this "age of business," Harding died before his reputation collapsed after the disclosure of numerous scandals beginning in late 1923. He appeared to be in perfect health at his inauguration in 1921, a total contrast to the outgoing Woodrow Wilson. Yet Harding died a year before his predecessor, plunging the nation into a state of mourning not seen since the death of Abraham Lincoln.[59] Stricken while on a speaking tour of the West, Harding became ill in Seattle and died in San Francisco a few days later. While Harding's illness was at first attributed to tainted seafood, his doctor later claimed the president died from a stroke. The family's refusal to permit an autopsy gave rise to speculation concerning an alleged plot against the president. Sensational rumors were later spread that Mrs. Harding, having found out about her husband's love affair with a younger woman, had poisoned him.[60] Harding, who began his presidency in the myth of the "smoke-filled room," left with the more sensational myth of being poisoned by a vengeful wife.

Soon after Harding's death, a wave of corruption was exposed that completely destroyed his reputation. Much bribery and corruption were linked to his underlings, some of whom went to jail or committed suicide. This episode was a cruel irony because Harding had always stressed loyalty to his friends and associates. The two most important scandals involved the Veterans Bureau and the Interior Department. Charles Forbes, head of the Veterans Bureau, which had responsibility for control, management, and constructions of veterans' hospitals, was convicted of taking bribes. In the Teapot Dome Scandal, Interior Secretary Albert Fall was ultimately sent to jail for taking bribes in leasing government-controlled oil reserves at generous rates to two prominent oil executives. Attorney General Harry Daugherty was investigated for possible wrongdoing in the divestiture of confiscated German assets but was never convicted. Although no crime was ever linked directly to Harding, the misdeeds of dishonest subordinates destroyed his reputation in the historical record.

Although personally discredited by the scandals, Harding's policies remained popular with the voters. His untimely death passed the mantle to Vice President Calvin Coolidge, who ran in 1924, pledging to continue the Harding policies. The rapid decline in interest concerning the scandals, the return of business prosperity, as well as the business mind-set of the nation led to an overwhelming Republican victory in that year. Coolidge's presidential bid was partly a referendum on the Harding presidency. "The election of 1924 was actually a repetition of 1920—it demonstrated a continued public desire for 'normalcy' (which in 1924 meant the Harding policies)."[61]

Looking beyond the scandals, the Harding administration is difficult to evaluate because many of its achievements were subtle and intangible. Unfortunately better remembered for the political scandals, Harding also left behind a business recovery that lasted through 1929. Rather than being a political nonentity, Harding actually set the political agenda for the rest of the decade. He was not an activist president, but the public and Congress did not support new activist programs during the decade. The Harding administration successfully contained the friction and the bitterness of the Wilson days and eased the transition to a prosperous peacetime existence. The period 1921 to 1923 was one of crisis and readjustment and Harding's stable leadership provided a bridge to the "Coolidge prosperity."

Having entered the presidency during a period of great economic and social turmoil, Harding guided the nation toward more domestic peace. A peacemaker by nature, he tried to solve problems by recruiting the "best minds" for his administration. He never abandoned his faith in limited government and free enterprise as the best way for America to progress, and the return of prosperity seemed to vindicate his philosophy of government. But just as the nation was finally settling down from the travails of the early 1920s, Harding was rocked by a series of scandals involving some of his closest associates. His presidency ended in turmoil, coming full cycle from the turbulence that marked its beginning.

3

The Triumph of Calvin Coolidge

LIKE HIS UNFORTUNATE PREDECESSOR, Calvin Coolidge embraced a strong pro-business philosophy that emphasized limits to governmental action, support for laissez-faire capitalism, and a return to the days of William McKinley, when government played only a small role in society. He presided over a more prosperous economy than did Warren Harding and remained a popular president throughout his nearly six years in office. He was a more astute judge of character and his administration was never tarnished by scandal. Ultimately, however, Coolidge also lost much of his good reputation when the economic depression broke out less than a year after he left the presidency, raising questions about his policies while in office.

Like Harding, Coolidge is better understood through his values and conservative philosophy than through a host of presidential actions. From both his childhood years in Vermont and his conservative, Puritan family background, he acquired a philosophy of human nature and the proper role of government from which he never deviated. In college, in his early political career, and later in the presidency, he exhibited a clear pattern of conservative thought, which was popular with the voters until the Great Depression led to a broad public reassessment of the proper role of government.

The Coolidge presidency did not produce achievements that are easy to measure. Apart from a limited program, he preferred the government to step aside and let the private sector (especially the business community) have its way. This type of presidency was extremely popular while the prosperity of the decade continued but fell out of favor after the start of the Great Depression. As president, Coolidge tried to restore calm to the nation after the turbulent Wilson years and the notoriety of the Harding scandals. To the public, he came to represent stability, unity, and harmony. He was usually described as intelligent, tough-minded, knowledgeable, and—amazingly in such a cynical profession—an idealist.[1] He was a good administrator and an astute judge of people, and his administration was free of scandal.

The conservative philosophy that dominated Coolidge's political career is partly attributable to his birth and upbringing in the small town of Plymouth Notch, in rural Vermont. Plymouth Notch was not a typical American city. It had no extremes of wealth, every man was reasonably educated, and it had escaped most of the typical social problems of that time.[2] Moreover, it retained a strong Puritan influence even in the late nineteenth century. Born on 4 July 1872, Coolidge's full name was John Calvin Coolidge, but to distinguish him from his father, who had the same name, he was called by his middle name. His father had worked at several jobs, including teaching and running a dry goods store, and provided a moderately comfortable living standard for his family. From his father, one of the leading citizens of the town and a lower-level political figure in the Republican Party, Calvin Coolidge inherited an interest in politics.

As a young man, Coolidge exhibited the same personality traits that often described him as president: unbelievably shy, cautious, quiet, and alert. He received a major shock at a young age when his mother died, and he commented afterward that "life was never the same for me again."[3] Coolidge was an intelligent young man, although he did not blossom as a student until he attended Amherst College. "A lot of people in Plymouth can't understand how I came to be President," he later declared.[4] Actually, he had a "strong mind and a lively set of brains," claimed the famous journalist William Allen White.[5]

One of the most important values of his later presidency, thriftiness, Coolidge learned from both his family and his home town. His family was of early Puritan stock and exhibited the Puritan traditions of thrift, frugality, and industry. His father's frugality was reinforced by local values: New England, where Coolidge grew up, was regarded as a "civilization based on thrift." Coolidge absorbed this value so completely that he was described as thrifty "with his words, his emotions, and his money."[6] Later, as president, he placed great emphasis on this Puritan quality when making decisions on spending public money.

Coolidge attended Amherst College, where he was an excellent student, ultimately graduating cum laude. While he was in college, Coolidge's professors reinforced his already conservative Puritan philosophy. Defending the Puritan idea of success through hard work, Coolidge declared that "people are entitled to the rewards of their industry. What they earn is theirs, no matter how small or how great."[7] This view of the sanctity of property later became a major theme throughout his presidency. At Amherst he also learned to cherish the works of one of the heroes of American capitalism, Alexander Hamilton, who became a personal icon to Coolidge. Although Coolidge never publicly advertised his scholarly qualities, he received an excellent education at Amherst, where he learned to read in French, German, Latin, Greek, and Italian. (Later his critics would declare that he could be silent in five different languages.)[8] He was able to read some of the classics in Greek and Italian, including Dante's *Inferno* in the original Italian. He also participated in a nationwide contest among college seniors to write an essay on the cause of the American Revolution; he was awarded first prize, but he was so modest that he did not tell his father until long afterward.[9]

Coolidge studied law after graduating from Amherst and soon became active in the local Republican Party. His career path was becoming clear to him, and in his new political activities he would be influenced by the Puritan values passed down by such luminaries as Jonathan Edwards, Cotton Mather, and John Calvin, as well as by the economic and political philosophy of Alexander Hamilton. Well read with a broad-based education, Coolidge clearly was a man of some ability. He was later described in a 1967 study as culturally the equal of Franklin Roosevelt and William Howard Taft and a more logical thinker than any twentieth-century president except Herbert Hoover and John F. Kennedy.[10]

Coolidge began his political career in late-nineteenth-century Northampton, Massachusetts, where politics was regarded as extremely honest for that time. The state, following the standard set down by such well-known figures as the Adams family and Senator Charles Sumner (of the Civil War period), had a higher standard in politics than did many other states of that era (especially the Ohio of Harding's time). Not surprisingly in such an environment, Coolidge developed a reputation for extreme honesty and integrity. He soon became the county chairman of the local Republican Party, and by the early 1900s he was regarded as a rising young figure within it. In his first attempt at elective office in 1906, the aspiring young politician was elected to the Massachusetts House of Representatives. A contemporary described him at the time by saying, "like a singed cat, he is better than he looks."[11] To bolster his income as he began his political career, Coolidge also served as vice president of his savings bank.

While only a newcomer to elective office, Coolidge already had deeply held positions on the role of government in the economy, on the proper place of workers and management, and on the importance of wealth. "What was of real importance to wage earners," he said, "was not how they might conduct a quarrel with their employers but how the business of the country might be organized as to ensure steady employment at a fair rate of pay." [12] He believed that a healthy business community was the key element in providing prosperity for the workers. Coolidge also expressed an early belief in a benevolent plutocracy. In line with his faith in a wise overlordship by the affluent, he believed that wealth was sacrosanct and expressed a reverence for the dignity of wealth. Government should play only a limited role and not attempt to make people wealthy or to help them advance in a capitalist society. He instinctively opposed widening the activities of government in ways that would transform it into the militant champion of the common man over business.[13] Even early in his career, the views that guided his economic policies as president were firmly established.

Coolidge's career advanced in 1912 when he was elected to the Massachusetts state senate. His rising power in the party was evidenced by his elevation to the presidency of that body in 1914. Described as a "scholarly conservative," he declined to accept any political favors involving money in order to keep his reputation untainted. Neither was Coolidge a fanatical ideologue. A loyal Republican and a consistent conservative, he would work with Democrats and progressives if doing so did not hurt the Republican Party or the vital interests of his conservative backers.

Coolidge's career moved upward again in the next few years, as he became lieutenant governor and then governor of Massachusetts. By this time a very clear picture of the rising politician had emerged, which would describe his later personality as president. He had learned when not to say too much in public, citing "the value of a silence which avoids creating a situation where one would not otherwise exist." [14] He was considered to be a poor orator but was thought to be sincere. A contemporary described him as "never hurried, never off his guard, never excited." [15] He was gathering valuable experience with each rung he climbed up the political ladder and was regarded as a shrewd politician with the ability to sense political trends and follow them.

Coolidge first became nationally known during the Boston police strike of 1919. In that strike-filled year, the Boston police force struck to gain approval for a union and for higher wages. Coolidge called out the National

Guard to help break the strike and later insured that the striking police would never be rehired. He regarded the police walkout not as a strike but as a desertion of duty and claimed that the policeman's role was not that of a laborer but of a defender of peace and order. The public in Boston feared a general strike, which had recently occurred in Seattle. Coolidge's strong stand against the strikers made him a hero and his oft-repeated comment that "there is no right to strike against the public safety by anyone, anywhere, anytime" won widespread approval with the public.[16] Even President Wilson sent congratulations "to the man who defied Bolshevism and won."[17]

Coolidge's role in the Boston police strike launched a brief presidential bid in 1920. His "dark horse" candidacy bore fruit when he was picked by the delegates at the Republican Convention to run for vice president with Warren G. Harding. His nomination was a surprise. The bosses actually favored another candidate for that office—Senator Irvine G. Lenroot of Wisconsin—but the delegates "revolted" and picked Coolidge instead.[18] Coolidge, who had not sought the vice presidential nomination, was victorious in the Harding landslide of 1920. A skilled politician from his many years in Massachusetts government, he now learned the "game" of national politics while serving as vice president. At Harding's insistence, he attended the regular cabinet meetings, although, in line with the traditional role of the vice presidency, he played no major role in the administration. While serving in his new post, the future chief executive was described by a contemporary as "an experienced politician of many years, possessing a definite political philosophy, [and] a shrewd judge of men."[19]

Coolidge was elevated politically once more in 1923, when Harding suddenly died. Coolidge was at his father's home in Vermont when he received the news that he had become the president. His father, a notary public, administered the oath in a scene that was widely publicized. Later he was sworn in again by a federal judge from Washington, D.C., when he was informed that the original swearing-in might not have been legal. From the outset, the Coolidge presidency was clearly going to be a nonactivist, pro-business administration. Before he had been president for five months, he declared in a public speech that "the chief business of the American people is business."[20]

It was immediately obvious that there were vast differences in style between former President Harding and his successor. As president, Coolidge was far less gregarious than Harding and he even tried to turn this silence into a political asset. He declared, "Four fifths of all of our troubles in this life would disappear if we would only sit down and keep still."[21] When running for president in 1924, he stated, "I don't recall any candidate . . . that ever injured himself very much by not talking."[22] Coolidge was silent when it served his ends, usually in public, but loquacious, even "gabby," in private gatherings. One associate claimed that Coolidge's hobby was "conversation," albeit in less public settings.[23]

On the substantial issues of the day, Coolidge essentially continued the Harding agenda. He had inherited a prosperous economy, and his principal aim as president was to help the economy keep expanding. A devout believer in pro-business policies, he clearly identified the welfare of business with the welfare of the nation. His presidential agenda was intended to foster business prosperity in as many ways as possible. He indicated his strong support for business in his oft-quoted comment, "Those who build a factory build a temple of worship. Those who work in a factory, worship there."[24] He also stressed the Puritan work and spending values for the country. "Work and save, save and work," he urged and he never thought that bad things would happen if people worked and saved.[25] Government was nonproductive and should not play a significant role in people's daily lives. Investment in government not only was sterile but also drained the productive force of the nation's capital, which was needed for full economic activity. Business alone could produce wealth and national well-being, he concluded.

Coolidge also promoted a limited role for the government because he believed the American political and social order was basically sound and worked best when left alone. He considered those who criticized or attempted to alter the political system misguided or even dangerous radicals. Private enterprise was the backbone of society and would lead Americans to economic independence, prosperity, social stability, and general individual development. In a society of individual enterprise, Coolidge believed the function of government was to act positively only in a crisis. Its role was not to run things but to help things run themselves. He did not have a crusading mentality, like former President Woodrow Wilson, believing instead that man had to claim his own rights and rewards. This idea of minimal government was clearly what the public wanted at the time and helps explain Coolidge's popularity during the 1920s.

Coolidge strongly opposed the progressive idea of direct democracy and active government. Direct democracy would lead to popular excesses and unsound financial legislation, resulting in "disorder and the dissolution of society." He opposed the progressive emphasis on regulatory commissions, whose bureaucracies he considered an abomination and an example of "destructive activism." Coolidge cynically defined a bureaucracy as an institution that "set up the pretense of having authority over everybody but being responsible to nobody." If the American people could not secure perfection in their own economic life, "it is altogether improbable that the government can secure it for them." [26]

Along with this minimal role for government, Coolidge favored a "free hand" for business. He believed in a business system unhindered by government regulations or legal obstructions, and in the free accumulation of wealth. "Business should be free," he said, "because the prosperity and the ethical and intellectual welfare of the whole nation depended upon its profitable operations." [27] The accumulation of wealth was important not only because it led to large payrolls but also because it was the chief support of science, art, learning, and charities. To facilitate a healthy business climate, the government should cut taxes on the rich, allowing them to properly invest the money. If business did something improper, it could correct its own abuses without government intervention. The government should not harass business and should provide no more regulation than absolutely necessary. Coolidge's pro-business philosophy fitted the popular mood of the 1920s, a time when the nation placed its faith in the businessman and the free-enterprise system while expressing apathy toward political action and rejecting society's "obligation" to the individual.

Coolidge implemented this policy of a limited role for the government from the outset of his presidency. He was slow to take antitrust action and determined to weaken the regulatory commissions. These policies were backed by the public, which wanted a rest from crusading government, and by a Congress that was as conservative as the president. Even for matters on which Coolidge favored action, his unaggressive attitude toward Congress worked against him. (He generally despised the members of Congress, calling them "timid" and "spoiled," and expected little from that body.)[28] His approach to legislation was similar to that of the nineteenth-century presidents, who would occasionally introduce bills but not challenge Congress when faced with opposition. This attitude was clearly shown by his unsuccessful attempt to reorganize the railroad industry into nineteen separate systems to improve service and solve their financial problems. The plan was rejected by Congress and Coolidge did not pursue it further.

One of Coolidge's earliest challenges as president was to deal with the scandals inherited from his predecessor. An excellent judge of personal character, he soon cleared out the unsavory members of the Harding administration. The most serious scandal, Teapot Dome (concerning bribery over the lease of government-controlled oil reserves), involved some of the highest-ranking officials in the administration. To clean up the oil scandal, Coolidge appointed Harlan Fiske Stone as attorney general and Owen Roberts as special counsel; both men distinguished themselves so well that eventually they wound up on the United States Supreme Court. Interior Secretary Albert Fall had already resigned and Navy Secretary Edwin Denby was soon asked to resign. Ultimately Fall was convicted of taking a bribe and became the first cabinet officer in history to be sent to jail. The "Ohio Gang," lower-level cronies of Harding from his home state, were also carefully weeded out. More troublesome was the removal of Attorney General Harry Daugherty, Harding's closest political adviser, who was linked to possible corruption in the sale of confiscated German assets. Reluctant to dismiss Daugherty because he had been so close to Harding, Coolidge finally asked for Daugherty's resignation when the former attorney general failed to completely clear his reputation. (Daugherty was never actually convicted of any crime.) So well did Coolidge clean up the Harding scandals that he was never linked to them himself and they did not become a problem for him in the 1924 elections.[29]

Coolidge kept in office a number of Harding's leading cabinet officials. Of these, Mellon and Hoover had the greatest influence domestically on his administration. Mellon was particularly influential: Coolidge regarded him as the "soul of the party." He was responsible for implementing many of Coolidge's business policies, especially regarding tax and budget matters, where he was given more support than he had found during the Harding administration. Hoover, not as close to Coolidge, continued as an aggressive advocate of expanding American business interests abroad. With the key members of the Harding team still on board, Coolidge was ready to implement much of the former president's agenda.

Coolidge was careful not to go beyond a limited number of initiatives because of his conservative political philosophy. Along with his views on the ill effects of an active government and the need to give business a free hand, Coolidge also emphasized that the Constitution put effective limits on the activities of the president and on government. He interpreted the Constitution literally in a way that limited the powers of government.[30] He addressed himself only to problems clearly provided for in the Constitution and by judicial interpretation of it. Believing that the Constitution did not authorize the president to deal with problems that belonged to other jurisdictions, he was a statesman of the late-nineteenth-century kind.

Working within this Constitutional framework, Coolidge made clear from the beginning that his would not be an activist presidency. "Don't hurry to legislate," he declared.[31] Instead, his highest priority was in promoting the prosperity of business. In a society of individual enterprise, he declared "the role of government was to act positively *only* if things went dramatically wrong." The president, he added, should not "speak, veto, or spend unless absolutely necessary."[32] The government should encourage business because it was the instrument most likely to lead America to economic independence, prosperity, social stability, and general individual development. Former President Taft agreed with Coolidge's nonactivist philosophy, stating that "the country was delighted to have a rest" and "with approaching and present prosperity the people wanted to be left alone."[33] Both Coolidge and Congress were receptive to this observation; between 1923 and 1929 the record of Congressional inaction was remarkable.

In his annual message to Congress in 1924, Coolidge laid out a blueprint of his future presidential policies. Declaring "our main problems are *domestic* problems," he especially emphasized the importance of tax reduction and frugality in government. His key recommendation was that Congress should cut the emergency wartime surtaxes and lower income taxes. He also backed a number of lower-priority measures, such as an antilynching measure to protect black people and a child-labor amendment to the Constitution to protect children. He supported aid such as medical benefits to veterans, but not a bonus. He backed limited aid to farmers through a tax reduction and support for farm cooperatives, but he opposed subsidies. Except for his tax measures, he had limited success in steering his agenda through Congress.[34]

The president's highest priority in 1924 was tax and debt reduction, a matter of controversy with some groups in Congress. In line with his Puritan upbringing, Coolidge believed that debt was almost sinful and should be retired as soon as possible. Federal taxes were too high and threatened the nation's prosperity. Congress, however, was reluctant to act on tax cuts at this time and cited several major objections to the president's proposal. Was it better to lower the national debt than to offer lower taxes to the rich? Were the tax cuts excessive and was it not better to try to lower the tariff instead in order to help Americans? Not until 1926 did Coolidge get his way on tax cuts.

Coolidge also failed in his attempt to sell Muscle Shoals to private investors. The sale of this government-built and operated nitrate-producing complex in northern Alabama had been discussed earlier during the Harding presidency, but no action had been taken largely because of opposition by Senator George Norris of Idaho, who saw an opportunity for government-owned utility and fertilizer operations in the region. When Norris unsuccessfully proposed the building of a government-owned fertilizer plant at Muscle Shoals, Coolidge opposed the project as "the opening wedge for socialism."[35]

Coolidge took a political risk in the election year of 1924, when he vetoed various measures intended to aid the nation's veterans. To make up for lost income during time served in World War I, Congress had agreed to establish a twenty-year paid-up insurance policy at a cost of $2 billion. At the end of this period (in 1945), the plan provided for a $1,000 bonus for the former servicemen. Coolidge's veto of this bill was overturned by Congress, an action that was in contrast to his successful veto of another bill that would have increased pensions for veterans of previous wars.[36] He opposed these measures as a drain on the treasury, and he felt a better way to help veterans was to cut taxes.

Coolidge was on the same side as Congress that year when it passed the Johnson Immigration Bill, tightening the quota system of 1921. Immigration restriction was popular with Congress and the public during the 1920s, partly as a result of the Red Scare of 1919–20. The temporary 1921 act passed during the Harding administration did not restrict immigration enough and was amended. In line with strong nativist sentiment in the United States, the new 1924 act sharply cut the annual quotas for Southern and Eastern European countries. One aspect of the new law opposed by both Coolidge and Secretary of State Mellon was the total ban on Asian immigration, a move sure to antagonize Japan. Ever reluctant to challenge Congress except in the most extreme cases, Coolidge signed the new immigration act anyway.

Coolidge began his campaign for a new term in 1924 at a time when domestic matters were going well. The business community was prosperous and the difficulties of the wheat farmer abated temporarily when a partial failure of the Canadian wheat crop raised wheat prices. To help on the trade front, more credit was extended to Europe to enable it to buy more American exports. The pieces were falling into place for the reelection of the president.

Just prior to the conventions, an issue potentially damaging to Coolidge had arisen concerning a new program of government aid to the farmer. The McNary-Haugen Bill proposed government purchases of eight surplus commodities at an average of prewar prices, which was above the current market price. The government would then sell the products abroad at whatever the market price. The farmers would pay a transaction fee on the products bought by the government but hoped the increases of farm prices at home would exceed the amount paid in the transaction fee. The program was defeated in Congress in 1924 but reappeared throughout the decade as the farmers' situation continued to worsen. Coolidge consistently opposed the McNary-Haugen Bill, both as a subsidy plan that could unbalance the budget, and as a violation of his laissez-faire economic philosophy. Was the program government-sanctioned price fixing, which would cause a fundamental change in American life? Was this a battle to redefine the role of government? Was the sturdy independent farmer about to become a ward of the government? This issue reappeared after the 1924 elections and became a continuing source of controversy during Coolidge's second term.

With the farm debate temporarily defused and the economy booming, Coolidge was able to dispose of his Republican rivals for the nomination rather easily. His main concern at the convention was to choose a suitable running mate. Coolidge offered the second spot to Senator William Borah, a much-respected progressive whom the president personally liked and who had similar views on economy in government. When Borah refused, Governor Frank Lowden of Illinois was chosen by the delegates to run for vice president but declined. (Lowden's refusal to accept the nomination after being chosen by the convention was the first time this had happened since 1844.)[37] The convention then chose Chicago banker and former budget director Charles G. Dawes to run with Coolidge.

Coolidge's reelection bid was aided immensely by the bitter divisions in the Democratic Party. Al Smith, governor of New York, and William McAdoo, treasury secretary under Wilson (and his former son-in-law), engaged in a seemingly never-ending contest for the nomination. Smith represented the eastern, urban, and non-Old Stock wing of the party. He was trying to become the first Catholic to run for president representing a major party, a matter of controversy in the nativist, intolerant era of the 1920s. McAdoo represented the party's rural, southern and western wing, as well as its more traditional elements. The two engaged in a ten-day, 103-ballot contest, and ultimately the party turned to a third candidate, John B. Davis, who was a conservative Wall Street lawyer. To balance the ticket, the Democrats picked Nebraska Governor Charles W. Bryan, the brother of the former three-time presidential nominee William Jennings Bryan. The party was already so bitterly divided that it had seemingly committed political suicide even before the election took place.

The choice of Davis proved to be particularly unfortunate for the Democrats. A preeminent lawyer representing J. P. Morgan and Company, he could not attack Coolidge as a representative of big business. In his address before the convention, Davis stated, "The keynote of all Democratic policies should be to keep the road open for private enterprise and personal initiative," a position surprisingly similar to that of Coolidge.[38] Furthermore, Davis was a political unknown and had no support from the farmers, a group Coolidge had partly alienated by his veto of the farm-relief bill and for whose votes he had seemingly left an opening for his Democratic rival.

Along with the weaknesses of their candidate, the Democrats were also badly divided on a number of controversial issues. Unlike the Republicans, who were able to finesse the Ku Klux Klan and Prohibition issues, the Democrats were split on these and other topics. The party was especially at odds over a motion to condemn the Klan and, partly because of the influence of William Jennings Bryan, refused to take a stand. Delegates from the eastern states were generally of immigrant or Catholic background while many of the delegates from the southern and western states were either Klan members or represented states where the Klan was particularly strong. The Democrats were also split over the League of Nations, Prohibition, and the "Catholic" question, putting the party in a hopeless position for the 1924 campaign.

To counterbalance the two conservatives running on the major parties, Senator Robert LaFollette of Wisconsin was nominated as the candidate of the Committee for Progressive Political Action, which represented a coalition of progressives, farmers, unions, and radicals. (LaFollette had opposed creating a full-scale permanent progressive party, concerned this might hurt progressive candidates running on the two major parties.) LaFollette was a progressive Republican and a well-known reformer going back to the Theodore Roosevelt era. He pledged to "destroy the power of business monopoly over the political and economic life of the American people." He attacked "the control of government and industry by private monopoly" and pledged more action through the antitrust laws. He further promised to end the use of injunctions in labor disputes and guaranteed the workers' rights to collective bargaining.[39] Because LaFollette was the only progressive in the race, it is not surprising that Davis and Coolidge spent more time attacking him than each other. Coolidge was particularly harsh on LaFollette, calling him a dangerous radical who would turn America into a "communistic or socialistic state."[40]

The progressive movement of 1924 was much weaker than its earlier counterpart of 1912 and the fears that it would divide the Republican vote as Theodore Roosevelt had done in his earlier progressive candidacy proved to be unfounded. Senator LaFollette had far less appeal to the voters than Roosevelt had twelve years earlier, partly because of personality differences between the two progressives and partly because the country was much more conservative in 1924. LaFollette's political appeal was also lessened, particularly among the urban masses, by his appearing to especially represent the rural areas rather than focusing on the problems of the cities.

Many factors combined to make Coolidge's position impregnable in 1924. He was aided by the prosperous economy and his obvious good character. Coolidge had not been blamed for the scandals, which he had dealt with very skillfully. His two rivals in the 1924 elections had failed to generate much enthusiasm from the voters. The business sentiment in the country was strongly for him, believing "it [still] needed to be left alone to recover from the war strains and governmental interference in business."[41] To protect his strong position, Coolidge shrewdly adopted the strategy of speaking as little as possible without giving offense. (His more boisterous supporters argued that the choice to the voters was "Coolidge or chaos" and urged the country to "Keep cool with Coolidge.")[42] The general feeling was that Coolidge had no desire for any reforms and both the public and business community did not want them either.

One of Coolidge's greatest assets in the campaign was his strong personal qualities. Believing in his honesty and small-town philosophy, the public rallied around the Coolidge candidacy. George Harvey (a leading Republican) said that Calvin Coolidge would be elected or rejected by the people "not for what he has done, but for what he is."[43] A leading scholar of the period added that "after the ups and downs of the Wilson and Harding administrations, most Americans were ready to settle for the genius of the average." [44] Coolidge's calm, inactive approach resonated well with the voters. "For a nation that was tired of having the ship of state rocked, Coolidge was a reassuring skipper." [45]

Coolidge's victory was a foregone conclusion, considering both the prosperity of the times and his strong personal appeal. Most Americans felt secure with Coolidge as president and one observer noted, "He inspires a deep, nationwide confidence that all will go well with the country while he is in the White House." [46] By running a "me-too" campaign in nominating a conservative, the Democrats gave the voters no reason to change from the conservative Coolidge, and the president's victory was assured. On election day, Coolidge received more votes than Davis and LaFollette combined.

His stature having grown markedly since assuming the presidency in mid-1923, Coolidge began his second term amid an economic boom now in full swing. His Republican Party, with overwhelming majorities in both houses of Congress, was dominated by "regulars" and businessmen, although there was a small, vocal, progressive bloc that continued to agitate for more aid to farmers. With the remainder of his presidency to be focused on tax cuts and preventing the passage of the McNary-Haugen farm-relief program, Coolidge appeared to have the necessary support in Congress. In his annual message to Congress in 1925, Coolidge spelled out the agenda for his second term. He particularly stressed the need for economy in government and tax reduction. "The government can do more to remedy the economic ills of the people by rapid economy in public expenditures than by anything else," he asserted. [47] Regarding agriculture, he favored only limited government activity and strongly opposed price fixing. On the still-unresolved Muscle Shoals issue, he favored selling the property only if the new owner would produce nitrogen for fertilizer. By the end of his presidency, Coolidge achieved the most important parts of his agenda: passage of the Mellen tax cuts and defeat of the McNary-Haugen Bill.

One of Coolidge's objectives that was easily implemented was the transformation of the regulatory commissions. He picked people who opposed a strong federal policy, best exemplified by an appointee who proclaimed that the Federal Trade Commission had been a "publicity bureau to spread Socialist propaganda." [48] Coolidge (and his predecessor Harding) changed the function of the regulatory commission from regulating business abuses to encouraging business freedom. The progressive Senator George Norris claimed that this new policy of choosing commissioners amounted to an indirect repeal of the regulatory legislation.[49] Coolidge generally succeeded in pulling in line the regulatory agencies, and they hardly performed their duties during his administration.

Coolidge's policy toward antitrust action indicated a similar pro-business bias. The government had a mediocre record in winning antitrust cases, and low penalties were imposed when the government was successful. In the case of Alcoa Corporation, the Coolidge administration demonstrated both a friendly attitude toward business and loyalty to Treasury Secretary Mellon, who was a major shareholder. When Attorney General Harlan Fiske Stone was getting too aggressive in investigating Alcoa for possible antitrust violations, Coolidge elevated him to the Supreme Court and replaced him with a more pliable cabinet officer. In an unusual development, his first choice was rejected by the Senate as being too much a tool of business and became the first nominee to be rejected for the cabinet since 1868.[50] Not surprisingly, given all his support for business, Coolidge was regarded by the business community as the "ideal" president.[51]

In 1926, Congress passed the Revenue Act and gave the Coolidge administration its greatest legislative victory. Under this comprehensive tax law, people at all income levels received benefits. The gift tax was repealed and estate taxes were cut in half, with a maximum rate set at 20 percent. The inheritance tax was reduced and the surtax on high incomes was cut substantially, the maximum rate being lowered from 50 percent to 20 percent. The biggest tax cuts were given to those with incomes of more than $100,000. Treasury Secretary Mellon unofficially increased the extent of the tax cuts by initiating cash refunds, credits, and abatements to wealthy individuals and corporations that amounted to $3.5 billion by the end of the decade.[52] The benefits were not only for the wealthy, because 70 percent of income taxes in 1927 still came from those earning more than $50,000. Americans with incomes of less than $3,000 paid less than 1 percent of the total income taxes. A married person with an income of $7,500 (a very substantial sum) paid only $70 in federal income taxes under the new law. The overall effect of the new tax policy was to excuse approximately 98 percent of the population from paying any federal income tax at all.[53] Because three-quarters of 1 percent of the population paid 94 percent of the tax, Mellon claimed that the income tax had become a class rather than a national tax.[54]

Coolidge had no comprehensive solution to the most pressing economic problem of the period, the plight of the farmer. By the mid-1920s, farmers came to rely upon the McNary-Haugen Bill as the best remedy for low farm prices. Coolidge vetoed this bill in 1927 and 1928 and instead favored a more modest solution. He encouraged farm cooperatives to market products, and he pushed for more government credit even though this did not meet the farmers' most pressing need for higher prices. Coolidge defended his limited efforts by contending that the farmer should act like a businessman and not be a burden to the taxpayer. He was strongly against the price fixing and subsidy features of the McNary-Haugen Bill, fearing that foreign retaliation and a great expansion of agricultural products domestically would follow passage of the bill.

Coolidge was not optimistic about any overall economic solution to the agricultural crisis. He declared that "farmers never have made money [and] I don't believe one can do much about it. . . . The life of the farmer has its compensations but it has always been one of hardship." [55] The president preferred to help the farmer by lending money to cooperatives, which he hoped would voluntarily curtail production, but he opposed more extensive aid as a violation of his laissez-faire philosophy. To implement his farm program, Coolidge favored the Curtis-Crisp Bill, which provided low-interest loans to farm cooperatives with controls on production and would create a Federal Farm Board with $250 million to loan to cooperatives to keep nonperishables off the market when surplus production threatened to depress prices. In spite of the president's support, the Curtis-Crisp Bill was defeated in Congress.

Ultimately Coolidge felt that the best way to help all segments of the economy was to continue his pro-business policies, which he believed would bolster the economic expansion. He stressed minimal interference with business, as well as no significant intervention to help farmers or workers. Expanding business was crucial because this would help everyone. Not a more active government but frugality in government, elimination of every kind of waste, and a general raising of the standards of efficiency were the keys to a healthy economy, he believed. In the last two years of his presidency, Coolidge pursued policies aimed at continuing the expansion—policies that would later be questioned when the stock market crashed soon after he left office.

By 1927, the problem of overspeculation and extension of credit in the economy was becoming a source of concern and raised the possibility of intervention by the Federal Reserve System. The government had an obvious stake here since the vast installment buying of securities created stock market profits, which the federal government taxed to reduce its debt. On at least two occasions in 1927 when the Federal Reserve System was inclined to contract credit by raising the rediscount rate, Coolidge and Mellon successfully opposed it. The credit supply remained cheap and plentiful, feeding the expansionist and speculative boom. The president stated that 1927 would be a year of "continued healthy business activity and prosperity," while Secretary Mellon added that "the market is not yet overextended." [56] Such reassuring comments by Coolidge and Mellon bolstered the stock market, which then climbed even higher. Coolidge also rejected a federal role in overseeing the stock market, stating that regulating the New York Stock Exchange was New York's business and not a responsibility of the federal government.[57] Without a substantial tightening of credit by the Federal Reserve System, an absence of caution by administration leaders, and no federal effort to check for improper practices in the sale of stocks, the bull market steadily advanced. So strong was the pro-business sentiment at that time that, even if Coolidge had wished to change the course of the economy, he would have faced formidable obstacles from Congress and the public.

The booming stock market and the prosperous economy (except for agriculture) led to great popularity for Coolidge and made another term as president seem likely. However, in the summer of 1927 while on vacation in the Black Hills of South Dakota, Coolidge shocked the nation by declaring, "I do not choose to run for President in 1928." [58] At first some believed that he would accept a draft while not actively seeking the nomination, but soon the realization set in that Coolidge would step aside in 1928. The secretive Coolidge had not even told his wife before he made his decision public. Some of the reasons believed to be behind his retirement were the death in 1924 of his son (for whom he was still grieving), frustration with fighting Congress, personal health reasons, fears over possible future problems in the economy, and perhaps exhaustion with the job. Coolidge personally explained that he did not want to be in office too long. He stated, "It's four years ago since I became President. If I take another term, I will be in the White House till 1933. [I feel that] ten years in Washington is longer than any other man has had it— too long." [59]

Wall Street was among the sectors disappointed with the president's decision to retire. It liked both his political philosophy regarding organized wealth and attaining money and his policies of "masterly inaction," and it felt he was the symbol of business prosperity. Three days after Coolidge's withdrawal, the *Financial Chronicle* wrote, "However much or little Mr. Coolidge individually may have had to do with the prosperity of the past four years, he is credited with having been the backbone of that prosperity." [60]

Coolidge's decision to step aside allowed Herbert Hoover to become the Republican nominee for president in 1928 and the new titular head of the party. Coolidge was not enthusiastic about his former commerce secretary's nomination, saying, "That man has offered me unsolicited advice for six years, all of it bad." [61] Much of this advice, in contrast to that of Treasury Secretary Mellon, had been to curb the stock market speculation. In the 1928 race, Coolidge played a minimal role in Hoover's victory and campaigned very little for his successor. He did not criticize Al Smith, the Democratic candidate, and rarely praised Hoover. In Coolidge's limited role in the campaign, "he backed Hoover with just enough to satisfy the amenities." [62] Whatever Hoover's differences with Coolidge, the Republican victory of 1928 was regarded as an endorsement of the Coolidge philosophy of government, which stressed conservatism and the primacy of business leadership. It also endorsed the idea that the function of government was to promote business health as the best means of fostering national well-being.

Coolidge retired in early 1929, still a popular leader. His pro-business policies had coincided with six years of business expansion and he had restored public confidence in the presidency. His was a reassuring presence while in office. "In a nation of bustling chaotic cities, he symbolized the traditional order of the New England village [and] to a nation rocked by scandals, he symbolized honesty." [63] He was a good administrator and kept his presidency free from scandal. As a humanitarian gesture, he had released the remaining political prisoners of the World War I era. His most esteemed accomplishment was holding down appropriations and applying the resultant surplus to reducing taxes and paring down the national debt. During the Coolidge years, the national debt was reduced from $22.3 billion to $16.9 billion. Government spending was kept in check to such an extent that the federal budget in 1929 was almost identical to that of 1923. [64] Rising levels of income and stock prices, which were labeled features of the "Coolidge prosperity," proved to him that his financial policy was a success.

However, Coolidge's laissez-faire theory of government insured that he would not aggressively attack the major economic and social problems of the 1920s. He failed to act on the problems that eventually led to the Great Depression, trusting instead in the marketplace to provide a remedy. At a time of great intolerance in the nation, he offered weak support for antilynching laws, ignored pressure for desegregation in the civil service, and refused to directly attack the Ku Klux Klan (preferring to wait for it to burn itself out). For the struggling farmers, he offered only limited solutions. Other than his tax cut measures, Coolidge was unwilling to recommend to Congress any major legislation of a positive stamp, a reluctance that, coupled with his vetoes of congressional acts, led to the smallest crop of important legislation since the nineteenth century.

Coolidge's administration was more successful in the short run than in the long term. He was called "the most widely admired political figure since Theodore Roosevelt at his peak. . . . People of every age, class, and region considered him a splendid President." [65] Yet, there was no great achievement with which posterity could identify Coolidge alone. His most notable accomplishments—debt reduction and tax cutting—were questioned with the coming of the Great Depression. He held to the Hamiltonian faith that the rich are indeed the "wise and good," and identified wealth with brains. His ideas were shared by the public and remained popular while he was in office and the business expansion continued. However, he lacked special insight into the coming financial collapse and the growing, unresolved problems in the economy would plague his successor.

Judged by the principal goals Coolidge set for his presidency, his administration was a triumph. The core of his philosophy was tax cuts and opposition to meaningful government assistance to farmers. He believed that lower taxes and reduced government spending would result in a freer, more democratic society. He hoped to return the country to a version of what it had been before passage of the Income Tax Amendment, a time of small and primarily local government. His opposition to the McNary-Haugen Bill was also a core element of his political and economic philosophy. He believed the bill marked a radical change in the relationship between government and the people and was even more threatening to freedom than the existing tax structure. By the end of his administration, the Mellon tax cuts and his successful vetoes of the McNary-Haugen Bill had preserved his vision for the future direction of the nation.

Coolidge had won the confidence of the public by the time he left office, and his political philosophy had triumphed. Walter Lippmann, one of the leading political pundits of the 1920s, commented, "the people like him, not only because they like the present prosperity, and because at the moment they like political do-nothingism but [also] because they trust and like the plain-ness and nearness of Calvin Coolidge himself." [66] Lippmann noted that the public was not discouraged by the paucity of important legislation during the Coolidge years. "Surely no one will write of these years since August 1923 that an aggressive president altered the destiny of the Republic. Yet it is an im-portant fact that no one will write of these same years that the Republic wished its destiny to be altered." [67]

4

The Search for World Peace and Stability in the Twenties

THE UNITED STATES'S APPROACH to foreign policy in the 1920s was largely determined by its disappointment with the events that followed World War I. For all the talk about "making the world safe for democracy" and creating a new world order, the progress of the Paris peace conference was sadly disillusioning. Old-world political rivalries and jealousies resurfaced, and Americans wondered what actually had been the true purpose of the war. The reluctance of the Allies to repay billions of dollars in loans to the United States reinforced an already growing mood in the United States to avoid future entanglements in Europe. While the United States was anxious to expand economic and cultural ties with Europe, it clearly was equally anxious to avoid any possible future military engagements.

As in its domestic policy, the United States took a turn toward "normalcy" in its foreign policy after the war. The Republican victories in the elections of 1918 and 1920 indicated that Americans preferred a more traditional, less involved foreign policy. However, there was not a total rejection of overseas involvement during the decade. The new policy was described as "involvement without commitment" and "a desire to avoid all old world political entanglements."[1] Within these guidelines, American foreign policy was actually quite involved during the decade, described by Senator Henry Cabot Lodge in 1924 as "a period when the United States as never before has been more active and its influence more felt internationally."[2]

During the 1920s, "noncommitment" rather than "isolationism" described American foreign policy. The United States was very much involved in the quandary surrounding European debts and reparations. The United

States took the initiative in bringing about an agreement of the major powers on naval strength and stabilized—temporarily—the power balance in Asia. It continued to exert great influence on the affairs of Latin America. As the decade progressed, American involvement with the League of Nations increased steadily, especially regarding activities in that body's various committees. In an attempt to prevent war, the United States championed the ill-fated Kellogg-Briand Pact. It also explored various programs to keep China from being exploited by the great powers. Surrounding all these moves by the United States was a firm resolve against any diplomatic commitments and a reluctance to accept international responsibility. The United States was isolationist only in the sense that it refused to participate in any international association of nations for the purpose of collective security. Because of the post-World War I atmosphere in the United States, American foreign policy in the 1920s refused to link foreign policy initiatives with political commitments.

One of the most striking developments in world affairs after World War I was America's great strength relative to other powers, a dominance that existed for the first time in history. Because of its unilateral disarmament policy after World War I, the United States was not the world's greatest military power during the decade, although it was about on a par with the world's great naval powers. However, because of changes brought on by the war, it now possessed the world's most powerful economy. As late as 1914, foreign investments in the United States totaled about $3 billion more than American investments abroad. By the end of the war, the United States had a $3 billion surplus investment in Europe, which grew to more than $8 billion by 1929. (This investment was separate from the approximately $10 billion in war debts that Europe owed the United States.) America had changed from a debtor to a creditor nation. By the end of World War I, the United States produced more goods and services than did any other nation, not only in total but also per capita, and was the richest nation in the world. By 1920 the national income in the United States was greater than the combined national income of Great Britain, France, Germany, Japan, Canada, and seventeen small countries.[3] Its economic position in the world had become so dominant that "perhaps the gap between the wealth of the United States and the wealth of the next richest country was greater in the 1920s than the difference in economic power between the world's two richest nations since the Middle Ages."[4] The United States had become too economically powerful to be uninvolved with the rest of the world.

After World War I, a consensus developed in America that would describe its foreign policy throughout the decade. The public agreed on the need to expand American business abroad and to preserve international peace and stability but showed only slight concern over the actual details of foreign policy. After the bitter fight over the League of Nations between 1919 and 1920, the public took little interest in foreign affairs until the rise of the Nazis in Germany and the expansion of Japan in the 1930s. President Warren G. Harding accurately grasped the political feeling of the American people and Congress when he officially kept aloof from many of the problems of Europe and the world. Unlike former President Woodrow Wilson, Harding clearly was a president who tied his foreign policy goals to political realities at home.[5]

Faced with a public that shunned overseas commitments, together with the United States's new powerful status in the world, Harding and Secretary of State Charles Evans Hughes were guided by pragmatism in their foreign policy. Harding supported an "America—First" program at home to make the United States more economically self-sufficient but he also wished to encourage a proper role in foreign affairs. Unlike his Democratic predecessor, he emphasized a greater reality in American foreign policy by talking more about the nation's legitimate national interests than about universal humanitarian ideals. This approach set a pattern in foreign policy that would persist through the Coolidge and Hoover administrations.

After World War I, the Senate and public opinion emerged as major obstacles to an activist foreign policy such as that envisioned by former President Wilson, who had sought a greater American role in the world. Long suppressed by Wilson, the Senate was in revolt against any form of "executive tyranny" and this situation cast definite limits on any presidential foreign policy initiatives. Public opinion also acted as a brake on diplomatic initiatives. Most people were apathetic, seeing no obvious foreign security problem and wishing to enjoy the good life.[6] They clearly desired to maintain the traditional inactive type of foreign policy and avoid involvement in all but the most pressing foreign policy issues. Should the various Republican presidents attempt to stray too far from their own nonactivist foreign policy philosophies, they would have to deal with the apathy of the public and the hostility of Congress.

The debate over the League of Nations exemplified this conflict between the nation's new importance in the world and its desire to avoid foreign obligations. After World War I, American public opinion turned inward, stressing "old-fashioned values" and the belief that the United States had "earned the right to be left alone." Former President Woodrow Wilson had not convinced the public that United States security was tied to a new international role for the country. Critics feared that the League of Nations would destroy the Monroe Doctrine, long a mainstay of American foreign policy. Would the League open the door to European involvement in Latin America and foster the rise of a new version of the "Holy Alliance" (a European consortium of the post-Napoleonic era that asserted the right to intervene in foreign nations)?[7]

The most telling point of the anti-internationalists was the fear that Article X of the League Covenant would engage the United States in future wars. This provision declared that member states were obliged "to respect and preserve against external aggression the territorial and existing political independence" of all signatories to the Covenant. Article X and the League itself were supported by President Wilson as a means of avoiding future wars and became major issues in the election of 1920. In a nation already reluctant to become heavily involved with overseas commitments, the League issue strongly divided the political spectrum.

This volatile debate on foreign policy forced Republican nominee Harding to stake out his positions very carefully during the campaign. Under great pressure from both wings of the Republican Party, Harding was deliberately vague about his true feelings on the League. To placate the anti-League segment, he admitted that he had reluctantly voted for the treaty with reservations (including the one to omit Article X) and stated that he was no longer in favor of joining the League.[8] The Republican internationalists, hoping that Harding would turn to their side, stressed that his election would make possible a revision of the League Covenant that would satisfy the American people. Harding encouraged this sentiment by proclaiming his support for some sort of "association of nations," although not Wilson's version of a strong League. He shrewdly collected votes from both sides of the debate, only revealing his true feelings after the election. Once installed in office, Harding announced that he believed the League of Nations was as "dead as slavery."[9]

Although it was unclear whether Harding's victory was a total or even a limited mandate against the League, a number of postelection developments insured that the United States would never join. Isolationist sentiment had mounted so rapidly by the spring of 1921 that Harding, even had he so desired, could not have secured senate consent for the treaty.[10] Throughout the 1920s, the most important roadblocks to U.S. membership in the League remained both public opinion and the Senate. Harding was unwilling to take up the cause for the League, declaring two days after the election that his victory symbolized that Americans had voted down the League. He promised that his administration would oppose membership in the League of Nations and would accept no overseas responsibility "except as our own conscience and judgment in each instance may determine." [11]

Harding's postelection comments reflected the caution he sensed in the public's mind. The United States would pursue such goals as world disarmament and peace but Harding stressed that the emphasis would be on national sovereignty rather than on world "super-government," something that was contrary to American traditions.[12] These sentiments won broad acceptance, and membership in the League was not strongly urged by either party after 1920. Democrats as well as Republicans became convinced that the voters had overwhelmingly rejected the League and that reviving the issue could lead to political disaster. Although Harding had hedged on the issue in 1920, the general consensus was that the voters had said "no" to the League.[13]

Having rejected the Treaty of Versailles, which included the League of Nations, the Harding administration faced the immediate problem of legally ending American involvement in World War I. Wilson, perhaps hoping that a Democratic victory in 1920 would lead the United States to agree to the Treaty of Versailles, had vetoed a joint resolution ending the war. This resolution tried to acquire for the United States all of the privileges but none of the responsibilities accruing to the victors in the war. In July 1921, with approval from the new Harding administration, a similar joint resolution was passed, declaring the war at an end. The United States then signed a treaty with Germany that reserved all rights granted the United States under the Treaty of Versailles.

With the war now officially over, the United States found itself confronted with a new set of challenges in Europe, Asia, and Latin America. American relations with the League of Nations were unclear and a ruinous naval race endangered peace in the Pacific arena between the United States and Japan. A similarly uncertain climate existed in Europe, where a new European conflict threatened to erupt from the bitterness engendered by disagreement over reparations and war debts. Meanwhile, to the south, maturing Latin American states were growing restive under the paternalistic American interpretation of the Monroe Doctrine.

Harding's secretary of state, Charles Evans Hughes, was guided by the principle of "achieving the possible" and unlike Wilson made no attempt to

remake the world at the risk of failure. Hughes had no interest in collective security mechanisms such as Article X of the League Charter, preferring instead
to achieve security with a minimum of commitment. He believed that the
American people and the Senate would reject military means to promote
peace and would refuse blanket commitments to deal with overseas crises.
Originally in favor of the League with reservations, Hughes decided against
membership; unlike former President Wilson, he was not willing to become a
martyr for the League.[14]

Having initially spurned the League, the United States gradually altered
its position to one of increasing cooperation with that body. The United
States originally feared that the League would develop into a "super-
government," primarily involving the nation in unwanted obligations. In May
1921, the ambassador to England, George Harvey, declared that the United
States would not "have anything to do with the League or with any commission or committee supported by it or responsible to it, directly or indirectly,
openly or furtively."[15] This philosophy soon was rejected by the United
States, and Secretary Hughes became the chief architect of a new, more active,
position. Having given up on his original hope that the United States would
join the League with reservations, he now stressed a policy of cooperation
without commitment. Under Hughes, the United States became an "unofficial observer" of the League, with its agents serving on several committees as
representatives of the United States but not as "official members."

This new relationship with the League reflected the view that the international organization played a useful role in solving European problems and that
the United States could become involved without entanglements, a position
that was politically acceptable to all but the most extreme elements in the Republican Party. The United States practiced "peephole" or "keyhole" diplomacy, wherein it sent observers to nonpolitical conferences sponsored by the
League. Gradually its role escalated from observer to participant on the
League's major committees. By 1922, American observers took part in de-
bates concerning League business but did not vote. By the middle of the
Hoover administration, the United States had five "unofficial observers" in
Geneva and had participated in forty League conferences.[16]

After rejecting membership in the League, the United States explored the
possibility of joining the World Court as another approach to peace. Also
known as the Permanent Court of International Justice, the World Court had
been established to supplement League machinery on supporting the postwar

international order. The World Court exemplified the Harding administration's attempt to establish a more direct relationship with Europe and the rest of the world during the early 1920s. Was this the "association of nations" that he referred to in the campaign of 1920? Harding claimed the United States could join the World Court and also be "wholly free from any legal relations to the League." [17]

During the 1920s, there were repeated unsuccessful American efforts to join the Court. Early in 1923, Hughes drew up some reservations that would preserve the United States' policy of noninvolvement in the League while allowing American membership in the Court. (The Court was separate from, not an agency of, the League.) In February, Harding urged U.S. membership on the Court but withdrew his support upon objections from Senator William Borah, a powerful member of the Senate Foreign Relations Committee. In the next few years, momentum built toward U.S. membership but ultimately all efforts failed. In 1924, both major parties endorsed in their platforms joining the World Court. Early in 1925, Coolidge urged membership on the Court but he backed down in the face of opposition from the Senate. That same year, the House of Representatives passed a resolution favoring American membership and the Senate followed suit in 1926. The issue was finally voted down years later in 1930 and again in 1935, when the Senate failed to rally the two-thirds majority required to ratify membership in the World Court, largely because of pressure created by the Hearst press.[18]

Unwilling to join the World Court or to make a total commitment to the League of Nations, the United States found another venue for pursuing peace: arms-limitation agreements, beginning with the Washington Arms Conference of 1921–22. Most Americans were concerned about the possibility of a naval arms race, which might lead to war or keep federal spending at a high level. Initiated by Senator Borah, one of the most bitter "irreconcilable" in opposition to the League, the administration called nine nations to Washington to discuss naval limitation and other issues pertaining to peace.

The pressures behind the convening of the Washington Conference came from several sources. Many senators and newspaper editors strongly backed the conference because the United States was already disarming and this action would force others to follow a similar policy. They did not wish a naval race against the combined British-Japanese fleets (somewhat bound by a naval alliance dating back to 1902), and an arms agreement was the only alternative to an American attempt to match the combined strength of these two naval

powers. The Senate was anxious to cut naval spending and the arms conference would maintain America's relative naval strength. On the eve of the conference, the United States decided on at least two major goals from the
conference: parity with the British navy and breaking the Anglo-Japanese alliance. Bearing in mind the bitter debate over joining the League of Nations,
Hughes consulted with the Senate as the conference began and all the treaties
were drafted with the wishes and prejudices of the Senate in mind. Hughes
did not wish to repeat Wilson's error of antagonizing that body by refusing
any contact while he negotiated the Treaty of Versailles.[19]

The Washington Conference, lasting from 12 November 1921 through 6
February 1922, was one of the most determined efforts of the decade to preserve peace. Nine countries from Europe, Asia, and North America participated (the United States, England, Japan, France, Italy, China, Holland,
Portugal, and Belgium), with the major roles being played by the three
leading naval powers (the United States, England, and Japan). These three
nations were guided by a desire to balance security interests while simultaneously limiting their enormous defense budgets.[20]

The most dramatic moment of the conference came in the introductory
speech of Secretary of State Charles Evans Hughes. Expected to make the
usual perfunctory address, he instead got to business immediately. "The way
to disarm is to disarm," he declared as he outlined his plan to limit the size of
the navies of the five major sea powers (the United States, Great Britain,
Japan, France, and Italy).[21] In the Five Power Pact, a ratio of 5:5:3:1.75:1.75
would limit the total amount of tonnage for capital ships (battleships and
heavy cruisers). The absolute numbers of tons would be approximately
500,000, 500,000, 300,000, 175,000, and 175,000 tons. Hughes announced that many ships would have to be scrapped, some already in existence and others still under construction or on the drawing board. So
extensive were the limitations that a British observer noted, "Hughes has sunk
in thirty-five minutes more ships than all the admirals in the world have sunk
in a cycle of centuries."[22]

Rather than just listing goals, Hughes laid out the specific terms of naval
limitation. A ten-year holiday on building capital ships, accompanied by the
elimination of such ships already built or less than 85 percent completed,
would reduce the levels of naval strength to an acceptable point. To reach the
suggested ratios between nations, the United States would have to sacrifice
approximately 815,000 tons to 583,000 for England and 448,000 for Japan.

Hughes's initial hope of obtaining limitations on all categories of naval vessels was unrealized because submarines and destroyers were exempted.

Skillful diplomacy was required to overcome objections from the other leading naval powers. England was being asked to surrender its centuries-old policy of keeping her navy at least twice as large as that of her nearest rival. But this policy was proving to be expensive and England was anxious to cut government spending. Burdened by debt, England had no desire for a new naval arms race and in early 1921 declared that it was willing to concede naval parity to the United States.[23]

Getting the Japanese to accept the "3" proved more difficult. The United States and England argued that their interests were worldwide and their navies would have to be spread over vast areas. Japanese interests, however, were exclusively in the Pacific area and would match the strength of the United States and England in this region. When Japan remained recalcitrant, the United States and England agreed not to strengthen their forces in the Philippines, Guam, Hong Kong, and other colonial areas under their control. Despite the smaller naval ratio, the conference actually "awarded" naval supremacy in the western Pacific to Japan.[24]

The Five Power Pact was only a partial solution to the problem of naval rivalries. The agreement did not cover all types of ships. Partly because of French opposition, no limitations were made on lighter ships, a decision that ultimately led to a new race in light cruisers, destroyers, and submarines during the decade. The American public, more hopeful than realistic, accepted the Five Power Pact as a substitute for the irksome necessity of naval expansion.[25]

The Four Power Pact, also negotiated at the conference, dealt with the possessions of four colonial powers in Asia (the United States, Great Britain, Japan, and France). This agreement pledged these powers to respect each other's possessions in the Pacific region. The signatories also agreed not to disturb the territorial status quo in Asia. Because Japan was regarded as the major threat in the region, the agreement was mainly designed to contain this expansionist power in Asia. There was no enforcement mechanism, however, and the Western nations hoped that appealing to honor and morality without commitment of any kind would prevent aggression.

The Four Power Pact also enabled England to solve the awkward problem of terminating its 1902 alliance with Japan in a diplomatic way. The alliance, renewed in 1911 and scheduled to expire in 1921, pledged England to back Japan if that nation were at war. Originally created to keep Japan from al-

lying itself with Germany or Russia, the alliance had become an unwanted al-
batross to British foreign policy. England, however, was anxious to avoid antagonizing Japan, a rising colonial power with interests in China, Taiwan, and
various Pacific islands. By allowing England a graceful withdrawal as part of
the Four Power Pact, the Washington Conference offered a chance to solve
her budgetary and "Japanese" problems simultaneously.

The Nine Power Treaty, the final major agreement negotiated at the
Washington Conference, dealt with the problem of China, which had long
been victimized by other countries. In this treaty, Japan and several Western
nations agreed to surrender special privileges in China. The Nine Power
Treaty essentially reaffirmed the 1900 Open Door policy of John Hay, the former U.S. secretary of state, leaving China intact as a sovereign nation and offering equal trading privileges for all. The signatory powers agreed not to take
advantage of China or to seek special commercial rights. The treaty, like all the
others negotiated at the conference, did not commit its signers to any kind of
action if one of them violated the agreement.

The Washington Conference, with a number of significant treaties negotiated, appeared to be a major triumph for American diplomacy and the cause
of world peace. Hughes stated that the naval treaty "ends, absolutely ends, the
race in competition in naval armament. . . . We are taking perhaps the greatest
forward step in history to establish the reign of peace." [26] Observers noted,
however, that since none of these agreements provided any means of enforcement, they could be abrogated by any of the parties. This lack of enforcement
mechanisms was in line with American determination to avoid legal commitments. President Harding saw this absence as a positive factor and defended
the treaties by saying the treaties constituted "no commitment to armed
forces, no alliance, no written or moral obligation to join in defense." [27] The
United States was relying on moral force rather than any direct means of enforcement that might lead to war.

By relaxing international tensions for a decade and creating a genuine
thaw that followed its ratification, the conference was a temporary success.
Had there been no treaty, it is most unlikely that Congress would have been
willing to spend the money for a greatly expanded fleet of battleships anyway.
Congress also would have been reluctant to increase spending for defense on
Guam and the Phillippines, regardless of the arms-limitation treaty. In negotiating the treaties, the practical Hughes demonstrated a keen "sense of the
possible" and a willingness to stay within its limits. Considering the political

climate at that time, the "sacrifices" of the United States at the Washington Conference were of warships and naval bases that probably would never have been built.[28]

Some of the gains made by the United States were ultimately frittered away by irresponsible policies in the postconference era. Hughes had gained British and Japanese agreements to reduce their battleship fleets in line with reductions, which the United States would have taken even without such agreements. The secretary urged the United States to build up the navy to maximum strength in accordance with treaty obligations. Unfortunately, the American people ignored his advice and abandoned his program of cooperative naval limitation in favor of irresponsible unpreparedness. The United States's lack of preparedness in 1941 (when Pearl Harbor was attacked) was not caused by its destruction of naval vessels in 1922 or of excessive naval building by Japan. The actual problem was that it was lulled into a false sense of security by the Five Power Pact and believed this treaty made further preparedness unnecessary.[29]

Ultimately some of the most important "gains" made at the conference by the United States and its Western allies were merely illusory. Rather than being contained, the Japanese actually strengthened their position in some areas. The Four Power Pact neutralized the islands, including both Guam and the Philippines, from which an offensive campaign could be launched against Japan. Although the Japanese recognized the Open Door policy for China, the United States refused to assume any responsibility under the treaty for enforcing this policy; it would be openly violated only a few years later. In an uncertain period of foreign relations, the absence of any enforcement mechanism proved to be decisive.

The fragile nature of this new détente became clear only two years later, when relations with Japan were complicated by the United States's new immigration policy. Hughes had urged Congress not to totally exclude the Japanese, claiming that doing so would erode the good will of the Washington Conference. He suggested either a small quota or a continuation of the "Gentlemen's Agreement," a previous voluntary ban on immigration. When the Senate refused to heed his advice and implemented the ban on Japanese immigration, Hughes lamented that Congress "in a few minutes had spoiled the work of years."[30]

The Soviet Union, which the United States regarded as an "outlaw nation" and a threat to world order, was not invited to the naval conference. The

Soviet Union had committed a number of offenses that isolated it from the other powers: it had quit the Allied cause in 1918, had fallen under Communist control, had repudiated pre-1917 Russian debts, and refused to compensate for confiscation of property. (This failure to repay past loans involved a loss of more than one-third of a billion dollars just to the United States and its citizens.) Soviet attempts to "Bolshevize" the world through its propaganda agencies and its surrogate Communist parties were regarded as threatening and helped lead to the Red Scare.

In spite of these differences, a human catastrophe in the Soviet Union temporarily brought about American involvement in that turbulent nation. In 1921, because of problems emanating from World War I, the Communist revolution, and the ensuing civil war, a great famine threatened starvation to millions of people in the Soviet Union. The Harding administration, unlike the Allies who conditioned aid to debt repayment, agreed to help Russia. Under Hoover, the American Relief Administration (ARA) spent $50 million in private and government funds on food, supplies, and seed plantings. While the ARA's twenty-two months of aid did little to ease American-Soviet relations, it did provide an opportunity for a closer look at the Soviet Union. Hughes publicly admitted that the ARA was a "peephole into Russia," which substituted for the consular reports denied the United States by nonrecognition.[31]

In the early 1920s, the Russian Communist leader Vladimir Lenin made repeated attempts to regularize relations with the American government. In desperate need of American goods and also hoping that American power could balance Japanese might in the Far East, Lenin indicated that Moscow was willing to make genuine concessions to the United States. In late 1923, Russia hinted that it was even willing to talk about its Washington debts but this overture, like all the rest, was coldly spurned.[32]

Although the United States withheld diplomatic recognition from the Soviet Union until 1933, the two nations did considerable business during the 1920s. After the United States lifted wartime trade restrictions with Russia (except on armaments) in the summer of 1921, the Soviets became good customers. The United States became involved in selling electrical equipment, helping to establish an automobile industry, and assisting in building a major dam in Russia. The United States permitted trade and even loans on a private basis and in 1923–25 its exports to Russia multiplied ninefold. The increasing economic ties to the Soviet Union, however, did not lead to a diplomatic thaw. Coolidge, as had Harding, favored the policy of both trade and keeping our official distance from Russia. He stated, "I do not propose to barter away for the privilege of trade any of the cherished rights of humanity."[33] Not until the presidency of Franklin Roosevelt was the policy of nonrecognition of Communist Russia, originated by Woodrow Wilson and one of the foreign policy mainstays of the 1920s, finally reversed.

United States relations with its own allies were awkward in the 1920s, as it attempted to collect billions in World War I-related debts. First through private and later through government loans, the United States had lent more than $10 billion to the Allies before, during, and after the war. The Allies had agreed to pay back these loans at 5 percent interest, but after the war they tried to persuade the United States to forgive the government loans (which were the main part of the debt).

The Allies raised many arguments for the forgiveness of the loans. They stated that the war had been a common cause in which they had done most of the fighting while the United States stayed mainly on the sidelines acting like a banker. The loans had been for munitions, not investments, and most of the money had been spent in the United States at war-inflated prices. The British cited their own example of canceling loans to their allies after the Napoleonic Wars and asked the United States to consider a similar policy. England argued unsuccessfully that Europe's unfavorable balance of trade with the United States made it difficult to repay the debts and that cancellation would promote European recovery. The United States was accused by the Europeans of acting like "Uncle Shylock" in trying to get its money back while the European nations could not reverse their heavy casualties.[34] The United States, however, was resolute and insisted on repayment. President Coolidge's comment, "They hired the money, didn't they?" expressed the prevailing attitude during the decade.[35]

The refusal of the United States to cancel the war debts led Europe to seek this money through German reparations. At the Versailles peace conference, Germany was forced to sign a war guilt clause and agreed to pay reparations at an amount that would be determined later. In 1921, the reparations commission levied the sum of approximately $33 billion plus interest on Germany. The first installment was paid but, after a temporary moratorium, German default followed in late 1922. France and Belgium thereupon invaded and occupied the Ruhr valley in Germany. At this point, Hughes decided upon action because the Allied debtors had determined to pay the United States only what they received in reparations from Germany. He was therefore receptive to a British suggestion that American experts participate in an investigation into Germany's capacity to fulfill her financial obligations.

The deadlock over reparations was eased when the United States suggested a two-part strategy. Under the Dawes Plan, Germany was granted a one-year moratorium on reparations payments, a cut of 80 percent in future annual payments, and an emergency $200 million loan from the United States, England, and France. The United States soon began the practice of extending private loans to Germany each year of several hundred million dollars a year. A cycle began that lasted throughout the decade wherein money originating in the United States was loaned to Germany, then paid to England and France in reparations, and finally returned to the United States to repay war loans. In 1929, the United States produced the Young Plan, which was to be the final word on German reparations. The original amount was greatly reduced and Germany was now asked to pay a total of $26 billion (covering principal and interest) over a fifty-nine-year period extending to 1988. This plan, which committed three generations of Germans to pay Germany's World War I reparations, was considered to be the long-sought "reasonable" solution to the much-debated reparations problem.[36]

The depression of 1929 upset the entire system of reparations and war debt repayments, undoing the solutions produced under the Dawes and Young plans. When the devastating economic collapse hit Europe in 1931, Germany suspended reparations and there was a growing realization that the debts would never be paid. Secretary Stimson favored a cancellation of the war debts and President Hoover urged either canceling the pre-Armistice debt (up to 1918) or the interest on the loans. Because public opinion would not permit either option, Hoover instead imposed a moratorium on debt and reparations payments in 1931. (Hoover had been urged to act by Germany's president, Paul Hindenberg, who feared that a Communist takeover in Germany might result from the financial crisis.)[37] Hoover's efforts were insufficient, and within two years Germany had canceled the reparations, provoking the Europeans to default on their debts.

Like the debt problem, the arms-limitation question also persisted throughout the decade. Enthusiastic for arms control because he wanted to further cut government spending, Coolidge helped initiate the Geneva Disarmament Conference in 1927 to continue the work accomplished at the Washington Conference five years earlier. Coolidge wanted the signatory powers of the Five Power Pact to consider limiting the number of ships smaller than the large capital ships dealt with in 1922. The conference was hastily organized and broke up with no agreement, leading Coolidge to turn his attention to another diplomatic objective, an agreement to outlaw war.

The desire to prevent another war, perhaps the major underlying issue of the decade, ultimately led to an international agreement in 1928 to outlaw offensive wars. The ill-fated Kellogg-Briand Pact originated with Salmon Levinson, a Chicago lawyer and peace activist who pushed for a ban on war in the early 1920s. He secured the backing of Senator Borah, one of the driving forces behind the Washington Arms Conference. In 1923, Borah introduced a resolution making war a public crime under international law, although he opposed adding enforceable sanctions. Later another peace activist, James Shotwell, a professor at Columbia University, backed a plan to eliminate war through compulsory arbitration but was similarly unsuccessful.

However unrealistic, the plan to outlaw war by treaty simply would not go away and ultimately was implemented through the combined efforts of Shotwell, French foreign minister Augustide Briand, and American secretary of state Frank Kellogg. When the plan was brought to the attention of the French diplomat by Shotwell in 1927, Briand offered to sign a treaty with the United States, with each side pledging never to launch a war. The foreign minister actually sought to lure the United States into the European alliance system to defend France. Kellogg rejected the overture but American public opinion would not let the idea die. On the suggestion of Senator Borah, the secretary of state then offered to sign if the agreement were extended to include many other nations. Briand was forced to agree, and ultimately sixty-four nations, including Germany, Japan, and Italy, signed the treaty to outlaw offensive war. Kellogg, who initially had opposed the treaty but later changed his mind and pursued it with the spirit of a zealot, was awarded the Nobel Peace Prize for his efforts.

Persuading the parties to sign the treaty was not an easy matter and Kellogg was forced to make important concessions. To avoid rejection by the Senate, Kellogg kept the text simple and omitted any means of preventing violations. To get French approval, he consented to her interpretation that the treaty permitted military action taken in self-defense or to honor her network of security arrangements. He also agreed to the British idea that it reserved full freedom of action in "certain British regions of the world." The United States added its own condition, claiming that it should not impinge upon the Monroe Doctrine. With all the exceptions being negotiated, critics called the

treaty to outlaw war as an instrument of national policy "the most comprehensive agreement ever created to legalize certain categories of war."[38]

Although a sincere expression of hope for an enduring peace, the Kellogg-Briand Pact seemed flawed for the task intended. Because there was no
authority to judge what was an "offensive" or "defensive" war and no enforcement procedure even if a nation were branded as the aggressor, the treaty
had no impact. It did not attempt to deal with the causes of war nor suggest
any machinery for settling disputes by peaceful means. It simply outlawed war
and relied entirely upon moral compulsion to prevent its outbreak. The treaty,
which reflected the hopes of the American people to do something about
world peace and yet to avoid any commitment for collective security, was approved by a doubtful Senate with only one dissenting vote. To gain assent
from the Senate, Kellogg had to give assurances that the treaty involved no
obligations of enforcement,[39] a key feature with all the previous security
arrangements negotiated by the United States during the decade.

It later became obvious that the Kellogg-Briand Pact had contributed
nothing to the cause of world peace. Outlawing war created the illusion of
safety, which seemed to eliminate the need for further direct participation in
world affairs. Future President Franklin D. Roosevelt declared at the time
that words without deeds were not enough, and that outlawing war led to a
false belief that something important had been accomplished.[40] Diplomat
Sumner Welles observed that the Kellogg-Briand Pact was "a happy and
decorous means of evading rather than accepting responsibility . . . a high
point in isolationist thinking . . . a fitting climax to foreign policy which even
in its least harmful aspects was totally negative."[41] The Kellogg-Briand Pact
nevertheless was accepted by many as "the final realization of a historic dream
even as the United States refused any sacrifice that might have given that
dream substance."[42]

The Kellogg-Briand Pact soon came under attack from many quarters
and its reputation diminished even further with the passage of time. Critics
wondered whether international good will alone could impose a ban on war.
Senator Reed, one of its sharpest critics, deemed it an "international kiss."[43]
One young naval officer observed, "There is no evidence, even in religion, to
prove that the world can outlaw war any more than it can outlaw the
weather."[44] Admiral William Pratt, naval adviser to the Washington Conference, declared that the belief that war could be abolished with a statement was
"to belie the facts of recorded history and to underestimate the human ele-

ment."[45] Henry Cabot Lodge Jr., son of the prominent senator and a future senator himself, said the pact was an attempt to get something for nothing.[46] Virginia Senator Carter Glass stated the pact was not worth a postage stamp.[47] Tragically, the critics were proven correct not long afterward. The stock market crash a year after the treaty went into effect set off a chain reaction that ended the short-lived global truce of the 1920s and any illusion of peace created by the pact.

In addition to peacemaking efforts for Europe and Asia, the United States attempted to improve relations with Latin America, which were under stress from problems involving American investments and the Roosevelt Corollary policy. Under the Roosevelt Corollary, dating back to the early 1900s, the United States had reserved the right to intervene in the affairs of South and Central America as well as in the Caribbean. Latin America was one region where the various nations actually wished the United States *would* practice an isolationist foreign policy. Although most Americans recognized major interests in the region, especially involving the Panama Canal, there was a growing movement to reverse the previous interventionist policy. When Harding became president in 1921, the United States had occupation troops in Haiti, Panama, the Dominican Republican, Cuba, and Nicaragua. Because many of the Latin American governments were weak, unstable, and financially shaky, the United States moved cautiously to reverse its policy but still managed to achieve some notable successes by the end of the decade.

Secretary of State Hughes was one of the principal initiators of the new, more enlightened, policy toward Latin America. While steadfastly holding to the U.S. right to be involved in Latin America, there was a clear trend during the decade to avoid intervention unless absolutely necessary. Hughes believed the United States could intervene in Latin America for legitimate reasons of self-defense or to protect U.S. citizens but not for purposes of aggression and domination. He tried to convince these countries that the United States had no intention of employing its power to their disadvantage.[48]

One example of this enlightened attitude toward Latin America was the renewed overture to Colombia, an effort to heal an old wound stemming from the 1903 U.S. intervention that had helped Panama win its independence from Colombia. An earlier attempt by the United States to apologize and pay compensation in 1914 had failed because Theodore Roosevelt's friends in the Senate regarded this as an insult to the former president. Roosevelt's death in 1919 removed an impediment to a deal and in 1921 the United

States agreed to pay Colombia $25 million, although it did not offer an official apology. The payment of the money was generally interpreted as an "apology" and led to an immediate increase in U.S. investments in Colombia.

The most serious problem in the region involved Mexico, which was threatening to seize foreign-owned land and mineral rights. Especially troubling was Mexico's desire to nationalize the extensive oil interests held by U.S. citizens in Mexico. (Mexico was the world's second-largest producer of oil in the 1920s, much of this controlled by U.S. interests.) Article 27 of the Mexican Constitution of 1917 provided that all subsoil rights belonged to the national state, reaffirming a long-standing earlier policy, which had only been changed in 1911 by a Mexican government trying to curry favor with the Americans. The United States refused to recognize the Mexican government unless it agreed to respect U.S. economic interests in Mexico. A 1923 agreement indicated that Mexico would back down but a newly installed government in 1925 once again threatened to seize foreign assets.

In 1927, the Coolidge administration was able to move relations with Mexico into a new and conciliatory phase. A brilliant step was the appointment of Dwight Morrow as ambassador to Mexico, where he was able to establish an excellent rapport with both the Mexican government and the Mexican people. As a goodwill gesture for the United States, he arranged for his son-in-law Charles Lindbergh to make a solo flight to Mexico City. Morrow persuaded Mexico to delay the seizure of the oil fields and to pay compensation for confiscated foreign-owned lands. Because of his great diplomatic success, Morrow has been called "the real author of the Good Neighbor Policy."[49]

Unlike the situation in Mexico, there was a temporary retreat to the older interventionist policy under President Coolidge in the case of Nicaragua. Because of its close proximity to the Panama Canal, Nicaragua was particularly important to the United States. Under President Taft, the United States began a lengthy occupation in 1912. It withdrew its forces in 1925 but, after a revolution that overthrew the democratically elected government, the United States returned 2,000 soldiers to Nicaragua. (One of the dissident leaders, General Augusto Sandino, later became an inspiration to the Marxist "Sandinistas" of the 1980s). The United States finally left Nicaragua in the closing days of the Hoover administration to end the longest intervention, which covered a period of more than twenty years.

One of the most telling blows to the old interventionist policy came from the Clark Memorandum, written in December 1928 but only released to the public in 1930 during the Hoover administration. The Clark Memorandum represented a complete reversal of the Roosevelt Corollary, formally renouncing the right of intervention under the Monroe Doctrine. President Hoover, who was more knowledgeable and more interested in Latin America than his predecessors had been, stated that he was not proud of the interventionist policy and declared "we do not wish to be represented abroad in such manner."[50] He proclaimed that it was American policy never to intervene in any other country's internal affairs and repudiated the idea of using force to sustain U.S. interests.[51] The early tentative steps taken by Harding and Coolidge were greatly expanded by Hoover's policy of "intelligent retreat" from Latin America. The Clark Memorandum, which did much to relieve Latin America's fears of further interference by the United States, would guide administration policy.

The Hoover administration demonstrated the new policy by removing American troops from Haiti and Nicaragua, where they had been stationed for years. Behind this new attitude toward Latin America was the realization by the public and Congress that there was no serious threat to the Panama Canal and that no naval threat from anyone in the Caribbean existed. Also by this time, the United States had lost much of its interest in imperial ventures after disappointing experiences in the Philippines and Puerto Rico and was tiring of its policing role in the hemisphere. Unfortunately, much of the good will earned by new U.S. policies during the 1920s evaporated with the outbreak of the Great Depression. The collapse of the American market weakened Latin America, and the United States was once again blamed for their ills.

In 1930, as the Great Depression threatened to destabilize international relations, the United States returned to arms limitations as a means of promoting peace. In that year, the five great naval powers met again and modified the 1922 ratios with Japan gaining a slight increase in authorized naval strength. Because neither the United States nor England had kept their fleets up to treaty size, these arrangements inhibited only Japan. Whatever progress toward "peace" was achieved by the treaty, a crisis in Asia the following year indicated how fragile this and all the other agreements of the 1920s actually were.

By the middle of the Hoover presidency, the limits of America's willingness to get involved in world affairs to preserve peace and order were tested by the Manchurian crisis. The Japanese government had invaded Manchuria in

1931 and formally annexed the area as a colony. The United States had few economic interests there and showed little concern, especially while it dealt with the Great Depression. Few realized the later significance of this attitude on the preservation of world peace: that the United States' lack of interest would encourage other aggressions by Germany, Italy, and Japan. Although Secretary of State Stimson favored a vigorous policy toward Japan, Hoover refused to consider any moves that might lead to war, specifically ruling out sanctions and embargoes as too risky. Ultimately the United States adopted a weak policy that included nonrecognition of the Japanese conquest of Manchuria without any additional steps. It would rely on moral force, hoping to avoid any direct involvement in the crisis. As expansionist governments in Germany, Italy, and Japan became more aggressive after 1931, the United States tragically learned that moral force had its limits.

The American response to the Manchurian crisis demonstrated the constancy of its foreign policy during the post-World War I period. The debate over the League of Nations had earlier indicated an American unwillingness to get actively involved in peacemaking efforts. A successful United States foreign policy depended upon "normal" conditions abroad. When the Great Depression destabilized the international scene and encouraged rogue governments to challenge world stability, the United States's "involvement without commitment" foreign policy proved inadequate.

5

A New Culture Emerges

THE DECADE OF THE 1920S was a time of remarkable cultural changes in American society. This was a period of amazing vitality, social invention and change, and the formative years of modern America. Because it became an urban nation for the first time simultaneously with a technological revolution that led to mass production and mass consumption, the United States saw a hastened breakdown of old habits and patterns of thought and the start of drastic changes in American lifestyles.

One of the most striking changes of the decade was the emergence of a new mass culture. Until the twentieth century, the country's social standards traditionally were set by small groups of preachers, politicians, lawyers, editors, and teachers, and later by the economic elite that spurred post-Civil War industrialism. From 1920 on, the tastes of the crowd became an increasingly important determinant in popular culture.[1] The new mass culture differed vastly from the traditional culture, which had been inspired by elite groups in society, and this change led to painful cultural conflict throughout the decade.

Before the great cultural shift of the 1920s, the white rural classes had been the majority. These people originally came from northern Europe, were Protestants, and usually were farmers or small businessmen. They believed in self-help, hard work, thrift, and personal sobriety, and they disliked bigness, diversity, the exotic, leisure, elegance, and personal indulgence. Restraint and moderation described their lifestyles. These rural people believed that their lifestyle fostered character and patriotism while life in the city bred vices.[2] By 1920, a strong mood of nostalgia for the "good old days" was felt by this once-dominant group and led to ever-increasing tensions with the rising urban majority. A wide cultural schism developed, which pitted the country-side versus the city and the Middle West and the South versus the East.

Alongside this rural-urban cultural divide was the increasing adulation toward the business community, largely a reflection of the very great expansion in the economy. Between 1918 and 1929, such factors as mass production, advances in technology, and increasing efficiency of labor led to a production gain of more than 60 percent, which far outstripped the increase in population. Because of the enormous extension of credit, advertising, and salesmanship, the consumption levels of Americans soared and this higher standard of living led to an ever-increasing faith in business. A contemporary writer declared, "Through business, properly conceived, managed and conducted, the human race is finally to be redeemed." Furthermore, business was called the "best science," the "truest art," the "fullest education," affording the "fairest opportunity," providing the "cleanest philanthropy," and offering the "sanest religion." The writer concluded that industry would be the "savior of the country."[3] Clearly the 1920s was a business age, when materialism and the good life largely replaced older ideas of reform.

During the materialist 1920s, the public at times needed to be persuaded to expand its desire for the new products available. Helping to stimulate the new mass-market economy was the new "science" of advertising, which was constantly creating new "wants" for the public. Through clever and sometimes misleading messages, advertisers succeeded in making products seem better than they were; advertisers became the alchemists of the business world in "making a silk purse out of a sow's ear."[4] Advertisers even began to use the popular theories of the behaviorist John B. Watson and the renowned psychiatrist Sigmund Freud in their efforts to connect with the consumer. Advertising became so extensive during the decade that it consumed more than half of the output of the printing presses.[5]

Also stimulating the desires of the public for more consumer goods was World War I, which helped to make the country tired of crusades and reforms and more interested in "the good life." The results of the war had been disillusioning, with the "crusade for democracy" seemingly turning into a struggle over colonies and reneging on war debts. The nation was tired of "important issues" and turned to heroes and daring events rather than reformers and great public servants.[6] As the earlier crises of the decade such as the League of Nations controversy and the Red Scare (which were in part extensions of World War I) passed from the scene, there was more interest in simply trying to enjoy life. Americans felt "a queer disappointment after the war and they sensed that life was not giving them all they hoped it would."[7]

Apart from this disillusionment, other factors contributed to new attitudes and a revolution in manners and morals. During the decade, the nation
faced momentous changes caused by the new status of women, the theories of
Sigmund Freud, the experiment in Prohibition, and the widespread availability for the first time of the automobile, radio, and movies. These changes were
especially associated with the urban lifestyle. Alongside an appreciation for the
new technological marvels, Americans struggled to retain the old rural sense
of community and autonomy. In spite of industrialism, a provincial nineteenth-century rural outlook continued and American life was still largely
dominated by small towns and frontier values.[8] While new values emerged in
the urban areas, the groundwork was laid for a historic rural-urban cultural
conflict.

Industrialism was the driving force behind a major change in the social
habits of the nation. When the workweek was shortened during the 1920s,
urban workers suddenly found themselves with more free time. By the end of
the decade, the workweek had declined from sixty hours to forty-eight hours.
The new economy also supplied new recreational outlets, such as the automobile, radio, and movies, all of which became wildly popular during the decade.
A declining cost of living made the enjoyment of these social outlets possible.
The average American, who had spent 60 percent of his income on necessities
in 1900, saw this figure decline to 50 percent by 1920, also gaining more
leisure time to spend the additional discretionary funds.[9]

The newly improved living standards caused the amusement and recreation industries to become big businesses almost overnight. Spectator sports
became extremely popular as new outlets for recreation, reflecting the greater
amount of leisure time available. One of the most striking changes was the
greater interest in participatory sports. "For the first time in our history," one
scholar wrote, "the crowds watching professional games are matched by the
large numbers of people thronging the golf courses, tennis courts, and playing
fields."[10] The increased prosperity of the period was enabling Americans to
enter the "age of play."

These changes in society, largely caused by the growth of business and
urban America, were reflected in the rise of new heroes that replaced older
icons of American society. Did the rise of big business with its huge bureaucracies and impersonal labor relations lead to doubts about the survival of individualism? Many of the newer heroes were individuals who overcame
adversity in an impersonal world and became a source of inspiration to the na-

tion. Did Americans feel uneasy with the new wealth and moral standards, seeking through heroes the old virtues of strength, courage, and probity?[11] "Politicians, military leaders, captains of industry, inventors, and explorers had long been icons of American individualism; now they battled for public attention with a new array of social heroes which included matinee idols, tennis players, and running backs of the Chicago Bears." So popular did these heroes become that "the appetite for vicariously participating in their lives proved nearly inexhaustible."[12]

Among the most popular of the new icons were sports figures. The 1920s was the golden age of American sports, with attendance at athletic events breaking all records and the champions of sport becoming known and loved throughout the land. "If St. Paul were living today," a prominent Methodist minister declared, "he would know Babe Ruth's batting average and what yardage Red Grange made."[13] During the decade, all the major sports were dominated by legendary figures whose fame would endure long afterward. By 1927, when he hit sixty home runs, Babe Ruth was a better-known American to most foreigners than was President Calvin Coolidge. Jack Dempsey, who lost his heavyweight title to Gene Tunney in the famous "long count," gave boxing its first million dollar gates. Harold "Red" Grange, the best college and professional football player of his time, in one spectacular college game in 1924 made runs of 95, 67, 55, and 45 yards the first four times he carried the ball. Bobby Jones and Bill Tilden took golf and tennis away from the country club set and gave their sports general appeal. Jones became the only golfer ever to win the "Grand Slam" while Tilden was the premier tennis player of the 1920s. In college football, Knute Rockne took an obscure Notre Dame University and turned it into the greatest college football powerhouse, compiling an amazing record of 105 wins and only 12 losses between 1919 and 1931.[14]

The greatest hero of the decade was Charles Lindbergh, a daredevil aviator who became the first man to fly solo from New York to Paris. Attempting to fly across the Atlantic Ocean had been a challenge to daredevils since the end of World War I. In 1919, two aviators had flown from Newfoundland to Ireland, but the distance was only about 2,000 miles compared to more than 3,000 for the Lindbergh flight. Several aviators had died in their attempt to fly solo from New York to Paris to claim a $25,000 award that had been offered since 1919. Even the famed North Pole explorer Admiral Richard Byrd had failed in his attempt. Lindbergh, who had flown mail over long distances in

...etermined that he could make the flight with the proper
...on, and the ability to stay awake for two days to control
...7, he arrived in Paris after thirty-three hours in the air
...cclaimed hero of the 1920s. Although Lindbergh ob-
...to cross the Atlantic by air, the novelty of his flight was
...York to Paris instead of leaving from Newfoundland
...a nation described as "spiritually starved" and "dis-
...s, scandal and crime,"[15] Lindbergh was the ideal
...nd possessing impeccable character, he seemed to
...the age. He was seen as testimony to the sound-
...character and a rebuttal of the intellectual criti-
...on of the age."[16]

...h's feat that he was elevated to nearly godlike
...s so intense that, "Except for the Armistice in
...thing in American history [was] compara-
...*World* declared that Lindbergh had performed
...n in the history of the human race."[18] In an
...light seemed to prove that individuals could
...ent magazine writer noted that Lindbergh
...en at the core, but morally sound and sweet
...Lindbergh its first "Man of the Year." For-
...ans Hughes declared that Lindbergh "has
...that is sordid, that is vulgar."[19]

...others would be found in the relatively new
...rm invented in the 1890s by several people
...f France and Thomas Edison, the movies
...vie industry became the fifth largest in the
...hundred million patrons attended the cin-
...equaled the total population in the nation.
...ape into newer worlds and gave an intimate
...lived. But the growing importance of the
...rms of entertainment. In the smaller cities
...sand people), the legitimate "live" theater
...or added movies to the program, and the
[20]

...led early in the century but saw its fortunes
...D. W. Griffith's two great epics, *The Birth*

Of A Nation (1915) and *Intolerance* (1916), respectable middle-c
cans generally regarded the movies as popular entertainment for t
population and beneath their notice, or potentially harmful to mo
be censored. Griffith's achievements demonstrated the artistic
and the storytelling power of motion pictures.[21] Soon after the v
panding motion picture industry emerged as the first mass cultural
America.

Along with the artistic quality of the directors and actors, var
cal breakthroughs served to popularize movies. Most important w
tion of sound to the production. Several inventors, including Tho
and Lee DeForrest, helped bring sound to movies, climaxing in
through film *The Jazz Singer* in 1927. The other development th
popularize films (in the summer months) was the introduc
conditioning to the theaters in the 1920s. When the experime
tried, the head of Paramount Studios, Adolph Zukor, admitted t
to the theater more to see the patrons' reaction to air-conditioning
film itself.

By the 1920s, the movies had become an integral part of tl
cultural scene, offering comfort and glamour at low prices. Ho
created a new elite of movie stars, displacing as public icons su
businessmen as John D. Rockefeller and J. P. Morgan. During
Charlie Chaplin was the biggest star and perhaps the best-know
world, his image of the tramp becoming the universal symbol of

Through actors such as Chaplin, the movies demonstrated
for social criticism. Satirizing the pompous and the powerful, Ch
how the solitary individual might survive in the face of modern so
tion and indifference. He became America's greatest screen con
one of the decade's severest social critics. He strongly opposed
mentality of the period, preferring more basic human qualities
and kindness. His films depicted an often unsuccessful struggle a
cial forces that attacked human dignity in modern society; the ord
could easily identify with him.[22]

The youth of the 1920s were the first generation to learn t
and morals from movies, and the lessons learned were not always
people with older, rural values. The movies' emphasis on sex, al
eral personal scandals involving screen stars, led to so much d
conservative groups that the studio heads installed Will Hays, H

master general, as their arbiter of morals. Hays established the "two feet on the floor" rules for bedroom scenes to substitute the suggestive for the explicit. He also emphasized that virtue must triumph in the story line, even if such a rule created often unrealistic endings. In his moral code for the movies, Hays stressed no excessive kissing, no ridiculing the clergy, no complete nudity, and no sympathy with criminals.[23] Yet in spite of Hays, the movies continued to display themes of sex and vulgarity, although they used greater subtlety.

During these early years for the film industry, many of the key positions were held by outsiders to American society. Because native middle-class Americans before World War I had considered movies disreputable, the positions of power in the movie industry— financier, producer, director, star— were left open to minority groups such as immigrants, Catholics, and Jews.[24] Ironically during the high tide of the anti-Semitic, anti-Catholic, and nativist sentiment in the United States of the 1920s, middle-class Americans were enjoying movies by people in these same groups, exemplified by Joseph P. Kennedy, Louis B. Mayer, Rudolph Valentino, Greta Garbo, and Marlene Dietrich.

The 1920s also saw the widespread acceptance of another form of entertainment, the radio, which like the movies became a major disseminator of the new mass culture. First invented in 1895 by the Italian Guglielmo Marconi, radio originally was used more for communication than for entertainment. In the beginning, it served mainly as a wireless telegraph for sending messages between ship and shore and was extremely valuable in rescuing shipwrecks. Even though Lee DeForrest's improved radio vacuum tube, the triode, made possible long-distance broadcasting in the early 1900s, radio was slow to catch on with the public. It was monopolized by the armed forces during World War I and, even immediately after the war, few people saw any practical benefit for radio in a mass market. In 1920, radio finally came of age, beginning with the first licensed radio station, WKTK in Pittsburgh; within two years, there were 576 licensed radio stations in business. Now seen mainly as a means of free entertainment for the public, the industry grew rapidly throughout the decade. In 1927, the Federal Radio Commission (forerunner to the later Federal Communications Commission) was created to enable the federal government to supervise this important new industry. So extensive was the appeal of radio that by 1930 approximately 40 percent of the families in America owned one.[25] An important factor aiding the growth of the industry was that it cost nothing to the listener because advertising carried the entire cost of radio broadcasting.

Unlike the motion pictures, radio came to be regarded as a source of both mass entertainment and news. It brought the world to everyone, with an immediacy never before known, and ultimately had such varied effects as changing music tastes and methods of political campaigning, and opening up rural America to better speech and a high level of humor. One early indication of its political significance was the broadcasting of the Republican and Democratic political conventions over the radio in 1920. Perhaps most significantly, radio broke down the isolation of the countryside. Along with the automobile and the movies, radio helped transform rural American in the 1920s by exposing it to the newly emerging urban culture.

One of radio's most important effects was to give people a common fund of experience and information, making Americans more alike than ever before. Because of its accessibility, radio was possibly an even more powerful medium of mass cultural diffusion than were the movies or the automobile. Radio was available to a much wider audience—to the ill and the infirm, the very young and the very old, and those who could not always go to a movie or ride in a car. It could be listened to in the privacy of one's home, and it was always there. The weather was never a concern. Also, it was "live," allowing the audience to listen to a sports event or a news happening as it occurred.

But perhaps nothing had a greater overall impact in changing the American lifestyle than the automobile. In 1869, the German inventor Nicholas Otto perfected the internal combustion engine, the crucial breakthrough in automobile technology. Sold commercially for the first time in the late nineteenth century, the automobile had a difficult beginning, with many manufacturers attempting to capture the market. The car industry struggled for years until the 1920s, when several basic demands were satisfied: cheap and reliable cars, good roads, accessible gasoline and repairs, and installment buying.

Building cheap and reliable cars was the most important need, and it was accomplished by the giant in the industry, Henry Ford. By 1914, Ford had perfected the mass production of cars by combining the system of interchangeable parts with his own breakthrough, the moving assembly line (which was inspired by the "disassembly" line of the meatpacking industry).[26] Other elements quickly fell into place to stimulate the industry, including the building of closed cars, which surpassed in popularity the open car by the middle of the decade. (The self-starter had been invented earlier, in 1912.) Ford began manufacturing his basic car, the Model T ("in any color as long as it's black"), in 1914. Steadily bringing down the cost, he dominated the market for years and correctly predicted that lower prices and a large volume of sales would bring the most profits. By the 1920s, Ford outproduced all the other car manufacturers and was one of the three richest men in America.

The effects brought about by the automobile revolution were so profound that Henry Ford later claimed to have invented the modern age. As much as any man of his day, Ford helped to destroy the social values of nineteenth-century America. The automobile opened up rural America to the outer world. In a nation of transients, had the car replaced the covered wagon to enable a restless people to stay on the move?[27] The building of closed cars helped change the morals of young people by giving them access to a "mobile bedroom" or a "mobile parlor" and moving them away from courting in houses under the watchful eyes of adults.[28] It also led to the rise of suburbs, because workers could now commute to their jobs. Even more significantly, the automobile, along with the movie and the radio, obliterated the isolation of the village and the farm and helped to bring the new mass consumption economy to the countryside. Rural America was now within reach of all the new developments of the age. The farmer could go to town for his entertainment (usually the movies) or to any store, or he could listen to the same radio programs at home as did the city people.

The dominant figure in the automobile industry, Henry Ford, was both a business mogul and a cultural icon to millions of Americans. The greatest of all the business heroes, he was credited with putting America "on wheels." From humble beginnings and limited education, he revolutionized the automobile business and brought down the price of cars to within reach of the average American. Frequently mentioned as a possible candidate for the presidency in 1924, Ford's combination of eccentricity and bigotry—as well as his business skills—turned him into an unusual role model. Flaunting his limited education, he proclaimed that "facts mess up my mind" and "history is more or less bunk." He even had the peculiar habit of eating grass sandwiches.[29] More serious was his prejudice, especially his hostility toward Jews. Despite his eccentricities and prejudices, he was a brilliant businessman who earned a worldwide reputation that extended even into Russia, which tried to recruit his services in organizing a Soviet automobile industry.

The increasing economic affluence in America stimulated by the rise of these new industries had an enormous effect on education. Affluence changed the education of the city youngster, allowing more students to attend high school. By 1930, approximately one-half the teenagers between fourteen and eighteen years old were in high school. Finishing high school was almost universal in the middle class and most of the children from working-class homes completed high school if they had at least average academic ability. The principal reason for more young people staying in school instead of going to work was that, for the first time, their families were able to support themselves without the youngsters' wages.[30] Affluence rather than compulsory education laws kept children in school and off the labor market. The trend toward staying in school extended to college, where enrollments doubled from 600,000 students in 1920 to 1,200,000 in 1930.

The new mass-production economy also affected American popular culture, although not in the way many had hoped. At first, some expected movies and radio would lift American cultural levels but the mass market dashed these hopes. In the quest for profits, this goal was abandoned; "art" in movies was replaced by "sex, sin, and sensation." The same pattern occurred in magazines and newspapers, which in their own quest for readers began to stress "sex" and "sensation."[31] The mass-circulation magazines carried few serious articles, choosing instead to deal with sports, fads, and leisure pursuits. (This trend was a reversal of the pre-World War I "magazine revolution," with its emphasis on muckraking stories designed to protect or enlighten the public.)

The black population experienced profound cultural change during the 1920s through the Harlem Renaissance. During and immediately after World War I, with the immigration of large numbers of black people from southern states seeking work in the big cities of the North, the black community of Harlem became a prosperous and important part of New York City and one of the most important centers of black culture in America. In literature, the theater, and music, black Americans reached new heights of cultural achievement.

By attracting so many distinguished literary figures, the Harlem Renaissance enabled a showcase of black writers to display their talents. James Weldon Johnson was both a historian and one of the leading inspirations of the Harlem Renaissance. Claude Mackay, an immigrant from Jamaica, was regarded by most critics as having been the most significant writer of the movement. Two other important writers were Countee Cullen, one of the major poets of his time, and Langston Hughes, the most prolific writer in the Harlem Renaissance and sometimes called "Shakespeare in Harlem."[32]

Beyond the literary world, other venues for black artists to display their talents were on the stage and in music, especially the new musical art form of jazz. On Broadway, various black composers collaborated to produce "Shuffle Along," the most successful show in New York during 1921–22. Perhaps the most enduring contribution was in jazz music, which was so popular with Americans that the entire period became known as the Jazz Age. Ferdinand "Jelly Roll" Morton was one of the pioneers, serving as the first jazz composer and one of the most innovative jazz pianists of all time. In 1920, jazz moved from its origins in New Orleans to Chicago, where it attracted a wider audience and soon became the music of black America. Louis Armstrong, possibly the best-known jazz performer of the 1920s, helped synthesize blues and ragtime music and became one of the fathers of jazz.[33]

This new music form took the country by storm in the 1920s and was hailed by both the general public and music critics. Even white musicians became involved, creating an offshoot called syncopated jazz, of which George Gershwin's "Rhapsody in Blue" became the most popular piece. Paul Whiteman was the leader of the most important of the white bands and became known for symphonic jazz, his version of this popular musical taste.[34] During the decade, the Harlem Renaissance spread beyond New York to many other large urban areas in the nation. By 1930, however, the movement was over, with the Depression making it more difficult for those in the arts and letters to ply their trade.

Women, like black Americans, also experienced profound cultural change during the decade. Prior to the 1920s, women were heavily involved in trying to uplift society through progressive campaigns. Between 1900 and 1920, women had been one of the dominant forces attempting to wipe out prostitution, abolish the saloon, and in general trying to raise the social standards of men. After World War I, women sought less to change the other sex and concentrated more on changing themselves.[35] The most important changes for women were outside the political world. Women gained the right to vote in 1920 with the passage of the Nineteenth Amendment, but many did not bother to vote and those who did generally cast ballots that followed the lead of their husbands, fathers, or other male relatives.[36]

In other areas such as education and employment, important trends were changing women's lifestyles. More women were entering college than ever before. By 1928, women at Columbia University outnumbered men for the first time. That same year, the number of working women was five times the figure in 1918. By 1930, more than ten million women were in the labor force (about 20 percent of the total), even in such nontraditional areas as business. One unfortunate byproduct of women's greater freedom in society was a steady increase in family instability. The rate of divorce, which was only 8.8 per 100 marriages in 1910, rose to 16.5 per 100 by 1928.[37]

An equally startling aspect of the "new woman" of the 1920s was her changing manners and morals. She was described as the "Flapper," a style identified by short hair, short skirts, and a deemphasis of the hips and breasts. (The term *Flapper* is nineteenth-century English slang for an unruly girl).[38] F. Scott Fitzgerald immortalized her in his early novels, depicting her as indulging in a seemingly endless round of drinking, smoking, and flirting. The Flapper represented a change from feminism of the earlier progressive era, which had focused on improving society. Her main interest now on herself, this new woman demanded the same social freedom that men enjoyed. The newly emancipated woman left home and asserted herself in the business world. She also began smoking and drinking in public for the first time. Women who had helped lead the fight for Prohibition now appeared in droves in the speakeasy. Drinking changed from a masculine activity to one shared by both sexes together as the previously "for men only" attitude was abandoned. "Under the new [system], not only the drinks were mixed but the company as well."[39] She began using more cosmetics and spurred the rise of the cosmetics industry, changes that reflected the new urbanism and the mass-market society. By the end of the Flapper era in 1930, women had established their rights in such masculine fields as drinking, smoking, swearing, sexual activities, and even disturbing the community peace.[40]

One of the most controversial changes involving women was the new attitude toward sex. Before World War I, a more male-oriented sexual code existed. Men were expected to succumb to the temptations of sex but only with a "special class of outlawed women," while women from respectable families were supposed to have no such temptations. The breakdown of the Victorian code, with its emphasis on feminine purity, began in the Greenwich Village society of pre-World War I New York City and accelerated during the 1920s. There was greater sexual freedom during the decade, reflecting the influence of Freud, the automobile, and the "sex and confess" magazines. As part of this upheaval in sexual values, there was more open dialogue between men and women. Modesty, reticence, and chivalry were going out of style, and women no longer wanted to be "ladylike" or pushed their daughters to be "wholesome."[41] Before settling down, younger women of the postwar generation appeared eager to abandon all social restraints on their behavior and enjoy the pleasures customarily reserved for men.

The 1920s was a time so preoccupied with sex that the topic was said to occupy the place in modern life that religion had occupied in the Middle Ages.[42] These changing sexual attitudes were reflected in a new type of dancing and music. The saxophone replaced the violin as the dominant instrument in the orchestra and the dancing itself was closer than ever before. The *Catholic Telegraph* of Cincinnati observed, "The music is sensuous, the embracing of partners—the female only half dressed—is absolutely indecent, and the motions—they are such as may not be described without any respect for propriety in a family newspaper."[43]

Much of the new sexual attitudes reflected the influence of the Viennese psychiatrist Sigmund Freud, many of whose writings predated 1900 but achieved a mass following in the United States for the first time in the 1920s. Freud stimulated a revolution in sexual attitudes by helping to overturn existing moral codes that he showed to be based on superstition. Freud's theories helped make psychology a national mania, introducing the nation to such ideas as libido, defense mechanisms, the unconscious and the subconscious, and repression and suppression. His theories on sex as a key human motivating factor, which is too often repressed by society, caused a new attitude toward sexual expression and resulted in a more open discussion of sex—by men and women.[44]

Freud's theories appeared to resolve many of society's most pressing problems. To many people, he provided a justification for rebelling against all accepted social conventions, especially sexual customs. Freud also offered a simple explanation for the personal and collective anxieties that affected American society in the postwar years. His ideas led to an attack on middle-class conceptions of modesty and self-control. Inhibition was denounced as the root cause of mental illness, while self-expression and self-gratification (even on sexual matters) were praised as the means to health and happiness.[45]

But the true meaning of Freud's theories was often misunderstood. He did not urge a revolt against all inhibitions and he never championed total sexual freedom as the requisite for health and happiness. In fact, he believed that civilization sometimes demanded restraint from pleasures, even sexual ones. The real purpose of his theories was to explain human motivation as primarily sexual in origin and thus to remove from the individual the burden of undeserved guilt and excess repression. Some people, mistakenly claiming that

Freud advocated free love, cited the danger of inhibitions, inferiority complexes, and introversion caused by the repression of sexual desire.[46] Others even interpreted history in Freudian terms, identifying repression as the cause of all the world's ills and describing American history as "three centuries of Puritanical repression, thwarting all that was healthy, spontaneous, life-reaffirming, and gracious."[47]

Because business was also one of the primary forces behind the social changes of the period, it —not surprisingly—also became a major literary theme. Bruce Barton, author of *The Man Nobody Knows,* was the best-known defender of the business civilization. His book, which put business in a religious context, offered a radical reinterpretation of Jesus as "the founder of modern business" and a "go-getter" who assembled the greatest little sales organization in history. He described Jesus as having been quite consistent with the business values of the 1920s. Jesus was an "advertising genius," the "greatest salesman of his age," and a "forceful executive." *The Man Nobody Knows* was the best-selling literary work in America during 1925 and 1926. The book fitted in with the pro-business climate of the times and, despite its provocative theme, was even praised by ministers.[48]

The most distinguished writers of the period, however, were harsh social critics who disliked the business culture of the 1920s. Sometimes called the "lost generation," these intellectuals were filled with disillusionment, rebellion, and alienation. They were disturbed by the savagery of World War I and the disappointing peace settlement afterward. They criticized the nations's dominant commercial culture, as well as nearly every important aspect of society during the 1920s.

World War I, which had led to so many changes in American life, emerged as a major literary theme in the 1920s. Most American writers saw the conflict as an unmitigated disaster. Ernest Hemingway in *A Farewell to Arms* wrote, "The war annihilated all reason, virtue and human compassion."[49] Leading progressive intellectuals of the prewar era had assumed that reason, clear thinking, and good ideas could transform social institutions for the better. In the postwar decade, such optimism disappeared from the major works of American writers and was replaced by devastating social criticism.

The postwar intellectuals launched a searching reexamination of all major American values and institutions. Few in number, they were highly vocal and their influence dominated both American literature and eventually the thought of the entire country.[50] They were believers in science, usually at the expense of faith in religion. These writers opposed attempts to regulate personal conduct, expressing a strong belief in freedom while attacking the old morality. They supported sexual freedom and open discussion of sex, while opposing censorship, Puritanism, and Victorianism. Their cynical attitude even shaped their views on history. They looked down upon all previous eras in history except certain "more enlightened" periods, such as ancient Greece, Renaissance Italy, France during the Enlightenment, and eighteenth-century England.[51]

The 1920s marked a literary renaissance in America that had been unmatched since the pre-Civil War days of Emerson, Whitman, and Thoreau. The best known of the postwar writers were F. Scott Fitzgerald, Sinclair Lewis, Ernest Hemingway, and Eugene O'Neill, three of whom later won Nobel Prizes in literature. This new generation of writers especially derided the American village and small town, linking it to bigotry and hypocrisy and generally criticizing the greed and shallowness of the period. They attacked life in these places and the heroes of their novels were depicted as being stifled by their home towns and forced to escape either to Manhattan or abroad.[52]

The two most effective critics of American culture in the 1920s were the journalist H. L. Mencken and the novelist Sinclair Lewis. The literary revolution was launched by Sinclair Lewis with *Main Street* (1920) and *Babbitt* (1922), in which the author revealed the ugliness of the American small town, the cultural poverty of its life, the tyranny of its many prejudices, and the blatant vulgarity of the social climber. After the publication of *Babbitt*, a flood of books by other authors reflected the intellectuals' dissatisfaction with the rule of America by the business class (symbolized by George Babbitt). Lewis, who became the first American to win the Nobel Prize in literature, extended his critique of American society when he attacked physicians in *Arrowsmith* in 1925 and ministers in *Elmer Gantry* in 1927.[53]

The leader of the decade's intellectual revolt was H. L. Mencken, who in 1923 began publishing *The American Mercury,* a magazine that featured articles of social criticism by important writers. The noted journalist Walter Lippmann called Mencken "the most powerful personal influence on this whole generation of educated people."[54] By opposing theologians, reformers, and educators, Mencken inspired an intellectual attack on politics, old-fashioned morals, and fundamentalism. When asked why he lived in a country he disliked so much, Mencken replied, "Why do people go to zoos?"[55]

Mencken had an especially sharp pen for his many adversaries. He loathed the small-town middle class, including among his targets politicians, farmers, members of the clergy, temperance reformers, Klansmen, and fanatics of whatever persuasion. He believed these groups represented hypocrisy, greed, religious intolerance, and political insincerity. In spite of his attacks on so many negative elements in society, he was criticized for having a somewhat shallow perspective and for failing to understand the shock that change caused to millions of Americans.[56]

So disenchanted were the intellectuals in the 1920s that some of them chose to escape to Europe; the most important of these expatriates were Ernest Hemingway and F. Scott Fitzgerald. As these writers exemplified by their own relocating abroad, their novels had a theme of rejection of dominant American values. They focused upon characters who were lost and despairing, who found no meaning in life beyond universal pleasures, and who rejected the world as it was but had no solution and no theory about what had gone wrong. These writers stressed that the war had overturned Western civilization, which had not yet righted itself.[57]

Although not an expatriate himself, Eugene O'Neill also examined the lives of people in despair who could not adjust to society. He focused upon the dark and violent side of mankind and his plays had a theme of violence or tension from potential violence, of the irrationality of men who appear on the surface to be civilized.[58] To writers such as O'Neill, an imbalance had occurred between the changing postwar world and everyday people seeking to find their proper place in society.

The intellectuals' revolt of the 1920s reflected the decline of the genteel culture, which had ruled over American values and ideals for nearly two centuries. A new American culture was emerging that reflected such major influences as the automobile, the movies, and the radio. The former genteel cultural order had been the instrument of the rural American middle class to teach the rest of society a code of behavior. Expanding urban and industrial centers, the ideas of Sigmund Freud, advances in technology, as well as the literary revolt were all challenging the relevance of the older, small-town values underlying genteel culture.

One aspect of this cultural struggle was the increasingly difficult position of the Protestant church, one of the pillars of genteel society. The dominant Protestant church saw two of its major philosophies, the social gospel idea and the fundamentalist creed, under assault. The church was facing challenges from the influx of Catholics and Jews and by the rise of modern science. Throughout the 1920s, there was a steady decline in religion, which appeared less relevant when put alongside the new developments in science and modern life.

One of the most striking indications of the new position of religion was the rise of the faith healer, Aimee Semple McPherson. The former missionary, teacher, and carnival barker attracted great numbers to her faith healings. An almost complete lack of dogma and theology, the promise of a close and easy relationship with God, and the lavishness of her church distinguished her from the plain tradition of historic Protestantism. She attracted all kinds of worshipers with an amazing blend of show business and faith healing. Denounced as a charlatan by many male religious leaders and social critics, McPherson was the first woman to control a powerful radio station as well as the first to preach over the airwaves. Her church reflected "the new materialistic, mass-consuming, sophisticated, pleasure-loving urban culture" and she found her greatest success in appealing to the uprooted who were trying to start new lives.[59] She also demonstrated the changing position of women in society.

The mainstream Protestant church reacted to all these changes in society by becoming more conservative and focusing its attention toward theology and away from its previous social gospel idea of reforming society. A serious problem was the growing clash between the conservatives and the modernists who questioned the literal interpretation of the Bible, including some of its most venerated creeds. The old small-town Protestant culture saw its religious, ethical, and moral values being flaunted at the same time its economic underpinnings were collapsing with falling farm prices. Rural, old-stock Americans, who were increasingly frustrated, bitter, conscious of their growing inferiority, and deeply sensitive to the destruction of their traditional values, sought new venues to defend their position. Unfortunately, one outlet for their frustration was to join the Ku Klux Klan and target the usual scapegoats: Catholics, Jews, and blacks.

After World War I, a cultural order that had dominated American life since the eighteenth century lost its hold on the minds of its adherents and a significant cultural break with the past occurred. The critics' fiercest ridicule was directed against the genteel effort to maintain small-town manners and habits as a guide for the newly emerging urban society. In the cultural disorder of the 1920s, brought on by the new technology, new media, and economic development, significant numbers of Anglo-Saxon Americans of every class and region fell back on racial and religious prejudices as their answer to the great cultural challenges of modern industrial America.

6

The Dark Side of the Twenties

THE 1920S WAS A DIFFICULT TIME for the United States, with new population trends and ideas testing the nation's core beliefs. A conflict broke out between the values of small-town rural Protestant America and the more diverse American society that was increasingly centered in the cities. In this struggle, almost every existing social institution was questioned. Although the traditionalists won several key victories, the forces of change were in the ascendency by the end of the decade.

A historic shift in the nation's demographic patterns was an underlying factor in these cultural changes. During the 1920s, the urban population exceeded the population living in the rural areas for the first time. This change reflected the continuous exodus of the farmer to the city, the migration of southern black people to the North, and the vast waves of immigration after 1900 (of which most people wound up in the cities). This population shift evolved into culture conflict, with those people holding to older rural values feeling threatened by the new city culture and fighting to retain their previous supremacy. Many rural leaders believed that the city was a center of debauchery, inhabited by people not of fundamental American values. To varying degrees, this urban-rural conflict was manifested in the rise of the Ku Klux Klan, anti-immigrant sentiment, Prohibition, fear of radicals, and a determined counterattack by the fundamentalists.

At the core of these conflicts was the greater resistance to change in the rural areas. Less isolated than the countryside, "the American city entered the twentieth century at least a decade or two before the rural part of the nation."[1] In spite of the major impact caused by such technological breakthroughs as the automobile and the radio, life for most people in rural America in the early 1920s was essentially unchanged from what it had been in the late nineteenth century. Especially in the rural areas, a feeling of deep anxiety existed in the United States after World War I. In spite of prosperity, the country felt deeply threatened from within and Americans did not retain their former confidence in democracy and religion. Fear of the Germans during the war had been transferred into a number of domestic concerns. There was a fear of the foreign-born, who had not yet adapted to American ways, and of the big city, where so many foreigners lived with values different from those of nineteenth-century America. Various efforts toward social change such as the new sexual freedom were condemned as un-American, with the more conservative Americans attempting to impose their values on American society. This resistance to change and insistence on conformity also involved the desire of rural church members to turn back modernism in religion and compel morality by statute. The protest of the tradition-minded American during the 1920s left its imprint upon practically every major social and political debate of the decade.

One of the earliest indications of a counteroffensive by rural America was the rise of the Ku Klux Klan, the best-known symbol of intolerance in the 1920s. In 1915, William Simmons proclaimed the Klan to be reborn amid a mass rally at Stone Mountain, Georgia. Its declared purposes were to uphold "Americanism," advance Protestant Christianity, and eternally maintain white supremacy. There were striking differences between the reborn Klan of the 1920s and its post-Civil War ancestor. The original Klan of the 1860s was for white supremacy only and admitted all whites. The new Klan was more diverse in its goals; admitted only native-born white Protestants; was strongly anti-foreign, anti-Catholic and anti-Semitic; and opposed "immoral" people such as adulterers and liquor interests as well as black people. It crusaded against all who offended the Klan's vision of a racially and morally pure America. Initially the Klan was kept going by the wartime crusade against Germany, opposition to alien Communists, and fear in the South of changes that would follow the return of black veterans.

Simmons, a professor at a small Georgia college, was unable to attract much of a following for the Klan in its early years; the group's membership by 1920 was only about 5,000, belonging to a few chapters in Georgia and Alabama. Only when Simmons teamed up with two clever promoters, Edward Clark and Elizabeth Tyler, early in the decade did the membership begin to soar. These two added a business mentality to the Klan organization, which was another difference from the post-Civil War Klan. They offered a percentage of the Klan's initiation dues to the recruiters, adding more incentive in the drive to attract new members, and kept a percentage of the dues for themselves. In exchange for taking over the actual management of the Klan, Simmons promised Clark and Tyler eight dollars of every ten-dollar initiation fee collected by their organizers.

The two promoters broadened the Klan's agenda to include a defense of traditional moral values and Biblical fundamentalism as well as new groups to oppose. At first a southern-based organization focusing on white supremacy, the Klan tried to capitalize on the fear in the South about impending social change caused by the return of the one-half million black veterans who had served in the war and by the massive emigration of another one-half million black people who had emigrated to the North. When these fears of a major change in racial attitudes went unrealized, the Klan turned to its other targets: Catholics, bootleggers, Jews, immigrants, and people deemed immoral.

The Klan's assault on Catholics, Jews, and foreigners was different from previous bouts of intolerance against specific minorities in the United States. The Know-Nothings' campaign against the Irish in the 1850s and the crusade against the Chinese in California in the 1870s targeted groups living in close proximity. The Klan's strength lay mainly in the rural areas of the South, the Midwest, and the West where, except in Louisiana, the Catholic and Jewish populations were small and innocuous and the foreigners were an insignificant number. Did these attacks mask a more widespread twentieth-century social malaise, with the Negro, the Jew, the Catholic, and the immigrant serving as convenient and unfortunate scapegoats? Did the Klan actually reflect opposition to many aspects of the new urban culture: its social mixtures, its intellectuality, its liberal politics, and its new standards of ethics and morality?

The Klan was based in the small towns, drawing most of its recruits from the less-educated and less-sophisticated part of the population. It drew upon a sense of desperation felt by Protestant townsmen of native stock who felt both eclipsed by the rise of the city and mocked and exploited by the country's social and economic elite. The Klan's greatest selling point became the protection of traditional American values and it especially opposed the New Immigrant from southern and eastern Europe, blaming him for causing a moral breakdown. The weakening of traditional religious and moral values of small-town America was said to be exemplified by the widespread violations of Prohibition, the new sexual freedom, and the growing acceptance of the theory of evolution. These "immoral" values seemed to threaten the foundation of fundamentalist Christianity and created new opportunities for Klan recruiting.

The Klan's growth was greatly aided by the Protestant church, which supplied respectability and a good part of its local leadership. Essentially, Protestant fundamentalists constituted "the backbone of the Klan."[2] Of the Protestant churches, the most sympathetic to the Klan were the Baptists, Methodists, and the Disciples of Christ. The Klan attracted millions of supporters by its anti-Catholicism, along with its promise to restore morality and to bring Christian righteousness to society. In a new form of racism, the Klan preferred Anglo-Saxon whites over other whites and became vehemently anti-Catholic for the first time. One of its leaders stated, "The Klan stood for the same things as the Church, but we did the things the Church couldn't do" (such as boycotting Catholic businesses, intimidating Catholic individuals, or attacking bootleggers).[3] By 1921, the Klan had shifted its focus of activities away from black people and now specialized in attacking white people, who became its principal victims in all parts of the country.

Under its most influential leader of the decade, Hiram Evans, the Klan spelled out its doctrine of prejudice and moral uplift for the nation. Evans stated that "the Nordic American today is a stranger in large parts of the land his fathers gave him." He criticized the melting pot as a "ghastly failure." On the issue of job competition, Evans stated, "While the American can out-work the alien, the alien can so far under-live the American as to force him out of all competitive labor." He called prejudice against foreign ideas "a protective device of nature against mental food that may be indigestible." The Klan stressed "loyalty to the white race, . . .and to the spirit of Protestantism which has been an essential part of Americanism ever since the days of Roanoke and Plymouth Rock." Furthermore, "Americanism could only be achieved if the pioneer stock is kept pure." In his vehemence against Catholicism, Evans declared that "Rome shall not rule America." He added that Protestantism was more than just a religion. "[It] was the expression in religion of the same spirit of independent self-rule and freedom which was one of the highest achievements of the Nordic race."[4] Obviously, the Klan represented a troubled group of Americans who were recruited mainly from the countryside, were conscious of their growing inferiority, and were deeply sensitive to the destruction of their traditional values by the new culture of the cities.

By 1921, many forces in society were set in play that fostered the rise of the Klan, including economic depression, Prohibition, mass immigration, and the disillusionment with foreign affairs after World War I. The agricultural depression of 1920 strengthened the movement because the farmer's economic frustration was diverted into Klan hatreds. Furthermore, fear of the "new Negro" in the South after World War I motivated the Klan to try to keep the Negro "in his place." All these frustrations of rural white Americans and the many social and economic problems of the early 1920s led the Klan into its "golden age." In 1920, the Klan was represented only in small-town America, especially in the South, where there was a final effort to preserve the values of the community against change. But in 1921, the Klan began to greatly expand its membership outside of its original base in the South. By the end of that year, it claimed to be operating in forty-five states and enrolling 1,000 members a day. By 1924, 40 percent of its members were from three states (Indiana, Ohio, and Illinois); meanwhile, 25 percent were in the Southwest (from Louisiana to Arizona), 16 percent were from the old Confederacy, 8 percent were in the rest of the Midwest, 7 percent were in the Pacific Northwest, and 3 percent were in the North Atlantic and New England area.[5]

At the same time that the Klan's national appeal was growing, an internal power struggle developed, causing a major change in its leadership. In 1922, Clark and Tyler were ousted and Hiram Evans, a dentist from Texas, became the new national leader, replacing the somewhat ineffective founder, William Simmons. (Clark later went to jail for mail fraud and violation of the Mann Act.) Evans ended the previous financial incentives, which under the old system had made the recruiters rich, instead placing them on salary.

One of the most important changes under the new leadership was the greater emphasis on politics. The Klan shifted from terror to more active political involvement and such traditional Klan punishments as lynchings and floggings were replaced by getting pro-Klan candidates elected to high political positions. In Oklahoma, an anti-Klan governor was impeached by a Klan-dominated legislature. In Oregon, the Klan won the governorship and enough seats in the legislature to ban parochial schools. (This action was later overturned by the courts.) In Colorado, the Klan elected two United States senators. In Indiana, the Klan elected a senator and the governor and dominated the state legislature. Under Evans, Klan membership reached a peak of five million by the middle of the decade and was so powerful that it could defeat an attempt to condemn it at the 1924 Democratic Convention. (William Jennings Bryan successfully deflected an effort by the convention to condemn the Klan, replacing it with a resolution that merely supported toleration of all groups.)[6] From about 1922 to 1925, the Klan was a major force in American politics and rural life and the United States had never had a stronger "hate organization." In an amazing display of its strength in 1925, the Klan paraded 40,000 members down Pennsylvania Avenue in the nation's capital.[7]

That same year the Klan began a rapid decline, partly because of problems within the organization. A. E. Stephenson, the Klan leader in Indiana, which had 350,000 members and was the most powerful state organization in the country, was convicted of kidnaping and murder. Believing he had been abandoned, Stephenson "blew the whistle" on many of his cohorts and caused some of the Klan-elected officials to be indicted for fraud and bribery. (In one trial in which a Klan official was acquitted of murder, his defense attorney was future United States Supreme Court justice Hugo Black.)[8] With all these revelations, the Klan lost its claim to be preserving America's morals. The spillover from Stephenson's downfall helped lead the entire organization to a nationwide decline, from which it never recovered.

Throughout the remainder of the decade, the Klan steadily grew weaker and by 1929 its power and glory were almost gone. The nomination of the "Catholic candidate" Al Smith exemplified the decline in Klan influence in the Democratic Party. The Klan fell largely because of a series of self-inflicted wounds. As one historian of the Ku Klux Klan writes:

> It was not the Klan's principles which had been responsible, for had it selected its members more carefully and grown more slowly, it might have found a permanent place in the lodge world of America. It was the combination of violence, politics, and exploitive leadership which destroyed its power. The Klan's leaders were out for money and ruled irrationally and dictatorially in its pursuit. The fight over the spoils wrecked the organization in nearly every state and practically every community.[9]

The Klan's decline reflected both its internal weaknesses and a more settled atmosphere in American society. Its appeal to religious values was weakened by the immorality of its leaders, so that eventually the public was repelled. Many of the social and political fears on which it had capitalized had faded: no massive race rebellion had occurred, the immigration policy had been tightened, and the U.S. economy was in the midst of a six-year expansion. By 1929, the Klan had no more than 100,000 members and had returned to its original base in the South. To expand its membership, it decided to change its principal targets once more. The Klan, which had shifted its hostility from black people to Catholics and aliens during the early 1920s, began to focus on labor unions, liberals in government, and anti-Semitism by the end of the decade.[10]

Another movement that became prominent during and immediately after World War I, paralleling the rise of the Klan and drawing from some of the same sources, was Prohibition. Apart from the morality aspect, the arguments for Prohibition were extensive. Proponents even claimed that nearly three thousand infants were smothered in bed each year by drunken parents.[11] Drinking was associated with such unpopular groups as the immigrant masses, the rich, and especially the saloon-keepers, who (allegedly) ran the city machines and controlled the votes of the whisky-loving immigrants. Drinking was also linked to the German brewers and their "disloyal" compatriots who drank ale and beer.[12] Because the greatest support for drinking was in the cities, the urban areas were regarded by the Prohibitionists as their chief enemy.

In their fight to outlaw drinking, rural Prohibitionists joined with urban-based progressives who also hoped it would lead to better moral character, individual improvement, and national greatness. The progressives saw Prohibition as one way to uplift the working class and deflect the danger of class unrest and the rise of radical groups like the socialists and the IWW. Would it help eliminate poverty and protect the family? Would it curb unemployment and also lessen physical abuse of women and children? Would it purify politics by removing the breeding ground for corrupt bargains between political bosses and the immigrant?

One of the most severe indictments by the Prohibitionists was the charge that the liquor industry stimulated crime. The saloon-keeper, confronted by overcompetition, was practically forced to disobey the liquor laws and to ally himself with vice and crime in order to survive. The Sunday closing laws, which reflected the moral standards of middle-class Americans, ran directly counter to the values and desires of most city dwellers, especially the Irish and Germans. The saloon-keeper not only found it profitable to cater to the Sunday demand but had to remain open to keep from losing his customers and going out of business.[13]

The Prohibitionists also outlined a long list of other, more unsavory activities allegedly committed by the saloon-keeper. He was accused of selling adulterated drinks or cheap liquor in expensive bottles; of encouraging hard drinking by patrons; and of selling drinks to women, children, and known drunkards. To further enhance his income, the saloon-keeper entered into partnerships with prostitution, gambling, and even petty crime (such as allowing pickpockets to operate in the saloon). He paid protection money to the police to keep these arrangements going. He even helped run up votes for the political machines and a formidable alliance was created when he delivered votes and money to the machines.[14] To the Prohibitionists, the saloon had become the modern "den of iniquity."

Allied with the urban Prohibitionists were southerners who raised the questions of race and class conflict. They believed that liquor debauched both black people and lower-class whites, kept these groups poor, and prevented the South from developing. They also believed it led to crime and immorality and worsened the race question. With the southern Prohibitionists, along with sympathetic rural groups in the Midwest and West and urban progressives, a coalition was forming to make America "dry."

The growing strength of the Prohibitionists was the culmination of a movement whose roots ran deep in American history. Colonial Georgia had outlawed drinking (albeit temporarily) in the 1730s. The modern era of Prohibition goes back to the 1851 "Maine Law," which made that state the first in the nation to completely outlaw drinking. By 1900, the movement had expanded and five states had total Prohibition while many others had local-option laws. During the early 1900s, the cause was greatly strengthened when the progressive reformers joined the crusade. In 1913, the temperance forces were strong enough in Congress to pass the Webb-Kenyon Act, which prohibited the transport of liquor into dry areas (while en route to wet states), enacted over President Taft's veto. By 1915, every state had at least local-option laws and eleven states had total Prohibition. Two years later, twenty-seven states, mainly in the South, the Midwest, and the West, were dry and many others had local-option laws.[15] The Prohibitionists now concentrated their efforts behind a drive for national Prohibition.

The movement to outlaw drinking at the national level made its breakthrough during the World War I crisis. The opponents of drinking, led principally by the Protestant churches, won significant support in Congress in the 1916 elections and became especially strong during World War I. The war helped the Prohibitionists because of the increasing hatred of German beer brewers, the need for grain used in making alcohol, and a desire to maintain military discipline and virtuous character among the soldiers. In 1917, Congress prohibited in the Lever Act the further manufacture of liquor for the duration of the war. The Eighteenth Amendment was passed by Congress the next year, prohibiting the sale, manufacture, or transportation of alcoholic beverage. (It did not outlaw buying or drinking alcohol.) In January 1919 the amendment was ratified by the states, and nine months later the Volstead Act was passed to enforce the law.

The beginning of Prohibition (in 1920) symbolized the victory of small towns over big cities; of evangelical Protestants over Catholics, Jews, and Lutherans; and of old-stock Anglo-Saxons over the New Immigrants.[16] The main supporters of Prohibition were in the South and West; they were farmers, residents of small towns, the Methodists and Baptist churches, Republicans (except in the South), and married women. At first, few anticipated massive resistance to the new law. Navy Secretary Josephus Daniels declared "the saloon is as dead as slavery."[17] William Jennings Bryan predicted that, as the virtue of the country asserted itself, the number of citizens with a fondness for beer and hard drink would "certainly decrease."[18]

But almost from the beginning these predictions proved false and enforcement became a problem. Although Prohibition reduced the amount of drinking of hard liquors by an estimated 50 percent,[19] a total ban proved impossible. Most people did not believe it was a truly a "crime" to drink, and if caught there was no legal penalty for drinking. Illegal stills and smuggling stymied the law and by 1925, only an estimated 5 percent of illegal liquor smuggled in (either by boat or by sled across the Canadian border) was stopped. Even doctors were involved in the violations. The Volstead Act did not prohibit prescribing liquor for medical purposes and family doctors could write prescriptions (for alcohol) for those suffering from "thirstitis." Doctors were also permitted access to six quarts of whisky and five gallons of alcohol per year for "laboratory" purposes, some of which undoubtedly wound up in circulation.[20] There was an inadequate number (only three thousand for the entire country by 1930) of poorly paid Prohibition agents, of whom approximately 10 percent were ultimately fired for corruption.[21] Both the states and the federal government were reluctant to spend more on hiring new agents, and some states either refused to pass or later repealed their own "baby Volstead" acts. Instead, Congress chose to increase the penalties for violating the Prohibition laws, making juries less likely to convict. By 1924, a political understanding had been reached by the national government—strong support for the law but not enough money to enforce it.

One example of the lack of success in enforcing Prohibition was what occurred in the city of Detroit, which became the "liquor capital" of the nation
(liquor was mostly smuggled in from Canada). The illegal liquor business in
Detroit was estimated at $215 million annually and was the second-largest in-
dustry in the city after automobiles. The police chief of Detroit said there were
1,500 saloons when Prohibition went into effect (in 1920) and by 1925, the
number had risen to at least 15,000 places selling liquor in the city.[22] Because
of problems in Detroit and other parts of the country, in 1929 the assistant attorney general in charge of enforcing Prohibition said that in the United
States liquor could be bought "at almost any hour of the day or night, [in]
urban or rural districts, [in] the smaller towns or the cities."[23]

Ironically, although one of the arguments in favor of Prohibition had
been that it would prevent crime, the opposite effect occurred. Bootlegging
produced the chief income for gangs, which infected the large cities. (The
term "bootlegger" comes from a practice in some of the southern states,
where the "moonshiner" sought to avoid paying a federal tax on manufactured distilled spirits by hiding the small liquor bottle in the leg of his boot.)[24]
By 1927, Al Capone in Chicago was operating a $60 million business and had
a private army of nearly one thousand hoodlums who "rubbed out" rival
bootleggers who infringed on Capone's "territory." Gangsters in many large
cities either took over the government or were permitted to create their own
"private governments"; they also moved into legitimate businesses and labor
unions.

By the end of the decade, Prohibition still appeared to have the support of
the majority of the nation but its strength was eroding. The depression of
1929 increased pressure for repeal. Was the high rate of crime, crooked politics, and other social maladies too high a price to pay for continuing the experiment? In the Wickersham Report of 1931, former attorney general
George Wickersham and his panel concluded that the social and political costs
of Prohibition outweighed the benefits.[25] The report did not recommend repeal, although this was a clear inference in the study. This finding, coupled
with a growing national sentiment for repeal of the amendment—fueled by a
concern over the contempt for law enforcement that was bred by the ban on
drinking—showed that the days of Prohibition were numbered.

Another crusade that came out of the fundamentalist counterattack
against the modernists was the attempt to reverse America's historic Open
Door policy on immigration. Throughout the nineteenth century, the

nation's optimism and passion for economic growth encouraged this policy. But U.S. attitudes toward immigrants began to change when the Old Immigrant from northern and western Europe was replaced in the annual arrivals by the New Immigrant from southern and eastern Europe. By the early 1900s, confidence about the nation's ability to absorb a steady stream of immigrants from diverse backgrounds had given way to a new pessimism about assimilation and the resilience of the social order.

To old-stock Americans, the sheer number of immigrants was sufficient to cause alarm. Between 1900 and 1917, nearly 14.3 million people arrived in the United States, averaging in some years more than one million. By 1910, 15.2 percent of the population was first—or second-generation American (68 percent of whom were living in the cities).[26] In 1920, on the eve of the historic shift in immigration policy, there were nearly 14 million foreign-born people (including 8,046,000 New Immigrants) out of a total population of 105,700,000 in the United States.[27] With such a radical shift in the nation's ethnic background, many Americans had "a fear of being overwhelmed and of suddenly finding one day that they are no longer themselves."[28]

Not only the volume but also the cultures and lifestyles of the newer immigrants seemed threatening to the old-stock Americans. Most were Catholics and Jews from southern and eastern Europe and possessed different core values. They were not used to free enterprise, industrialism, competition, self-help, and social mobility, and were not accustomed to government promoting moral ideas such as Prohibition. A culture conflict developed, as old-stock Protestants living in rural America had difficulty accepting the manners and values of the cities, with their diverse ethnic groups, relaxed ethical codes, and easy political virtues. The nation became hostile to the New Immigrant and wished to preserve the old American ethnicity before it was too late. These feelings led many Americans to doubt whether the traditional Open Door policy on immigration should continue.

As with Prohibition, World War I had also stimulated a reexamination of the immigrant "problem." Congress had earlier taken initial, unsuccessful steps to lock out the immigrant. It passed literacy tests in 1899, 1909, and 1917 (requiring that a person be able to read in English or any other language to qualify for admission), which were vetoed respectively by Presidents Cleveland, Taft, and Wilson. In 1917, Congress passed a literacy test for the fourth time and then overrode Wilson's veto. (Between 1899 and 1909, more than one-quarter of the immigrants arriving were unable to read in any lan guage.)[29] During the war and immediately afterward, interest also focused on the policies of repression, Americanization, and deportation. One form of this new hostility was a ban in many states on aliens obtaining licenses in medicine, pharmacy, engineering, and other professions. Even more ominous for the immigrant, there was also a general acceptance of closing the "open door"; the American public no longer favored unrestricted immigration. The wave of postwar strikes (many in industries with a large number of "hyphenated Americans"), racial conflict in the cities, and the equation of aliens with political radicalism during the Red Scare, now intensified the drive to shut out the New Immigrant altogether.

World War I and its aftermath had shaken America's confidence in its ability to absorb large numbers of immigrants, and raised questions about possible divided loyalties among immigrants and about whether they could ever be assimilated. Walter Hines Page, wartime ambassador to England, stated after the war, "We Americans have got to . . . hang our Irish agitators and shoot our hyphenates and bring up our children with reverence for English history and in the awe of English literature."[30] Even President Coolidge echoed these sentiments, stating, "America must be kept American."[31] In less polite terms, the secretary of the St. Petersburg, Florida, chamber of commerce declared that "The time has come to make this a 100% American and gentile city, as free from foreigners as from slums."[32]

This growing crisis was precipitated by the great numbers of immigrants who entered the United States immediately after World War I. Immigration had slowed during the war, but the floodgates opened soon after. More than 800,000 people entered the country in the period between June 1920 and June 1921, about 65 percent coming from southern and eastern Europe. Alarming reports were being received from consuls in Europe that millions were planning to leave and a panicky Congress rushed through an emergency restriction on further immigration. Even the former champion of open immigration, the business community, was now shifting to the camp of the restrictionists. The increased technological efficiency in business had reduced the need for unskilled workers at the same time that the industrialists were becoming more nativist because of the Red Scare.[33]

By this time, many factors were combining to strengthen the nativists and make restriction inevitable. The economic depression of the early 1920s had cut off most of the financial support for Americanization (especially from business) and the Red Scare had dried up much of the sympathy for the immigrant. The beginning of Prohibition linked the immigrant to crime because nothing in the immigrant culture made drinking seem unethical and his tendency to violate the Prohibition laws made him seem both "criminal" and immoral. The American Federation of Labor maintained its former policy of strong support for restriction as a means of protecting jobs and supporting wage scales. The open racism of the Klan, the fears harbored by old-stock Americans, and the growing hostility of business were laying the groundwork for the nativist laws of the decade.

Adding to the nativist pressures were the writings of the "scientific racists" such as Madison Grant, the intellectual leader of the movement. Although Grant's *The Passing of a Great Race* came out in 1916, he became popular only in the early 1920s. More than anyone else, he taught the American people to recognize within the white race a three-tiered hierarchy of Mediterraneans, Alpines, and Nordics; to identify themselves as Nordics; and to regard any mixture with the other two groups as a destructive process of "mongrelization." [34] Grant contended that race was the determinant of civilization and that only Aryans had built great cultures. [35] Stoddard Lothrup, Grant's main disciple, expressed special concern over the rapid rise of the "yellow" and "brown" races. He agreed with Grant that the white man's salvation rested with the Nordics and that the immigration of inferior white races would mongrelize the Nordic. [36] These racist views were reinforced by the popular novelist Kenneth Roberts, author of *Northwest Passage*. Roberts was also a firm believer in the Nordic theory and believed that a continuing deluge of Alpine, Mediterranean, and Semitic immigrants would inevitably produce "a hybrid race of people as worthless and futile as the good-for-nothing mongrels of Central America and Southeastern Europe." [37]

The growing popularity of eugenics (the study of the improvement of races) was aided by the new technique of IQ testing, which was adopted by the United States Army during World War I and whose results were released after the war. Proponents of the test believed it did not reflect environmental factors and therefore could be used to measure the intelligence of native-born Americans, as well as Old and New Immigrants. The test results indicated that foreign-born soldiers of northern European background scored almost as well as American-born Caucasians, whereas those of Latin and Slavic background averaged significantly lower. Eugenicists cited these findings as proof of the inferiority of the New Immigrants. [38] Were they of a "serf" mentality, too backward to progress? The eugenicists tried to show that even the Italian Christopher Columbus had Nordic blood and, if he did not, perhaps more credit should be given to the Nordic sailor Leif Ericson, who had reached the New World five hundred years before Columbus.[39]

A New Immigration group especially targeted by nativists was the Jews, the most hated of all the non-Nordic Europeans. Unlike the case of black people, there is virtually no history of violence against Jews in America and the discrimination of the 1920s took more subtle forms such as instituting unofficial quotas for admissions of Jewish students at prominent universities. Even Harvard University expressed fears of becoming the "new Jerusalem" and instituted a quota.[40] Part of this anti-Semitism was rooted in the "100 percent Americanism" slogan of the war years, which aimed to make everyone conform to mainstream Protestant values. Prominent German Jews came under suspicion during the World War I crisis, as did Jewish radicals, socialists, and Bolsheviks during the period of the Red Scare. Would Jewish immigrants spread Bolshevist ideas in the United States after World War I and undermine the traditional society favored by old-stock Americans?

Two of the most important sources of anti-Semitism were the famous industrialist Henry Ford and the Ku Klux Klan. Ford published anti-Semitic smears in his newspaper, *The Dearborn Independent*. Expressing fear of the "international Jew," Ford supported the ideas in the infamous forgery *Protocols of the Elders of Zion*, which allegedly "proved" the existence of a Jewish plot to rule the world.[41] A rare case of violence against Jews was the Leo Frank lynching in Georgia in 1915, which was followed two months later by the founding of the Ku Klux Klan amid an atmosphere filled with anti-Semitism in that state.[42] For the first time in American history, there was substantial organizational support for anti-Semitism—through the Ku Klux Klan. These feelings took root early in the decade during a time of depression, disillusionment, and uneasiness over a changing America—in spite of being condemned by such prominent Americans as former presidents Woodrow Wilson and William Howard Taft. The social uneasiness was steadily building, and conditions were ripe for Congress to pass a new round of nativist legislation.

In the early 1920s, the government was "alarmed to the point of panic" when the wave of immigration was unabated by the literacy tests and felt compelled to adopt new immigration policies.[43] The wartime literacy test had failed to stem immigration and 52,000 immigrants per month were entering the country for most of 1920. In 1920–21, 119,000 Jews had entered the country and added to the pressure for restriction. Congress responded to widespread public support for a new immigration policy by ending the historic Open Door policy in several stages. The temporary plan of 1921 limited European immigration to a total of 350,000 people. Based on the 1910 Census, it limited the annual quota of each European country to 3 percent of the number of its nationals in the United States at that time. Countries in northwestern Europe obtained the largest quotas, while those in southern and eastern Europe had much smaller quotas. The new law set the first sharp and absolute numerical limits on European immigration, with the greatest effect intended for the New Immigrant. Although the law was enacted to discriminate against southern and eastern Europe, quotas for these areas were consistently filled while those for northern and western Europe went begging and the "problem" continued.[44]

Congress responded with a 1924 law, which had a much greater impact upon the immigration process. Until 1927, the 2 percent plan would be in effect, further tightening restrictions upon the New Immigrant. This plan based quotas on the number of European nationals in the United States in 1890, a time when the New Immigration had only begun. Thus the quotas for southern and eastern Europe declined significantly while the northern and western European quotas were less affected. Among the countries experiencing the greatest change were Italy and Poland; Italy's quota was reduced from 42,000 to 4,000, while Poland's fell from 31,000 to 6,000. The overall cap on immigration would be 164,000.[45]

The 1924 law provided for a second phase to begin in 1927 (later changed to 1929), calling for a new means of fixing quotas and a lower immigration total of 150,000 per year. This total would be parceled out in proportion to the distribution of national origins of the white population of the United States in 1920. The new system preserved the national origins principle, which favored northern and western Europe. Family exceptions were permitted only for wives and minor children of American citizens, not aliens. Once again, only Canada and Latin America were excluded from the law's provisions and maintained unrestricted immigration.[46]

By the mid-1920s, the antiforeign crusade was declining and some of its leading champions were in disrepute. This changing mood of the nation was reflected in Madison Grant losing support as interest in eugenics declined, Henry Ford publicly apologizing for his anti-Semitism, and the Ku Klux Klan falling apart. By this time, prosperity had helped to stem the Klan and other "haters" and Americans were now more confident and self-assured. The nation was tired of crusading, especially because the restriction laws were in place and the problem was being "solved."[47]

The campaign to preserve America as it was and resist the forces of change entered another venue in 1925 with the Scopes trial, which tested the legality of teaching evolution in the public schools. The evolution debate demonstrated that the urban-rural conflict was not only between Protestants and Catholics but also an internal struggle between modernist Protestants and fundamentalist Protestants. The modernist wing took a symbolic rather than a literal interpretation of the Bible. By 1900, most urban Protestant ministers had accommodated their beliefs to the evolution theory but, in the rural areas where society was more insulated, the older views still prevailed. In rural areas and small towns, especially in the mountain areas of the South, many Protestant ministers continued to oppose Darwin's evolution theory. They were strengthened by popular anger against Germany (the home of modernist religion) and against attempts to accommodate religion to scholarly criticism of the Bible such as denying the miracles, and by the Red Scare (which linked atheism and antireligion sentiment to Communism).[48]

The fundamentalist movement was essentially a protest against some of the leading elements of the modern world such as industry, cities, and science. Its adherents feared that Darwin was undermining a literal interpretation of the Bible, a trend that would inevitably destroy the underpinnings of Christianity. This "back-to-basics" approach to religion drew most of its recruits from Baptists, with some support from Methodists and Presbyterians, and found a home in rural areas where religion was their principal stimulating experience. A variety of forces after World War I increasingly aroused the fundamentalists, including the steady influx of Catholics and Jews in the country during the early 1920s and the continuing decline in religious belief, partly attributable to the influence of such controversial thinkers as Darwin and Freud. Adding to the church's uneasiness was the growing importance of science. Major breakthroughs in the use of electricity—as well as the new groundbreaking theories of radioactivity, quantum physics, and relativity—led to increasing prestige for science, seemingly at the expense of religion.[49] The overall effect of these social and scientific changes was a substantial decline in the self-confidence of Protestantism, so that conditions were ripe for a counteroffensive.

The Protestant church was also having grave internal difficulties during the decade. The earlier social gospel idea that had energized the church before

World War I had faded. By the mid-1920s, the battle over social Christianity had been won largely by the conservatives, who insisted that the ministry confine its attention to theology and avoid involving the church in the world of economics and politics. The social liberals in the church now joined the modernist movement, which sought to reconcile the new views of science and psychology with traditional religion, an activity that usually weakened a literal interpretation of the Bible and cast doubt upon some of the most venerated creeds of the Protestant faith. This internal struggle weakened the church and the more secular view of religion caused the evangelical fundamentalist wing of the church to lose much of its Sunday attendance.[50]

In the early 1920s, as they saw these trends developing, the fundamentalists took the offensive in their attempt to outlaw the teaching of evolution in the public schools. The fundamentalists, whose deeply ingrained religious values had affected the struggles over Prohibition and immigration and had shaped the outlook of the Klan, were also at the root of the Scopes evolution trial. Would evolution crush the Bible and upset the moral order of society? Was fundamentalist Protestantism's literal interpretation of the Bible, which included the creation of the earth in six days, no longer possible? Would acceptance of man's evolution from lower species destroy the faith of the nation's youth, break down standards of morality, and create a wave of crime and immorality? The fundamentalists had been protesting evolution for years without success until World War I, the Red Scare, and the stressful nature of the period gave them a chance to be heard.

The fundamentalist attack on evolution was bolstered enormously when William Jennings Bryan joined the movement. Bryan, who was an evangelical as well as an active politician, joined the crusade against Darwin soon after World War I. In the conflict between a literal interpretation of the Bible and science, Bryan sided with the Scriptures. He declared, "It is better to trust in the Rock of Ages than to know the age of rocks; it is better for one to know that he is close to the Heavenly Father than to know how far the stars in the heavens are apart."[51] Bryan became a fanatic on the issue and under his leadership the campaign to coerce the teaching of the Biblical account of man's origin in biology classes quickly caught the attention of the nation. Northern and western states failed to respond to Bryan's crusade, but he found a strong following in the South. The first important victory for the anti-evolutionists came in Tennessee, where, with the help of Bryan and a powerful fundamentalist lobby, the state legislature outlawed the teaching of any theory that denied the Biblical story of man's origin. Governor Austin Peay signed the bill, believing that the law would never be enforced.[52] Critics saw the law as a threat to free speech and academic freedom and the stage was set for a historic confrontation.

When the American Civil Liberties Union arranged for a test case involving the young biology teacher John Scopes, the matter went to trial. The Scopes trial attracted national attention partly because of the famous lead attorneys William Jennings Bryan, the fundamentalist champion, and Clarence Darrow, the foremost trial lawyer in the nation and a confirmed agnostic. At the trial, Bryan announced that it would be a "duel to the death" between Christianity and evolution.[53] The Scopes trial seemed to represent all the divisions in American society during the decade. To many, the case symbolized the countryside versus the big city, the West and the South versus the East, Anglo-Saxonism versus multicultural America, Protestant versus the other religions, and traditional Protestantism versus modernists and the others.[54]

Initially, the momentum shifted toward the prosecution. At the beginning of the trial, the presiding judge, who was a fundamentalist himself, contended that the only issue before the court was whether Scopes had violated the law, which he obviously had done. The judge's ruling frustrated the defense's effort to show that the law was either incorrect or foolish. The defense rescued itself when it put Bryan on the stand as an "expert" witness for fundamentalism. Forced to admit that he had not read widely in science, philosophy, or education, Bryan weakened his credibility.[55] When he was also forced to stand behind some of the more amazing stories in the Bible as being literally true, he appeared to be naive or silly. The judge ended this line of questioning to save Bryan further embarrassment but also refused to let Bryan vindicate himself the next day by testifying again. The trial ended with Scopes being found guilty and fined $100. The Tennessee Supreme Court threw out the fine on a technicality, thereby preventing his attorneys from testing the constitutionality of the law. The victory for the fundamentalists proved to be short-lived. Ridicule was brought upon the anti-evolutionist position and, although the law in Tennessee was not repealed until decades later, it would not be enforced either. Bryan died five days after the trial ended; with his death, the heart went out of the movement, which quickly subsided.

Race as well as religion and ethnicity was another aspect of society seeking its proper form in the changing America of the 1920s. After the race riots of the immediate postwar period, in the first half of the 1920s there was a steady rise in black nationalism, partly a reaction to the increasing concern over race and culture by the Anglo-Saxon types trying to preserve an older America. The Anglo-Saxon crusade to slam the door on immigrants and to keep racial and religious minorities in their places had helped to inspire black separatism. This new black assertiveness also stemmed partly from the black veterans' World War I service, a conflict that had been heralded as a struggle for "liberty and democracy" and had led blacks to demand greater freedom.

Feeding on this dissatisfaction in the black community and on the poor state of race relations was the black leader Marcus Garvey. Having come to the United States from the island of Jamaica in 1916, Garvey became the first black leader to win a mass following. This "Moses of the Negroes" rejoiced in being totally black—in having no white ancestors in his past. His appeal was mainly to the poor and the middle class, of which many had migrated from the South and now lived in the big cities.

On the eve of American entry into World War I, Garvey founded in Harlem the United Negro Improvement Association (UNIA). This organization ran such diverse businesses as a chain of grocery stores, a laundry, a publishing house, and a restaurant. The most important of Garvey's operations was the Black Star Steamship Line, a venture designed to promote trade among Africans and their descendants throughout the world. By 1920, the UNIA claimed upwards of two million members in eight hundred chapters and four continents.[56] In return for monthly dues, UNIA members received modest health insurance and death benefits plus the emotional satisfaction of promoting racial solidarity.

Black pride, solidarity, and self-determination were Garvey's main themes. He stressed a black nationalism and a "back to Africa" program, was proud of his blackness, and saw history and religion through a black perspective. He became an implacable enemy to another black leader with similar ideas, W. E. B. Dubois, who generally appealed to more educated blacks. Garvey told his audience to glory in their blackness and African heritage and advocated the necessity for racial purity with the same vehemence that the head of the Ku Klux Klan had promoted white supremacy.[57] Garvey was reluctant to attack the Klan and in fact supported the racial ideas of the Klan but with a black viewpoint. Garvey's uplift movement for blacks focused upon black solidarity and African heritage. American blacks would achieve power and dignity, he said, when they had reclaimed Africa from the white man, which would be best achieved by building a strong, independent economic base in the United States. His overall objective was somehow to unite the black people of the world under common goals.

Garvey made powerful black and white enemies as his organization grew. He denounced the NAACP, declaring that its goal of integration represented "the greatest enemy of the Negro" because it retarded self-reliance and nationalism.[58] Fearing that UNIA represented a threat to their organization, which stressed integration and antidiscrimination, NAACP leaders denounced Garvey with an intensity usually reserved for the Klan.

By the middle of the decade, the Garvey movement was in serious trouble. J. Edgar Hoover of the FBI, perceiving Garvey's UNIA as a dangerous source of unity among urban blacks and as great a menace to the social order as were Communists and anarchists, kept UNIA under constant surveillance. Garvey was not a good businessman or administrator and irregularities were found with UNIA. The organization declined after Garvey was sent to jail in 1925 for mail fraud (he was released and deported in 1927); in addition, most black people either were too poor to sustain the group or backed the NAACP goals of integration and nondiscrimination. Garvey had shown that the black community could unite, but better organization was needed to sustain such a movement.

Another lingering source of uneasiness was the fear of radicals, an outgrowth of the Red Scare, which had abated by the early 1920s but left behind a concern throughout the decade. The case of Sacco and Vanzetti, who were Italian immigrants and anarchists, aroused the fear of both foreigners and radical ideas and was regarded as the "one case of the decade which roused the liberals from their long slumber."[59] The case involved the robbery and murder of a guard transporting money in 1920; law officers following a tip arrested Sacco and Vanzetti soon afterward with weapons in their possession. The judge at their trial was assumed to have been hostile toward radicals and (allegedly) said he wanted to "get those guys hanged."[60] In 1927, after seven years on death row, endless appeals, and investigating panels, the two were executed. Many believed that Sacco and Vanzetti were innocent victims of the "Red Scare" and that their execution was a reflection of those troubled times. In the early 1960s, the journalist Francis Russell reexamined the case. Applying modern ballistics tests that were not available in 1920, he concluded that the gun found on Sacco had killed the guard but that the tests regarding Vanzetti's weapon were inconclusive.[61] In spite of the new evidence, the fate of Sacco and Vanzetti left a lingering perception of innocent victims trapped by a wave of intolerance. Was the "innocence" of Sacco and Vanzetti (or at least Sacco) another in a long series of myths of the 1920s?

The case of Sacco and Vanzetti is another indication of the troubled character of the decade. During this coming of age for the nation, older ideas were being tested as the nation underwent a difficult transition. Of the major controversies of the period such as immigration restriction, the Klan, Prohibition, and Protestant fundamentalism, all had in common a hostility to the new urban society that was emerging and a desire to arrest change through persuasion, coercion, or statute. Eventually all these efforts by the defenders of an older America were defeated. In 1933, the Eighteenth Amendment was repealed and the Klan was little more than a dim memory. Immigration restriction was frustrated (the law did not apply to the western hemisphere) when Mexicans, French Canadians, and Puerto Ricans (all mostly Catholics) poured in. After the Scopes trial, there was little attempt to enforce the anti-evolution laws not yet repealed. At first successful, the political fundamentalists in the 1920s were ultimately defeated in trying to resist change. They successfully helped elect one more small-town president in 1928 over the Catholic Al Smith. But the Great Depression of 1929, which raised questions about the traditional laissez-faire economic theory, also ushered in a future president, Franklin Roosevelt, who was more tied to the cities and their increasingly diverse populations.

7

The Rise and Fall of Business

IN THE 1920s, business attained a stature it is unlikely to ever reach again. In an era of continuous economic expansion, the business community had the overwhelming approval of both the government and the general public. Its natural adversaries, the labor unions, were in a period of decline and the sentiment of the age was "the business of America is business." Until the 1929 stock market crash, the business community was in its golden age.

The decade of the 1920s was the last one in which laissez-faire was the guiding theme of the economy. Government regulation was almost nonexistent and, with few exceptions, only "friendly" pro-business laws would pass through Congress. The three Republican presidents and the judiciary were overwhelmingly in support of business. Only after the 1929 stock market crash did government begin to intervene in the economy more actively. At first only limited, government involvement increased substantially during the early 1930s as the nation failed to recover quickly from the Great Depression.

The 1920s, which began with a business depression in 1920–21, ended with a more serious one beginning in late 1929. When the economy recovered fully from the first depression, a six-year business expansion followed, which was only ended by the worst economic collapse in the nation's history. During this decade of economic extremes, certain groups advanced greatly while others declined or benefitted only slightly. The general prosperity of the age (in which most people shared in varying degrees) covered up key weaknesses in the economy; these weaknesses became more obvious after the stock market crash of 1929.

One of the most important economic influences on the decade was World War I. After the war there were some obvious economic difficulties in the conversion to a peacetime economy, and a wave of inflation, serious labor con-

Of A Nation (1915) and *Intolerance* (1916), respectable middle-class Americans generally regarded the movies as popular entertainment for the working population and beneath their notice, or potentially harmful to morals and to be censored. Griffith's achievements demonstrated the artistic possibilities and the storytelling power of motion pictures.[21] Soon after the war, the expanding motion picture industry emerged as the first mass cultural medium in America.

Along with the artistic quality of the directors and actors, various technical breakthroughs served to popularize movies. Most important was the addition of sound to the production. Several inventors, including Thomas Edison and Lee DeForrest, helped bring sound to movies, climaxing in the breakthrough film *The Jazz Singer* in 1927. The other development that helped to popularize films (in the summer months) was the introduction of air-conditioning to the theaters in the 1920s. When the experiment was first tried, the head of Paramount Studios, Adolph Zukor, admitted that he went to the theater more to see the patrons' reaction to air-conditioning than to the film itself.

By the 1920s, the movies had become an integral part of the American cultural scene, offering comfort and glamour at low prices. Hollywood had created a new elite of movie stars, displacing as public icons such legendary businessmen as John D. Rockefeller and J. P. Morgan. During the decade, Charlie Chaplin was the biggest star and perhaps the best-known man in the world, his image of the tramp becoming the universal symbol of Hollywood.

Through actors such as Chaplin, the movies demonstrated their power for social criticism. Satirizing the pompous and the powerful, Chaplin showed how the solitary individual might survive in the face of modern society's isolation and indifference. He became America's greatest screen comic as well as one of the decade's severest social critics. He strongly opposed the business mentality of the period, preferring more basic human qualities such as love and kindness. His films depicted an often unsuccessful struggle against the social forces that attacked human dignity in modern society; the ordinary person could easily identify with him.[22]

The youth of the 1920s were the first generation to learn their manners and morals from movies, and the lessons learned were not always acceptable to people with older, rural values. The movies' emphasis on sex, along with several personal scandals involving screen stars, led to so much criticism from conservative groups that the studio heads installed Will Hays, Harding's post-the United States, determined that he could make the flight with the proper plane, good preparation, and the ability to stay awake for two days to control the plane. In May 1927, he arrived in Paris after thirty-three hours in the air and became the most acclaimed hero of the 1920s. Although Lindbergh obviously was not the first to cross the Atlantic by air, the novelty of his flight was that he went from New York to Paris instead of leaving from Newfoundland and that he went alone. In a nation described as "spiritually starved" and "disillusioned by cheap heroics, scandal and crime,"[15] Lindbergh was the ideal hero. Handsome, modest, and possessing impeccable character, he seemed to be above the materialism of the age. He was seen as testimony to the soundness of American youth and character and a rebuttal of the intellectual criticism of the "moral degeneration of the age."[16]

So acclaimed was Lindbergh's feat that he was elevated to nearly godlike status. The public excitement was so intense that, "Except for the Armistice in 1918 and V-J Day in 1945, nothing in American history [was] comparable."[17] The New York *Evening World* declared that Lindbergh had performed "the greatest feat of a solitary man in the history of the human race."[18] In an increasingly complex world, his flight seemed to prove that individuals could still make a difference. A prominent magazine writer noted that Lindbergh "has shown us that we are not rotten at the core, but morally sound and sweet and good." *Time* magazine made Lindbergh its first "Man of the Year." Former secretary of state Charles Evans Hughes declared that Lindbergh "has displaced everything that is petty, that is sordid, that is vulgar."[19]

In a nation starved for heroes, others would be found in the relatively new motion picture industry. An art form invented in the 1890s by several people including the Lumiere brothers of France and Thomas Edison, the movies came of age in the 1920s. The movie industry became the fifth largest in the United States and an estimated one hundred million patrons attended the cinema each week, a figure that nearly equaled the total population in the nation. It offered the spectators an easy escape into newer worlds and gave an intimate knowledge of how the other half lived. But the growing importance of the movies adversely affected other forms of entertainment. In the smaller cities (with fewer than two hundred thousand people), the legitimate "live" theater wilted, the vaudeville houses closed or added movies to the program, and the Chatauqua lecture circuit declined.[20]

The movie industry had struggled early in the century but saw its fortunes revive during World War I. Before D. W. Griffith's two great epics, *The Birth* flicts, unemployment, and agricultural distress soon followed the Armistice of November 1918. The difficult transition partly reflected the fact that by the end of the war one-quarter of the civilian labor force was engaged in war industries. A confusing economic situation unfolded, marked by an economic decline followed by a temporary recovery only to be followed by another more serious downturn. The first economic decline was short-lived and by the spring of 1919 an expansion began that lasted well into 1920. The economy reversed itself again in late 1920, and by the next year the nation experienced one of the most serious downturns in its history. Prices fell drastically, nearly five million people were unemployed, more than 100,000 bankruptcies occurred, and 453,000 farmers lost their farms.[1] Not until the second half of 1922 did the nation begin to recover from this downturn.

One major group that suffered greatly after World War I and essentially missed out on the golden age of the 1920s was the farmer. While U.S. farmers had expanded production to take advantage of the needs created by World War I, they were hit by a severe drop in demand and lower farm prices as early as 1921. Although farm prices rallied temporarily by the mid 1920s, farmers were never as well off as they had been only a few years earlier. U.S. farmers were once again competing with European farmers and the worldwide prices for commodities dropped as production increased. Complicating the problems and helping to oversaturate the market was the vast increase in U.S. domestic production as more machinery was utilized on the farm. Farm bankruptcies increased from 21 per 100,000 in 1920 to 120 per 100,000 during 1924–26. The value of farm land, on which rested much of the farmer's accumulated wealth, dropped from $78 billion in 1921 to $58 billion in 1927.[2] The number of farmers continued to decline and the acreage of land being cultivated for crops decreased for the first time in American history.[3] These difficulties reduced the share of agriculture in the national income from 16 percent in 1919 to 10.7 percent in 1921 to 8.8 percent in 1929. The farmers' purchasing power declined 25 percent by 1921 from wartime levels and did not fully recover for many years.[4]

One possible remedy that the farmer began to favor was dealing with cooperatives, both in the selling of crops and in the purchase of supplies. In general, cooperative associations failed to correct the excess of supply and demand. The inability of these voluntary organizations to control output with so many individual producers was further complicated by the fact that much of the market was international. The farmers' inability to raise agricultural prices ultimately affected the entire American economy because at least one-quarter of the nation's employment was in farming during the 1920s.

Along with declining farm prices, the farmer also complained of a lack of adequate credit. In an attempt to remedy these problems, the government set up a program in 1923 to make loans to farm cooperatives for the period between the planting season and the actual marketing of crops. This program would give agriculture the same sort of working capital long enjoyed by business concerns when they borrowed from commercial banks. Farmers no longer had to dispose of their crops to money lenders to raise cash, even if the marketing conditions were not good. This improvement in credit conditions, however, did not solve the farmer's most serious problem, an oversupply in the marketplace.

Like agriculture, industry was also affected in the postwar period, when a serious decline in production occurred simultaneous to a severe price deflation. The effects of the depression on labor were especially serious. The number of workers engaged in manufacturing fell by nearly one-quarter between 1919 and 1921, accompanied by a substantial decline in wages. Factory labor's difficulties were ameliorated by a sharp decline in the cost of living. At the end of the deflationary period in 1921, those who were still employed were slightly better off than they had been before because the increase in purchasing power was greater than the fall in actual wages.[5]

In contrast to labor's difficulties, employers were far better off than workers during the economic downturn. The overall decline in production and corporate profits was offset by the large wartime surpluses they had accumulated and they were even able to maintain dividends at wartime levels. The effects of the price deflation were mollified by a sharp drop in the prices for commodities, a trend that led to wider profit margins for finished products than had existed before or during the war. Clearly the principal victims of the depression were the farmers, who saw their purchasing power decline by approximately 25 percent, and labor, which experienced extremely high unemployment and wage cuts.[6]

In late 1922, the economic cycle turned and recovery from the postwar depression began. The American economy now entered a period of expansion that, with only minor interruptions, continued until the crash of 1929. This renewed prosperity was based largely on consumer spending in the private sector, aided by a dramatic fall in prices that more than compensated for wage cuts during the recent downturn. Much of this increased consumer spending was in automobiles and in the greater availability of electrical appliances such as refrigerators and radios.

One of the most significant new developments affecting the national economy after World War I was the shift in the financial status of the United States from a debtor nation to the greatest creditor nation in the world. Before 1914, the United States had never invested abroad as much as foreigners invested in this country. It had made up the difference by exporting more than it imported, especially agricultural products and raw materials. But at the beginning of World War I, this traditional economic relationship was reversed. Now Europe could only pay its obligations to the United States if it sold more to the United States than it imported or if it received additional loans or investments from the Americans. The United States was reluctant to end its traditional trade surplus with Europe and in fact made such a change more difficult with the passage of a high tariff law in 1922. The solution that emerged was for more American loans to be extended. After the Armistice, the United States government continued its wartime policy of loans to the Europeans and even encouraged loans by private institutions.

The United States maintained its policy of both a trade surplus and substantial overseas investments with Europe throughout the decade. The Dawes Plan of 1924, which clarified the issue of German reparations, also restored international confidence and paved the way for more extensive U.S. loans and investments abroad. American loans to Europe during the 1920s ultimately totaled about three billion dollars, making possible a United States export surplus as well as European recovery and expansion. These loans to Europe became a crucial factor in international economics and, if they were slowed or stopped (as happened in 1929), international finances would be seriously disrupted.

Each of the three Republican presidents of the period was dedicated to helping the business community. President Harding, who set the pattern for the decade, staffed his administration with strong pro-business advocates best exemplified by his treasury secretary, Andrew Mellon. The administration's basic policies were to reduce taxes as much as possible, especially on the higher brackets, while maintaining a budget surplus and reducing the national debt. President Harding's statement that "what we need in America is less government in business and more business in government"[7] clearly showed the administration's priorities.

His successor, Calvin Coolidge, was the most pro-business of the decade's Republican presidents. Coolidge retained Mellon in his post and continued the policies begun by the Harding administration. He particularly stressed the reduction of government spending in areas that business did not want, such as social reforms, and he tried to minimize the role of the federal government. Both Harding and Coolidge successfully resisted policies that were strongly opposed by business including farm subsidies, measures to cope with unemployment, and extended controls over business and public utilities.

Herbert Hoover continued this pro-business trend both as commerce secretary and later as president. He encouraged the creation of associations that promoted business cooperation rather than competition. He tried to eliminate waste and provide better understanding through collecting and publishing statistical data. Hoover's policies led the business and financial community to see that, like his two predecessors, he would place no obstruction on their activities.

These Republican presidents operated within an environment that was receptive to their business policies. The business community was aggressive in trying to keep the support of the public by successfully enlisting the mass media on its side. Behind this support was the overwhelming fact that business leadership seemed to have "delivered the goods," that the system worked, and that in no previous era in history had there been so much wealth in one country.[8] As a result of this economic climate, business usually had its way on major policy matters. In 1920, the railroads were returned to private ownership despite some pressure to continue public operation. Under the leadership of Treasury Secretary Andrew Mellon, a new tax policy was enacted that lowered or eliminated certain types of taxes. The Federal Trade Commission, created by Woodrow Wilson to police the business community, was now converted into an ally of business.

As part of this friendly government attitude, business was encouraged to form trade associations to help itself. The purpose of these trade associations was to cope with markets for goods that had not expanded sufficiently and to avoid ruinous competition. Industries that had previously been competitive became partly monopolistic, and the government, which had formerly opposed all organized efforts to "restrain trade," gave its approval. Each of these trade associations had its own code of "fair practices" and the machinery for enforcing it. Trade associations worked best where there were so many small firms that there was a need to restrict overcompetition but were not essential in those industries where one or two giants dominated the field and set industry prices. These arrangements were accepted by the United States Supreme Court in the Maples Flooring case of 1925.[9]

Of even greater importance to business was the scientific management theory of Frederick Taylor, explained earlier in the century but widely used now for the first time. Taylor outlined guidelines for the more productive uses of both management and workers. Management would work more efficiently if there were a shift from one-man rule to a team of skillful bankers and personnel managers. "No great man," Taylor contended, "can (with the old system of personal management) hope to compete with a number of ordinary men who have been properly organized."[10] During the 1920s, there was a steady shift in the actual running of the company from ownership to management (with Henry Ford being the only major industrialist to hold out against this change). The chief advantage of Taylor's plan was that it permitted a number of managers to handle situations too complex for one individual.

Taylor also changed dramatically the position of the ordinary laborer in the factory. Originally the factory worker was a craftsman who supplied the equipment, trained helpers, and controlled the actual work. The labor force was in charge of the rate and quality of production. This system tended to keep production down because under the piece rate system, an increase in production would actually lower wages by prompting the owner to lower the piece rate.[11] As long as the skilled workers controlled the work procedures, the growth in the labor force was the most direct cause of the rise of industrial output. The challenge was to make the worker more productive, a goal that could be accomplished only when management learned and controlled the work process.

Taylor's system was to separate the thinking and the doing of the work. First, management had to learn how to do the work; elaborate time and motion studies of labor were undertaken. The changes that resulted from these studies altered the long-standing relationship between workers and management and helped lead to a "production revolution." All the decisions would now be made by management. The worker would merely follow orders and a greater labor efficiency would be achieved. The Taylor system took skilled jobs and broke them down into the simplest operations, leading to the hiring of less-skilled and cheaper labor.[12] This system of reorganizing management and changing the role of the worker was not practiced until the 1920s because it required expensive machinery to be fully implemented and was not cost-efficient until business had become very big.

Having learned to use management more efficiently, business made another crucial breakthrough when it learned how to use chemistry joined with electricity to revolutionize other industries. New electrochemical operations were used widely in the automobile, motion picture, radio, and telephone industries, as well as in the manufacture of refrigerators, washing machines, and other household appliances. Improvements in parts and processes made possible through the application of chemistry and electricity increased the efficiency of gasoline motors and even the production of gasoline itself.

Increased use of electricity also had a great effect on the operation of the factory and the home. The factory no longer had to be near the coal fields or the river. The water wheel and the steam engine, which had powered America's first industrial revolution, were effectively replaced. Instead, electricity made possible the more efficient "straight-line" system of production involving the use of the conveyor belt and the assembly line, enabling business to cut production costs. So extensive had the use of this new power source become that, by 1929, close to one-half of the nation's manufacturing plants used electricity. Even the private sector was caught up in this trend. More than sixteen million homes involving about 63 percent of the population had been wired by the end of the decade, creating a huge market for electrical appliances.[13]

However, industry's reluctance to share the new wealth with labor created the serious problem of inadequate purchasing power to buy these consumer goods. In the uneven prosperity of the 1920s, corporate profits consumed the largest share of the new wealth while industrial wages remained at a standstill after 1922. A substantial part of these profits went into new plants and equipment and thus into still more production of goods that the workers could not afford to buy.[14]

The poor distribution of income became an obvious problem as the production capacity of American industry steadily grew during the decade. The rich were getting richer much faster than the poor were becoming less poor. In 1929, the wealthy or well-to-do, earning $10,000 or more per family or $5,000 or more per individual, were only 2.4 percent of the population. The comfortable, earning $3,000 or more per family or $1,500 per individual, were 19.6 percent of the population. The poorer families, earning less than $1,500 per year per family or less than $750 per individual, were 78 percent of the population. The generally accepted minimum working-class budget for the decade called for $2,000 a year for a family of four. Yet by 1927, the average industrial wage had risen to only $1,304, the difference being made up by working women. The average family had 1.6 income earners, which brought family income up to the $2,000 minimum and enabled families to barely get by.[15] Because the boom of the 1920s was built mainly on sales of durable goods whose production was growing much faster than workers' incomes, a potentially explosive economic problem was created.

The "solution" to this problem was installment buying, which made possible a rapid growth of the consumer market for cars, radios, furniture, and electrical appliances for the home. It also made the economy more unstable and risky. If the incomes of consumers did not increase at the same rate as their purchases on credit, there would be a limit to the growth of installment debt. When this limit was approached (by 1929), effective demand for durable consumer goods sold on installment would cease growing at the previous rate, and the entire economy would feel the consequences.

This risky economic trend of installment buying was relatively new in the United States. Until soon after World War I, houses were usually the only items that respectable people bought on credit. (Even cars were bought with cash until 1919.) To create a greater mass market, installment buying began for cars; two-thirds of all car sales were on time payments by 1927. This trend in automobile purchasing broke down the old reluctance to buy on credit, and the practice then spread into new areas. By 1928, 85 percent of furniture; 80 percent of phonographs; 75 percent of washing machines, 70 percent of refrigerators; and more than one-half of all sewing machines, pianos, and vacuum cleaners were bought on credit. So extensive had installment buying become that personal debts were rising two and one-half times faster than incomes. By 1929, providing consumer credit had become the tenth-largest business in the United States and approximately one-fifth of all retail sales now depended on credit.[16] The noted economist Joseph Schumpeter wrote, "It is an undeniable fact that during the Twenties, households habitually overspent their current receipts."[17] Buying on credit helped to put off the day of reckoning by unnaturally keeping up demand, but it also made that day worse when it came. When the consumers reached their credit limits by the end of the decade, installment buying could no longer support the economy.

Helping to bolster the economy by creating new "essential" products was the emergence of the automobile, motion picture, and radio industries, which became three of the largest in the nation during the decade. The most important of these new industries was the automobile, which replaced the railroad as the nation's largest industry. The number of cars produced annually rose from 1,518,061 in 1921 to 4,794,898 in 1929 and the number of motor vehicles (cars and trucks) registered rose from 10,463,000 in 1921 to 26,501,000 in 1929. There were 23,000,000 passenger cars in 1929, approximately one car for every six people. By that year, cars represented 12.7 percent of all manufacturers in America and the industry supplied 7 percent of the jobs and 9 percent of the wages for factory workers. About four million other workers drew their livelihood indirectly from vehicle production in such industries as steel, rubber, nickel, lead, plate glass, and gasoline.[18] During the 1920s, the automobile represented the fastest-growing industry in the nation.

The industry giant was the Ford Motor Company, which controlled 50 percent of the market by 1924, although it sold only the one basic, reliable, and very inexpensive Model T. Beginning in 1909, Ford transformed an industry that produced expensive, luxury vehicles for the rich into one that provided cheap, reliable transportation for the masses. Ford explained his overall goal for the company, saying, "I will build a motor car for the great multitude. It will be so low in price that no one making a good salary will be unable to own one."[19] Ford kept the costs down by offering one basic model to the public, declaring, "The customer can have a Ford [Model T] in any color he wants—as long as it's black."[20] By 1926, a major shift within the industry had occurred, with General Motors capturing 30 percent of the market (and passing Ford) through its variety of more upscale cars. Even though Ford converted from the basic Model T to the more sophisticated Model A in 1928, it failed to regain its earlier dominant position in the industry.

The growth of the automobile industry compensated for the decline in the other leading transportation industries: railroads and shipping. There was a debate immediately after the war whether the federal government should continue its operation of the railroad industry. The Plumb Plan authorized the government to nationalize the railroads but had little support in Congress. Instead, the Transportation Act of 1920 was passed, returning the railroads to private management but keeping them under strong government controls. The railroads became a less significant industry during the decade, steadily losing business to the newer transportation alternatives such as autos, trucks, and buses.

The shipping industry was in a similar struggle to survive during the 1920s. Most of the pre-1914 American shipping had been on lake and coastal traffic and this trade was being lost to the new competition from trucks. The

American shippers in the oceanic shipping business were unable to compete with foreign companies and could not remain solvent without a government subsidy. The Harding administration led a long and ultimately unsuccessful effort to obtain subsidies for the shippers. During the decade, the future of the American transportation industry clearly lay with the automobile industry, which was expanding rapidly without the need for any government assistance.

Explosive growth also occurred in the movie industry, which, like automobiles, reflected the nation's desire for more leisure activities. By the 1920s, the movie industry became the most popular indulgence in America and also one of the five biggest industries in the nation. During 1921–30, the total invested in the industry rose from about $78 million to almost $850 million. By 1925, there were 20,000 movie houses in the United States, selling more than 100 million admission tickets each week. In that year, about 700 feature films were produced and the industry employed approximately 300,000 people.[21]

The third of the new leisure industries, radio, came of age in 1920, when the first commercial radio station was licensed in Pittsburgh, Pennsylvania. Commercial radio had a slow beginning and, to attract audiences, sets were sometimes even given away free to those who would promise to stay home and listen. As the price of radios came down, the industry grew rapidly. By 1927, there were 732 broadcasting stations and at least 10 million radio sets in the country. To an increasingly entertainment-minded public, radio ownership increased greatly when it came to represent a major medium of entertainment rather than merely a form of communication. In 1920, fewer than one home in 10,000 had a radio set. By 1922, there were 60,000 in use, and by 1924 the number had grown to 7.5 million. The value of radio products sold in 1921 was only $11 million, but it increased to $412 million by 1929.[22] With this rapid growth, radio had become one of the great leisure industries.

Another industry that underwent vast changes during the decade was banking; it played a crucial role in the prosperity (and ultimately the collapse) of the economy. Traditionally one of the most conservative industries, banking became caught up in the speculative frenzy of the decade. The trend in this industry was to shift from more cautious investments such as government bonds into the riskier and (at first) more lucrative stock and real estate markets. A change in traditional corporate borrowing practices was causing a profit squeeze for the lending institutions. Rather than borrow from commercial banks, corporations found they could rely upon their growing profits or sell securities in a rising stock market to raise cash. Seeing that the demand for conventional loans was not enough to generate satisfactory profits, the banks began to invest heavily in the stock and real estate markets because both were doing very well.[23] In this new financial climate, the fastest-growing activities of commercial banks in the 1920s involved purchases of stocks, loans to finance others' purchase of stocks, and loans on urban real estate. This policy of the banking system to tie up so much of its resources either directly or indirectly in speculative investments increased uncertainty in the industry. A possible stabilizing institution, the Federal Reserve System, had little influence over the banks because the potential profits were so high that banks were undeterred by a hike in the discount rate (the amount charged by the Federal Reserve System to lend money to member banks). The new strategy of financial institutions involved a much greater risk than before but it was so profitable when the market was rising that even the usually conservative insurance companies greatly enlarged their stock and urban real estate investments.

While banks and most segments of the economy forged ahead in the 1920s, the position of labor unions steadily declined. During World War I, unions had gained such benefits as enlarged membership, federal government support for collective bargaining, and numerous agencies for adjustment of labor problems. However, they had not organized the basic mass production industries like steel and autos and many of the new union members were in defense-related plants, which were being demobilized. Many employers had accepted collective bargaining only as a war necessity imposed by the government and were anxious to end it, setting the stage for future labor-management conflict.[24]

Management's efforts to weaken organized labor after the wartime truce ended became known as the "American Plan," a strategy that included strong opposition to the closed shop and collective bargaining. Business believed these traditional goals of the labor movement violated the free use of private property and also limited the ancient right of workers to contract individually for the sale of their labor. One popular option for businesses was the open shop, which did not require all workers to join the union and enabled management to deal directly with workers rather than through the union. Business also stressed membership in a company union, which was more amenable to its goals. By the late 1920s, company unions had enrolled a million members by offering benefits the other unions did not such as health and safety insurance, grievance machinery, and by enrolling workers who were usually ignored such as black people, clerical workers, women, and recent immigrants.

Business also attempted to convert labor and the public to the business point of view; so successful was its appeal to the general public in the 1920s that "the overwhelming majority of the American people believed with increasing certainty that businessmen knew better than anyone else what was good for the country."[25]

Labor's problems increased through management's resort to the injunction to outlaw pickets, boycotts, and most of the weapons of striking workers. Business saw the injunction as a quick strike-breaker and obtained nearly one thousand of them in labor disputes during the 1920s, about as many as in the preceding forty years. The injunction helped to break the militant spirit of labor and put it in a much weakened position by the end of the decade. As a consequence, in 1928 there was the smallest number of strikes on record (only 629) and the following year there was the smallest number of strikers (only 230,463).[26]

Compounding labor's difficulties was a series of reverses suffered in the courts both during and immediately after World War I. In 1917, the Supreme Court upheld the idea of the "yellow dog contract" (which made employees promise not to join a union on condition of losing their jobs). In 1919, a federal court of appeals upheld a judgment for triple damages under the Sherman Act against the coal union for calling a strike. In 1921, the Supreme Court ruled that a boycott by the machinists' union to force unionization of a factory that made printing presses was illegal under the antitrust laws. That same year the Supreme Court also ruled that lower courts could limit picketing to "peaceful picketing"; to accomplish this goal they could require that no more than a single picket be stationed at each entrance to a plant. In 1922, the Supreme Court ruled in *United Mine Workers* v. *Coronado Coal Company* that a union could be sued and forced to pay damages for the actions of its members.[27]

In the most significant labor decision of the decade, *Adkins* v. *Children's Hospital*, the Supreme Court struck down a minimum wage law in Washington, D.C. In this decision, the Court declared unconstitutional a statute that fixed a minimum wage for women, declaring that it hindered the bargaining freedom between employers and workers. Before this 1923 decision, seventeen states and Washington, D.C., had enacted minimum wage laws, but after the Court's ruling many states began to repeal these laws.[28] By challenging protective legislation for workers, the Court created a favorable setting for business activities.

The difficulties faced by labor were clearly exemplified by the decline of the United Mine Workers, formerly one of the biggest unions in the nation. The union lost a strike in 1920 when a federal court granted the coal companies an injunction. This defeat, coupled with new machinery that cut employment needs as well as more work going to non-union mines, led to a decline in the union's membership from 500,000 members in 1920 to 75,000 in 1928.[29] The coal industry demonstrated how technology, along with the hostility of management and the judiciary, could lead to a precipitous decline in the status of unions.

The coal industry also exemplified the significant but uneven changes that technology was bringing to the economy. Rapid advances in technology led to growth in manufacturing output as well as displacement of workers, creating an unfavorable climate for union organizers. It was not easy to find new jobs while the total number of those engaged in manufacturing was shrinking. Between 1919 and 1929, the percentage of the total workforce engaged in manufacturing declined from 25.4 percent to 22.3 percent.[30] The number of union members fell from 5.1 million in 1920 to 3.4 million in 1929,[31] a consequence of the depleted union treasuries, the open shop and company union drive, the loss of so many strikes, and the disappearance of factory jobs. All of these factors led to a disillusioned union movement. Commenting on labor's difficulties, an American Federation of Labor (AFL) official wrote, "The AFL machinery has partially collapsed. AFL organizers have forgotten how to organize. They might be effective as lobbyists, legislators, or public speakers but their usefulness in organizing the disorganized has almost ceased." [32]

Labor's difficulties also demonstrated the uneven prosperity of the decade, with business reaping most of the benefits of the 1923–29 economic expansion. For the business community, all the key economic indicators were positive during this six-year expansion. Production and productivity grew steadily; wages, prices, and salaries remained stable; costs fell; and profits rose. The rising profits were being spent on capital goods, leading to increased production and more profits. Business profits increased by 62 percent and dividends grew 65 percent, far outpacing the 21 percent growth in incomes and the 23 percent increase in the U.S. gross national product. In foreign trade, the 16 percent increase in imports was overshadowed by an increase of 20 percent in exports. With all the major economic statistics indicating great prosperity, stock prices rose 176 percent during this six-year period.[33]

Other factors also increased optimism in the business community and pointed to a healthy economy. The federal budget was balanced and the national debt was declining. Taxes were being reduced and government interference with business was at a minimum. Both business and public confidence were high as profit margins rose steadily and made possible an abundant supply of capital. There was a steady stream of new inventions and mechanical improvements and there was no shortage of labor or raw materials, both of which were relatively cheap. Slightly higher incomes, along with stable prices and an abundance of consumer goods on the market, led to a limited increase in the standard of living for wage earners.

But in spite of these favorable omens, a number of serious problems continued to plague the economy. Coal mining, agriculture, and cotton and woolen textile manufacturing were depressed industries. In coal mining, for example, 10 percent less was produced and nearly one-quarter of the miners lost their jobs during the decade. The nation's favorable balance of trade depended on U.S. loans to Europe being continued—at a time when the American stock market offered an ever more attractive alternative for investment capital. The demand for automobiles and other consumer durable goods, which was crucial in sustaining the expansion, was approaching the saturation point. The slow growth in workers' wages, necessitating an ever-increasing amount of installment buying, was a potentially ominous development. These factors indicated that there might be an end approaching to the prosperity of the 1920s.

To most Americans, the economy appeared to be in good condition and there was genuine surprise when a stock market crash occurred in 1929, followed by a more general economic downturn. By this time, Americans finally realized how serious were the two major economic problems: a poor distribution of income and a speculative frenzy that was out of control. Rather than being a cause of the Great Depression, the stock market crash actually was a symptom of a fundamentally unsound economy.

The most serious problem for the economy was an insufficient market for the vast quantity of goods being produced, a result of the poor distribution of income. During 1923–29, the share of the national income earned by the wealthy increased from 22.9 percent to 26.1 percent (about twice the level of post-1945 America). The wealthy did not spend most of their discretionary income on ordinary consumer goods, preferring instead to spend on investment (or speculation) and luxury goods.[34] The ordinary worker, with little or no discretionary income, was ultimately forced to go heavily in debt to buy needed consumer goods. When credit limits were nearing saturation by the end of the decade, the economy declined sharply.

Speculation, both in real estate and stocks, further undermined the economy; it also ultimately served as the catalyst for the stock market crash. Wealthy people and financial institutions engaged in excessive speculation during the decade, one example being the Florida land boom of the mid-1920s. This speculative boom exemplified a "feeding frenzy," as money chased real estate beyond any reasonable level of value until the bubble burst in 1926. Investment in Miami real estate, the central focus of the Florida boom, made it the fastest-growing city in the United States during the 1920s. Roughly 90 percent of those who made purchases in the Florida land boom had no intention of ever occupying the property or even owning it for very long. The real estate boom in Miami finally ended in September 1926, when land values had become totally unrealistic, causing this speculative bubble to burst.[35]

Such unchecked speculation in both real estate and stocks led to potential dangers for the economy. As the real estate boom grew around the country, real estate operators took their paper profits and bought stocks. The rise in stock prices helped to stimulate a wave of average Americans buying stocks on credit or margin. Before 1927, the stock market had been fairly priced but in that year the rising stock prices created their own momentum and a speculative frenzy began. In this "get rich quick" atmosphere, trading in stocks reached new heights. The volume of shares traded increased throughout the decade from 318 million in 1920, to 460 million in 1925, to 920 million in 1928, and to 1,125 million in 1929. By 1929, the majority of the 9 million investors were trading on margin. The value of margin loans from brokers increased from $2.5 billion in 1920, to $3.5 billion in 1927, to $6.6 billion by October 1929.[36] So extensive was this buying trend in the late 1920s that the vitality of the entire system came gradually to depend upon the steady rise of stock prices. When these prices finally collapsed, the whole structure came tumbling down.

Unfortunately, the power of the Federal Reserve System to deal with this problem of speculation was limited and its intervention could even inadvertently worsen the problem. In 1927, the economy slipped into a slight recession, causing the Federal Reserve System to lower interest rates and encourage loans. Because a large section of manufacturing had all the money it needed and no longer depended on the banks for commercial loans, the extra credit available was used largely for speculation.

Much of this extra credit was plowed into the stock market, leading to a 24 percent increase in brokers' loans on the New York Stock Exchange. (A broker's loan was borrowing from a broker to buy stock after the deposit—the margin—had been paid. Essentially, it meant buying a stock on credit.) Brokers received the money being loaned mainly from banks in what were known as call loans. The amount of money available for call money increased enormously during 1927–29. In both 1928 and 1929, the Federal Reserve reversed course and raised interest rates but failed to check the expansion of the call money market. Because the interest that banks received from such loans was still much higher than what they paid the Federal Reserve System, the problem continued. The call money also expanded because some large corporations (such as the Standard Oil Company) found they made more money from lending in that market than they could from their ordinary economic activities.[37]

Even the government policy of encouraging private loans to Europe, while advantageous in the short run, could not ultimately check speculation at home or stave off financial collapse. Throughout the decade (especially after 1924), large amounts of corporate profits were invested abroad, enabling foreigners to pay for the American surplus of merchandise exports. The danger was that a cut in the U.S. outflow of capital would lead to a decline in Europe's economy and hurt its ability to buy American goods. By 1928, these loans began to be cut back because greater returns could be had by investing in securities or call loans. The financial panic on Wall Street in 1929 caused a drastic cutback, which subsequently led to a downturn in Europe's economy and a further inability to buy American products. Thus the stock market crash affected not only the domestic economy but also foreign trade.

As the decade neared its close, the stock market speculation steadily gained momentum. The market value of all the shares on the New York Stock Exchange rose from $27+ billion on 1 January 1925 to $67+ billion on 1 January 1929.[38] Even a rise in interest rates failed to deter the speculators and investors continued to drive up the stock market. The rate for call loans on securities at the end of March 1929 was 12 percent and then steadily rose to between 15 percent and 20 percent later in the year. The increase in rates for call loans inevitably increased rates for margin loans as well. A few months before the crash, the brokerage houses raised their margin requirements to 50 percent. In spite of the increase in both the margin rates and requirements, investors continued to buy stocks, hoping that a rising market would compensate for these additional up-front expenses. Under these conditions, an economic downturn would put the margin traders in a precarious position, because they would have to put up more cash or risk having their stocks sold, raising the likelihood of a collapse of the speculative boom.

The speculative buying in 1929 had now become a frenzy and traders needed continually higher corporate earnings to support the ever-higher prices of the stocks. Despite the intense wave of speculation, which had been going on for at least two years, there was no consensus of experts that a collapse was imminent. Roger Babson, a financial guru to stock investors, had supported Hoover in 1928 because his administration would assure continuance of prosperity. Babson's prediction that Hoover represented good times and that "If [Al Smith] should be elected with a Democratic Congress, we are almost certain to have a resulting business depression in 1929" came to have an ironic twist.[39] (In a total reversal of his position in September 1929, Babson became one of the few experts to predict a crash.)[40] On 15 October 1929, Irving Fisher, who better represented a majority consensus, announced that stock prices stood on "what looks like a permanently high plateau" and that he expected to see the market "a good deal higher than it is today within a few months."[41] President Charles E. Mitchell of the National City Bank said a few days later, "I see no reason for the end of the year slump which some people are predicting."[42] Another prominent businessman stated at the time, "We are only at the beginning of a period that will go down in history as a golden age."[43]

Contrary to the usual folklore, stock prices did not suddenly crash without warning in October 1929. For several weeks, the market had been quite volatile and had been exhibiting a definite weakness. On 24 October 1929, the market sustained its first great shock, declining precipitously on what became known as "Black Thursday." Representatives of the big banks conferred and decided to buy stocks above the market price, which caused speculators to reenter and stock prices to partially recover by the day's end.

The crash of October 24 was the first panic on Wall Street ever to occur without the catalyst of a major business failure.[44] Most of the stocks that had gone down were speculative stocks and some observers regarded the decline as chastisement for speculators, calling it a "gamblers' " rather than an "investors' " panic. Seemingly knowledgeable observers minimized the danger from this crash. The famous British economist John Maynard Keynes stated the slump would benefit the world because it would liquidate unsound speculation.[45] Herbert Hoover commented, "The fundamental business of the country—that is the production and distribution of goods and services—is on a sound and prosperous basis."[46] Both opinions were wrong and further trouble lay ahead for the stock market and for the economy.

On October 29, known as "Black Tuesday," another panic occurred on Wall Street. Unlike the earlier one, which had focused upon the speculative stocks, this second panic dealt mainly with blue chip stocks. Within two weeks, the total value of all the stocks on the New York Stock Exchange had fallen by 49 percent. Before long, the financial panic on Wall Street created effects that reverberated throughout the economy. The predictions of the "experts" regarding the health of the stock market and the economy had been seriously in error.

Contrary to President Hoover's belief, the "real economy" was not healthy by the late 1920s. There was overcapacity in a wide range of crucial industries, especially autos, textiles, and construction, at the same time that money was being poured into further expansion. Car sales held up well until April 1929 and then declined sharply, causing big layoffs in the auto plants that summer. Earlier in 1928, the construction industry had begun to slump and by the following year had reached the levels of the deep recession year 1921. Another ominous development was a fall in factory employment during the last five months of 1929. Business inventories doubled that same year, an indication that consumers were unable to purchase enough to keep production at full capacity. The downturn in several key industries in the spring and summer of 1929 revealed that a recession had already begun. The crash of October 1929 was only the extension to the stock market of a faltering economy in which agriculture, construction, and autos were already in deep trouble.[47] If general business conditions had been "fundamentally sound" as President Hoover claimed, a revival probably would have followed the stock market crash after a relatively short interval.

Once the stock market collapsed, several factors prevented a return to normal conditions. The banks themselves were heavy investors in stocks and the sharp decline decimated the value of their assets. Worsening the situation was the banking industry's close business relations with many of the brokerage houses and other financial institutions also being caught in the downturn.

In October 1929 the banks had $8.5 billion out in loans to stockbrokers, the collateral for the loans being in stock. When the market crashed, the collateral was worth very little and the banks were nearly insolvent. When the market rallied temporarily, the banks quickly liquidated their stock holdings and the market declined further. Instead of fostering a rising stock market through call loans and stock purchases as they had before 1929, the banks now acted as a brake on any attempt by the market to recover. Banks were in a shaky condition, made worse by public "runs on the bank" and therefore less prepared to extend credit. The crash also had a psychological effect on investment, dimming any enthusiasm for expansion or establishment of new economic activities. Reflecting these shocks to the economy, the general public became fearful and not inclined to invest in the stock market or to make major purchases of consumer goods.[48]

The economy unsuccessfully tried to bounce back as business initially complied with governmental urging to keep production and wages near normal levels. After a temporary recovery, the economy went into a steep decline in mid-1930 that lasted for the remainder of the Hoover administration. Capital expansion by business was cut back as consumer spending declined dramatically, in part because of heavy losses in the stock market. With a smaller market for their products, manufacturers steadily decreased their production. This meant laying off workers or reducing workweeks or both, causing the downward trend to worsen. When production declined along with employment, the economy spiraled into a deep depression. An increase in consumer spending, which would have eased or even ended the depression, was not possible because of the astounding increase in personal indebtedness by 1929. This first generation of Americans heavily dependent on credit cut back on spending when faced with economic uncertainty, paving the way for the Great Depression.[49]

From the end of World War I to the crash of 1929, there was a clear pattern of problems in the economy, many of which went unresolved. Before October 1929, both the domestic and international economies were fundamentally unsound. When the United States cut lending abroad and erected higher tariff walls, Europe's economy weakened and was unable to increase imports from America. Adding to the problem was a domestic economy out of balance. The 1929 depression was primarily caused by a drop in consumption, an effect of the poor distribution of income and overextended credit, coupled with overproduction of consumer goods. Farmers had earlier lost all that they had gained during World War I and were left financially below prewar levels. Labor suffered from slow wage growth and significant unemployment, especially in the depressed coal mining and textile industries. By late 1929, these problems were able to trigger a serious drop in consumption, leading to an economic collapse. The economy had come full circle from the depression of 1920 and presented a monumental challenge to President Hoover.

The Tragedy of Herbert Hoover

IN MANY WAYS, Herbert Hoover was both an American success story and a tragic figure. He rose from humble beginnings to the presidency of the United States. His misfortune was serving at a time of great economic calamity and he lost both his popularity and reputation when he was unable to end the Great Depression. Hoover's philosophy of a limited role for the government, relying upon individual and voluntary cooperative efforts, could not solve the problems of the greatest financial breakdown in American history. Hoover's philosophy partly reflected his Quaker upbringing. A hard worker himself, he tried to build a society on the virtues of hard work, voluntary cooperation, commonsensical decency, and good neighborliness. He was an activist within limits, more willing than both Harding and Coolidge to have government intervene to solve problems but less involved than his famous successor, Franklin Roosevelt.

Hoover was more of a skilled administrator than a successful politician and he owed his political rise to success in various appointive positions, especially his tenure as secretary of commerce. More than just a day-to-day administrator, he evolved elaborate theories regarding the workings of the capitalist system with a special emphasis on encouraging a selfless, cooperative spirit in society. Hoover's career represented both the triumph and, ultimately, the failure of his economic theories. A brilliantly successful administrator who implemented his version of capitalism while serving in lower-level government positions, Hoover saw his ideas unable to cope with the Great Depression and overwhelmingly rejected by the public by the end of his presidency.

Hoover was raised in the Quaker community of West Branch, Iowa, and much of his personality and political philosophy reflected this upbringing. His Quaker background stressed "harmonies of spirit" and a cooperative social system.[1] He believed that people would work well together and that in rational discussion, minds can be persuaded to meet. The great emphasis on neighborliness and a voluntary spirit, which he turned to during the Depression, as well as a focus upon heroic individualism and a strong sense of self-reliance also stemmed from his religious background.

Hoover was born in 1874 into a fairly prosperous Quaker family. His father, who was a blacksmith and also operated a farm-goods store, died when his son was only six and plunged the family into poverty. Hoover later wrote of having learned "at the earliest and most impressionable age . . . the meaning of poverty from practical experience."[2] Four years later, after his mother died, he went to live with relatives in Oregon. In 1891, he was admitted to the "pioneer class" at the newly opened Stanford University, which began as a tuition-free institution. In preparation for his career as a mining engineer, he majored in geology. He also made his first plunge into politics at Stanford, getting elected treasurer of the student body in 1893. This was the last time he ran for office until 1928, when he was elected president of the United States.[3]

After his graduation in 1895, Hoover began a remarkable career that combined engineering and business. He worked and lived much of the next decade in such foreign locations as China, Australia, Russia, and England. He became wealthy from his engineering projects as well as from a consulting firm that he founded, and by 1910 he was worth $3 million. As early as 1907, Hoover declared that he had all the money he needed and wished to try something else.[4] He had enjoyed meteoric success in his business career and his future foray into government service would be equally spectacular.

Hoover's involvement in politics is surprising because he was personally shy and did not like to make speeches. In his early political career, he eschewed running for office and instead served in a number of appointive positions. Hoover had his first opportunity for public service when he was asked by President Woodrow Wilson in 1914 to help bring home the American tourists stranded in London with the outbreak of World War I. Later that year, Hoover was put in charge of Belgian relief activities, with which he claimed to have saved hundreds of thousands of lives. In the spring of 1915, he organized relief activities for two million people in northern France and later extended his relief activities to include Poland and Serbia. By 1917, he had helped feed more than nine million people in Belgium and France alone. By this time, his reputation was soaring and both Europeans and Americans regarded him as one of the "unique creations of the war." [5] His work in Belgium also helped him become in 1917 United States Food Administrator. In this position, Hoover demonstrated his superb organizational skills as he regulated the prices, distribution, and export of food. He persuaded Americans to ration food for the first time, inspiring the term "Hooverize," which meant to economize on food. The successful techniques used during his wartime service would later form much of his political philosophy both as commerce secretary and as president of the United States.

Hoover's responsibilities shifted when he was asked by President Wilson in November 1918 to transform the Food Administration into a postwar agency for the relief and reconstruction of Europe. This "second American intervention," he later said, had "saved civilization" and millions of lives.[6] The United States delivered about $5 billion worth of food to Europe after World War I, much of this through government loans along with some private and government charity. So idolized was he that streets were named after him in Europe, and he came to symbolize relief for those in need. He was considered to be the second most esteemed American in the delegation at the Paris Peace Conference after the war, overshadowed only by President Wilson himself.[7]

In 1921, Hoover further enhanced his reputation as a great humanitarian through his involvement in a massive relief effort to aid famine-stricken Russia, which was reeling both from years of fighting in World War I and a bloody civil war afterward. The situation had been complicated by the Bolshevik takeover, the Allied intervention in Russia at the end of the war, and a severe drought. When Europe refused to offer aid because it despised the Bolshevik government, the American relief effort became especially crucial. So desperate was the situation that, in 1921, the Communist leader Vladimir Lenin declared, "Without international aid, the government will perish." [8] Despite his own intense anti-Communist sentiments, Hoover justified his role in helping Russia by saying, "Twenty million people are starving. Whatever their politics, they shall be fed." [9]

In the period after World War I, Hoover's relief activities became legendary. The famous economist John Maynard Keynes said, "Hoover was the only one who emerged from the ordeal of Paris [site of the peace conference] with an enhanced reputation." [10] Supreme Court Justice Louis Brandeis stated that Hoover "was the biggest figure injected into Washington by the war." [11] Because of his outstanding accomplishments at home and abroad, Hoover's reputation as the "Great Engineer" and the practical idealist took firm hold in the public mind.

Hoover's growing reputation made him a possible presidential nominee in 1920 for both parties. He had never declared for either party, and he seemed to be a man above partisan considerations. In 1920, Franklin Roosevelt stated, "He is certainly a wonder, and I wish we could make him President. There could be no better man." [12] Not only the major parties but also a host of well-known reformers of the period such as Jane Addams, Ida Tarbell, and William Allen White backed him. When Hoover declared on 30 March 1920 that he was a Republican, the Democrats lost interest in him. Even though he was probably the best-known Republican in 1920, he had little support from Republican Party leaders and Warren G. Harding was nominated instead.

Hoover's unsuccessful fling with elective politics reflected both the appeal of his political views and the handicaps of his temperament and lack of political skill. He had gathered much support from progressives in 1920 because of his progressive viewpoint and his nontraditional approach to politics. Progressives approved of his pro-League position and his support for national planning. He was regarded as an advocate for labor and children and was considered sympathetic toward the "underdog." He had a record of efficient public service but expressed disdain for traditional politics, an attitude that made the Republican Party leaders wary of him.

Hoover's reluctant 1920 candidacy was both brief and unsuccessful. He did not actually campaign for the nomination and was quickly eliminated from the race. The previous year, Hoover had expressed personal doubts about entering active politics, saying, "I do not believe that I have the natural attitude or the politician's manner and above all I am too sensitive to political mud to seek public office." He further explained that he did not have the "politician's skill needed to arrive at such a job as the Presidency of the United States." [13] His poor performance in lining up support for his nomination seemed to confirm his critical self-opinion.

Over much opposition, Harding appointed Hoover to become secretary of commerce and for the next seven years he served as a strong member of the cabinet in two administrations. Many initially opposed his appointment because he was regarded as too apolitical, too progressive, or too international-minded. Hoover was considered too "activist" by some conservative

Republicans, while others queried whether he was actually a Republican. Some opponents felt he was too popular and too ambitious. To gain Hoover's appointment to the cabinet, Harding appeased the "Old Guard" Republicans by choosing Andrew Mellon as treasury secretary to serve as a more conservative counterweight to Hoover.

Early in his tenure as commerce secretary, Hoover published *American Individualism,* a comprehensive outline of his political and economic philosophy for post-World War I America. In this work, Hoover listed the major themes that would guide him as commerce secretary and later as president. He stressed cooperation, a sense of service, a governmental role of guidance rather than coercion, voluntary cooperation by all elements of society including business, and the leadership of selfless professionals. He was seeking a middle ground between ruthless capitalism and the authoritarian collectivism found in the Soviet Union. Idealism, he believed, could be balanced with self-interest to advance the American economy without resorting to the extremes of state socialism or cutthroat capitalism.[14] This philosophy explains Hoover's often mixed record in office as he sought a milder, more cooperative version of capitalism that would also sustain a growing economy.

To achieve these goals, Hoover stressed the need for a major change in America's value system. He called for cooperative individualism and de-emphasizing materialism in order to preserve the capitalist system, along with individual opportunity and the encouragement of selfless individual efforts for the collective benefit. He envisioned a mixture of traditional capitalism and a volunteer spirit by the public similar to the Quakerism of his youth. He hoped to transform traditional attitudes about private property and profit into a new sense of social responsibility with an emphasis on cooperation rather than on competition. To reach this goal, Hoover drew upon his wartime experiences as an administrator. He hoped a massive education and propaganda campaign would create a new public philosophy and enlist a core of volunteers to gain widespread support.[15] Hoover maintained a basic belief throughout his career, even during the Great Depression, that strong decentralized community organization was capable of elevating individual efforts for the community.

Hoover elevated the position of commence secretary while he served, and he became one of the strongest officials in the new cabinet. He brought to his new job ideas that also later guided him as president. With his unique brand of cooperative capitalism, he believed that expert skills could solve the nation's technical and economic problems. He called conferences on various problems to get input from experts on legislative remedies and to publicize the problems, hoping that Congress or the states ultimately would respond with appropriate legislation. Through this conference method, Hoover hoped to perfect a cooperative system without greatly expanding the federal legislative power or bureaucratic structure. He wanted to change the attitude of government relations with business from that of interference to one of cooperation. The success of these conferences ultimately would depend upon how much voluntary collective effort they inspired and their ability to generate reform through appropriate legislation.

Soon after becoming commerce secretary, Hoover urged President Harding to call a conference on unemployment, one of 250 conferences organized by Hoover while in the cabinet. The economy at that time was mired in a serious recession that lasted through most of 1922. The unemployment conference achieved little and almost none of its recommendations were followed, either by Congress or by Harding, who preferred to rely upon the natural business cycle to bring about recovery. Hoover was especially disappointed with Congress, which he deemed an ineffective body for dealing with national recovery problems; this attitude partly explains his later attempt to ignore Congress when the 1929 depression broke out.[16]

Because he saw labor as a significant unit within a cooperative society, Hoover was more sympathetic to unions than either Harding or Coolidge. He believed that all major industries should be unionized and should engage in collective bargaining. Strikes were sometimes necessary but were wasteful. Along with Harding, he helped pressure the steel industry to end the traditional twelve-hour day in favor of the eight-hour day. Hoover opposed the use of the injunction to end the big strikes of 1922, preferring instead cooperation between the parties.[17]

One of Hoover's other legacies as commerce secretary was his support for trade associations. These were the cornerstone of Hoover's economic "associationalism"—the major means to achieve both price stabilization and general economic prosperity—without coercive federal action. Hoover regarded the association as "cooperative competition," which might lead to an exchange of information about prices and such advantages as improved cost-cutting techniques within a single industry. This represented to Hoover a return to the wartime voluntary cooperation that he fostered only a few years earlier.[18] Hoover was clear that the associations did not represent any sort of price fixing, something he strongly opposed. Ultimately Hoover's association policy failed because these organizations were not accepted by all parties in the industries with the most cutthroat competition.

Hoover extended his theories of cooperation to the role of the United States in world economic affairs. He believed in a voluntary economic cooperation among nations to preserve peace and international stability. His world view envisioned a "commercial" League of Nations, which would produce a humanitarian world economy in which peaceful cooperation and economic expansion substituted for political and military confrontation.[19] His economic views inclined him toward a noninterventionist and noncoercive military policy, reinforced by his view that military action abroad usually created more problems than it solved.

According to Hoover's theory, this new mood of international cooperation would parallel the new cooperation and voluntarism in the United States. Adam Smith's classical economics would be replaced by voluntary national economic planning arising from cooperation between business interests and the government. In 1924, Hoover stated, "We are passing from a period of extreme individualistic action into a period of associational activities."[20] To bring this prediction to actual fruition, Hoover had to convince the American people that their own self-interest lay in responsible cooperation with each other. He wished for more cooperation and sharing of wealth rather than cutthroat competition and selfishness but he emphasized that voluntary means rather than public power be used to keep in line selfish businessmen and their trade associations.[21]

Hoover even tried to apply his theories to solving the agriculture crisis of the 1920s. (Although he served as commerce secretary, he did not confine his activities to this area and often meddled in the business of the other cabinet departments.) Hoover believed the solution to the farm problem lay in developing cooperatives, which would lead to substantial advantages in distribution and in elimination of waste. He supported the Capper-Volstead Act of 1922, exempting farm cooperatives from antitrust prosecution. He also helped draft the Agricultural Credits Act, which extended credits to cooperatives, country banks, and foreign buyers.

Hoover strongly opposed an alternative measure then being considered in Congress, the McNary-Haugen Bill, which provided for the federal government to buy the farm surplus for resale abroad at the world market price. Hoover believed the plan would merely encourage United States farmers to produce greater surpluses, causing the Europeans to retaliate with high tariffs and embargoes. Fearing that McNary-Haugen would lead to the destruction of the American economic system, Hoover declared, "I hesitate to contemplate the future of our institutions, of our government, and of our country if the preoccupation of its officials is to be no longer the promoter of justice and equal opportunity but is to be devoted to barter in the markets."[22]

Hoover's program for the farmer—intended to demonstrate the utility of economic theories based on cooperation—was more modest. He wished to encourage domestic consumption, to expand food exports, to increase the tariff on foreign agricultural goods, and to lower transportation costs on farm products and depressed commodities. The government would not take a major role because Hoover believed that farmers would regulate themselves under some degree of federal supervision. In spite of fears of possible antitrust violations, he encouraged cooperation among companies involved in or marketing the same or similar commodities. This plan for farm cooperatives was similar to the trade associations he proposed for industry.

To deal with the farmer's major problem, overproduction, Hoover favored the voluntary control of agricultural output. He urged the farmer to use cooperative production controls to deal with the surplus because unlimited agricultural production would lead to perpetual problems, regardless of any action the government might take through the tariff, domestic price fixing, or subsidies. Hoover strongly opposed a coercive role for the government in this matter and his influence was crucial to Coolidge's decision to twice veto the McNary-Haugen Act.[23]

Most of Hoover's attention was directed toward his primary responsibility as commerce secretary, the business community. Hoover tried to eliminate waste and inefficiency in business as well as set guidelines for newly emerging industries. To eliminate waste in established industries, he created the Division of Simplified Practice within the Bureau of Standards. Between 1921 and 1928, he resorted to his "conference method," sponsoring hundreds of conferences aimed at the elimination of waste, production, and distribution. With the help of four national radio conferences, Hoover developed guidelines for the new radio industry. Aided by expert advice from the well-publicized educational conferences that he called, Congress also passed legislation in 1926 for Hoover to organize the Bureau of Aeronautics within the Department of Commence.

Hoover's tenure as commerce secretary made him an influential Republican and he was considered a possible running mate for Coolidge in 1924. By the mid-1920s, he had emerged as the best-known Republican in Washington, excepting only Coolidge. A leading journal described Hoover's reputation in 1925, stating, "The plain fact is that no vital problem, whether in the domestic or foreign field, arises in the administration or the handling of which Mr. Hoover does not have a real—and very often—a leading part. There is more Hoover in this administration than there is anyone else. Except in the newspapers and the political field, there is more Hoover in the administration than there is Coolidge." [24]

Hoover's role in the Coolidge administration was enhanced when he was asked to head a relief operation along the Mississippi River. A great flood covered an area 1,000 miles long and up to 40 miles wide, leaving hundreds of thousands of people homeless and destitute. Hoover called this flood the greatest peacetime calamity in the history of the nation. His efforts in flood relief were described as "masterful" and added to his already high reputation. As a follow-up to his efforts, Hoover helped design the Mississippi Flood Control Bill of 1928, which would make the federal government responsible for building levees and for preventing and controlling floods on the Mississippi River.

In dealing with the Mississippi flood, Hoover applied his economic and political theories. As chair of the flood-relief committee, he raised millions in public and private funds. Ultimately, he provided relief for one and one-half million families in seven states. Hoover's committee provided technical information and equipment, but the work was carried out by grassroots leaders and local committees. The success of his flood-relief efforts reinforced his views on helping others, bolstering his conviction that Americans would "take care of one another in time of disaster." [25] Because most of the efforts had taken place at the local level, his faith in local efforts was reinforced and he later applied this approach to the Great Depression.

Hoover proved himself to be a good crisis manager during the flood-relief activities. As part of his efforts, he organized credit facilities and a program to break up the large land holdings and to provide land for both blacks and whites. Hoover became a hero after the flood, his reputation as the "Great Humanitarian" enhanced and personally more popular than ever. One flood victim remarked, "We think Hoover is the most useful American of his day. Why, he'd make a fine President." [26]

In spite of his reticent personality, Hoover had established himself as one of the dominant political personalities of the decade. He did not actively promote himself and he shunned the limelight as commerce secretary, but he nevertheless projected a favorable image of service, efficiency, and prosperity. He avoided the appearance of a politician, preferring to be seen as representing all segments of the country. By 1928, Hoover conveyed the public impression that he had never known failure.[27] His reputation was so formidable that he was considered one of the leading contenders for the presidency should Coolidge decline to run in 1928.

When Coolidge surprisingly decided to retire in 1928, Hoover's enormous reputation helped him win the nomination. He was chosen in spite of a lack of enthusiasm from Coolidge, Wall Street, and many within his own party. President Coolidge cynically remarked in May 1928, "That man has offered me unsolicited advice for six years, all of it bad."[28] Some critics cited his unimpressive party loyalty and nominal political experience while others objected to his elitist tendencies, derisively referring to him as "Sir Herbert." Some in the party questioned whether Hoover was a pacifist and, on the racial question, perhaps an opponent of segregation.[29] Yet so high was his stature with the public that his selection was somewhat inevitable in 1928 and he easily won the Republican nomination.

When the Democrats nominated Governor Al Smith of New York, the campaign of 1928 became one of personalities rather than issues. Both men had progressive themes to their campaigns and there were almost no major differences between them. Smith was weakened as a candidate by his stand on Prohibition and especially by his urban, Catholic background. In the campaign, Smith proved to be a poor candidate. He had earlier opposed woman suffrage, could not identify with the farmers, had a strong New York "urban" quality, and flaunted his Catholicism. His being a Catholic, a "wet," and having an urban background, antagonized the Protestant, rural, "dry" vote.

Smith's weaknesses were compounded by Hoover's many strengths. The economy was prosperous and had been expanding since 1923. No foreign crisis threatened vital American interests. Furthermore, Hoover's personal views were favorably regarded by the public. He was seen as an activist, campaigning for collective bargaining and farm cooperatives, attacking poverty, and leading the effort to bring relief to the Mississippi flood victims in 1927.

In the campaign, the differences between the candidates were fewer than the elements they had in common. They differed on Prohibition and religion (although Hoover himself never referred to the religious issue and called for religious tolerance). Both candidates were self made and were efficient administrators. Both had labor support and avoided appealing to such negative trends as the Red Scare and nativism. Each of the candidates defended capitalism and businessmen, and each could count numerous millionaires among their supporters. John J. Raskob, a wealthy businessman and one of the richest men in the nation, served as the Democratic candidate's campaign manager. Smith's strong New York accent was a problem, but was somewhat balanced by Hoover's boring delivery in speaking. (Hoover disliked giving speeches and delivered only seven major addresses during the campaign.) In the 1928 contest between the two candidates, Smith was not as liberal and Hoover was not as WASPish as usually assumed.[30]

One of Hoover's best assets in the election was his reputation. (The noted journalist Walter Lippmann called Hoover's reputation a "work of art.")[31] To the majority of Americans in 1928, Hoover was the immensely successful "super expert," a practical man of action who could be counted on to solve any problem. Hoover complained about the exaggerated idea people had about him. "They have a conviction that I am a sort of superman," he said. "If some unprecedented calamity should come upon the nation, . . .I would be sacrificed to the unreasoning disappointment of a people who expected too much."[32] Unfortunately for Hoover's reputation, the Great Depression later became such an event.

Contrary to the usual folklore, Hoover's Democratic opponent did not "lose" the election; rather, Hoover waged a masterful campaign and soundly won the election. Hoover's best campaign theme was the business prosperity of the period. He told the voters in his acceptance speech, "We in America are nearer to the final triumph over poverty than ever before in the history of any land. The poorhouse is vanishing from among us. . . . We shall soon . . . be in sight of the day when poverty will be banished from the nation."[33] (These words later came back to haunt him after the outbreak of the Great Depression.) Hoover obviously was the public's choice to maintain the nation's prosperity. On election day, he carried forty states, gained 58 percent of the popular vote (second only to Harding's 60.2 percent in 1920), and won 444 electoral votes to Smith's 87.

In the early months of his presidency, Hoover appeared to be the progressive activist that the Old Guard had dreaded. He attacked excessive fortunes as a menace to liberty and declared that business had become arrogant and must be checked. He stated that he wanted to lower federal income taxes on "earned" as opposed to "unearned" income. He also announced a plan to cut income taxes up to 20 percent for the rich and up to 67 percent for lower incomes (this plan ultimately was derailed by the outbreak of the Great Depression). In March 1929, he fulfilled a long-standing goal of congressional progressives when he ordered that all huge government rebates of incomes, estate, and gift taxes be made public. He also publicly divulged the efforts of politicians who lobbied on judicial or political appointments.[34]

Hoover took a far more progressive position on civil liberties and civil rights than had his immediate predecessors. He entertained many black people at the White House and made many (mid-level) black appointments to government jobs. He made available more money for Howard University and commuted the sentence of a black man who had been convicted of murder based on thin evidence.[35] Hoover publicly condemned lynching and favored giving tenant farmers and sharecroppers of both races the means to buy the land they worked. On civil liberties, he was against overzealous police activities and the harassing of leftist dissenters. His tolerant views were in sharp contrast to the intolerant tone of the decade.

As he had done while commerce secretary, President Hoover continued the use of conferences to study problems and pave the way for their resolution. By mid-1932, thirty conferences and commissions had made recommendations on such problems as illiteracy, housing, and child care. Government-applied pressure would then be used in calling for state or municipal action, similar to the method used by Theodore Roosevelt on the conservation issue in the early 1900s. Where voluntarism or state action could not solve the problem satisfactorily, Hoover generally favored federal legislation. On many of these studies, as in illiteracy and conservation of natural resources, Congress ignored his recommendations. Hoover proved to be a far more skillful administrator than politician, a problem clearly shown by his difficult relations with Congress.[36]

Until the stock market crash of 1929, agriculture was the greatest domestic problem facing the nation. One of Hoover's first actions as president was to call a special session of Congress to deal with the problem, out of which emerged the Agricultural Marketing Act, which created the Federal Farm Board. This act, which aimed at controlling surpluses and preventing excessive price fluctuation, was similar to the long-debated McNary-Haugen Act (without the provision for dumping the surplus abroad), which had been vetoed several times by Coolidge and opposed by Hoover. The Agricultural Marketing Act set up a $500 million fund with which to buy and sell agricultural products in order to raise prices. It could make loans to farm organizations and buy farm surpluses. Hoover particularly supported the idea of helping farm cooperatives included in the act, believing they would reduce acreage and stabilize prices. Also, farm cooperative ownership of the means of distribution—purchasing, storage, processing, and marketing—would cut out speculators and unnecessary middlemen. It anticipated the New Deal plan of farm supports for agriculture and constituted one of the most extensive programs for reorganizing the economy the federal government had ever undertaken.[37]

The Federal Farm Board, which implemented this program, turned into a Depression agency after the 1929 crash. By temporarily holding prices well above the market price, the board served as the Hoover administration's first relief agency. When the agricultural depression persisted, the Farm Board used up most of its $500 million fund and could no longer continue. By mid-1931, the board stopped buying wheat (it already owned one-quarter of the world's supply). The Hoover administration began to give away its huge surpluses of wheat and cotton to American charities and even to foreign governments.[38]

The Farm Board failed in its principal task of maintaining farm prices, largely because of its inability to restrain production. Hoover's expectation that the farmer would voluntarily cut production went unrealized. Although farm cooperatives were strengthened, the basic price and supply problems of the farmer remained. The failure of the program was a bitter disappointment to the president, who placed such great faith in cooperatives to solve economic problems. But in spite of its failure, the Agricultural Marketing Act marked the first significant program of government interference in agriculture and paved the way for a host of other economic programs during the Roosevelt administration.

The greatest crisis of the Hoover administration was dealing with the Great Depression, which began in October 1929 and ultimately engulfed all segments of the economy. Throughout the middle and late 1920s, stock-market speculation and banking practices had worried Hoover as commerce secretary. In 1925, Hoover had predicted that the Federal Reserve System's easy credit policy would bring inevitable collapse in the United States. In early 1926, he publicly warned against speculation in stocks. He repeatedly asked Coolidge to seek additional controls over private banking and financial practices (especially the use of common stocks as security for customer deposits). Only two days after taking office, Hoover conferred with Federal Reserve officials about restraining stock speculation.[39] Hoover's concerns were not

groundless and in October 1929 the stock market crashed, plunging the nation into the worst depression in its history. Unemployment ultimately rose
to more than 25 percent of the workforce. Hoover's philosophy on the limited role of government would be sorely tested in the remaining years of his
presidency.

In response to the Great Depression, Hoover remained true to his princi-
ples of minimal government action and reliance on voluntary private action.
He feared the American people might act like Europeans when confronted
with economic disaster, abandoning individualism and action through voluntary associations in favor of direct government aid. The advantages of remaining true to his philosophy were too important to be abandoned.[40] "Every time
we find a solution outside of government, we have not only strengthened
character but . . . have preserved our sense of real self-government," he declared.[41] Like Harding and Coolidge before him, he had faith in the hardiness
of the American character when faced with adversity, and in the basic soundness of the American economy.

When the crash occurred, the early expectation was for a temporary decline and the stock market actually made a substantial recovery within a few
months. In May 1930, the market was about where it had been a year earlier
and the prediction was for a relatively "normal" 1930. However, by early
1931, the economy was in serious decline and obviously would not return to
normal conditions any time soon. Hoover believed that a U.S. recovery was finally under way in mid-1931, when events overseas caused the economy to
decline once more. He especially blamed the breakdown of central European
banks for halting the U.S. recovery. In spite of Europe's financial problems,
Hoover believed the U.S. economy was recovering from its low point in
1932, when political uncertainly over the transition to Franklin Roosevelt
caused the economy to reverse course once more.[42]

Although the public blamed Hoover for the Great Depression, scholars
generally have excused him for causing the economic crisis. The controversy
over Hoover and the Depression mainly involves his response to the crisis.
Critics charged that he did too little and that he was a prisoner of his political
philosophy.[43] His supporters argue that his plan was working and that the recovery, already under way, was derailed by the crisis in Europe and by political
shocks in the United States such as the results of the elections in 1930 and the
nomination of Franklin Roosevelt in 1932.[44]

For a variety of reasons, Hoover tried to remain loyal to his political philosophy even after the outbreak of the Great Depression. Although not as closely identified with the laissez-faire idea as his predecessor, Calvin Coolidge, Hoover retained an abiding faith in the ideal of a limited role for the federal government. This system had given the United States a standard of living unmatched in the world. Even his experiences while living in Europe led Hoover to reject "statism" (the European system of heavy government involvement in society), which he believed was not as efficient as the American laissez-faire system.[45] His own life history confirmed his faith in the system. Throughout Hoover's adulthood, the United States had experienced three decades of prosperity and business expansion. In each of the downturns during this period (1907, 1914, and 1920), the federal government had done relatively little and yet the system self-corrected. Hoover believed that the American system had encouraged efficiency, individualism, enterprise, and personal success. He pointed to his own rise to the top from humble beginnings as proof that the system rewarded talent and hard work.[46]

Hoover's faith in the system made him reluctant to consider major changes in the role of the government. He believed that equality of opportunity would overcome or ameliorate inequities in society. Society owes its members not success but equality of opportunity, liberty, and justice. Even those from poor backgrounds such as his could succeed. He added, however, that laissez-faire must be tempered by economic justice and that society runs more smoothly when the strongest are sometimes restrained. With this caveat, he accepted the essential belief of William Graham Sumner, a major defender of laissez-faire economics in the nineteenth century, who declared that "life is a race that goes to the swift."[47] All of these ideas were put to the test by the Great Depression.

Because Hoover believed the American system was fundamentally in good order, he did not abandon his philosophy even during this financial crisis. He theorized that the Depression had its roots in World War I and was linked to war debts, lost lives, political instability that had "paralyzed confidence," revolutions abroad, disturbances in trade, and overproduction of key commodities. The crisis in the United States was temporary, more a "crisis in confidence" than a fundamental weakness in the system.[48]

Hoover's response to the crisis fitted into this theory of its causation and he tried to stimulate confidence without major changes in the system. Because he believed that the economy was basically sound, Hoover's "offensive" against the Great Depression was relatively mild. He called a "Conference for

Continued Economic Progress" in November 1929 with industrial and labor leaders in which he obtained voluntary pledges to avoid strikes; to hold to current employment, wage, and production levels; and to share work where possible. Hoover wanted the government to play an important role, but mainly at the lower levels. He asked the cities and states to speed up their public works in order to maintain employment and increase construction activity. He did not ask for additional funds for federal public works at first, believing that large-scale public works would not be effective in relieving unemployment unless planned in advance during a period of relative stability. With this strategy in place and the economy temporarily rebounding, Hoover declared in May 1930, "I am convinced we have passed the worst."[49]

Unfortunately, Hoover's optimistic prediction proved inaccurate, in spite of temporary cooperation from both business and labor. Business generally maintained production and wage levels until the summer of 1931. Labor agreed to forgo gains already won from management to permit lower production costs and a rise in profits that would stimulate the economy. But by mid-1931, both wage rates and production levels began to be cut due to reduced consumer demand. Hoover's expectation for a solution through voluntary cooperation from business and labor went unfulfilled.[50]

As the Depression worsened, Hoover lost additional public support with his unpopular views on relief for the unemployed. He initially hoped that business, private charity, and state and local government would offer relief to the unemployed. When this assistance proved inadequate, he was forced to consider a direct federal role. There were two kinds of federal relief considered during the Great Depression: direct relief known as the dole and indirect relief through public works jobs. Hoover remained opposed to direct relief even when unemployment soared during the Depression. He believed that locally financed self-help programs were more worthy of Americans than direct federal aid. Hoover generally remained opposed to most public works proposals throughout his presidency. He did support some that he considered "productive," as opposed to the "nonproductive," pork-barrel type. He made it plain that he was unenthused about federal work projects, declaring it was more important to cut expenses and have a balanced budget.[51]

Hoover's political philosophy helped turn the public against him on this controversial issue of relief for the unemployed. Although he supported aid to the farmer through the Farm Board, he was firmly against direct relief to the unemployed. Preferring private relief, he hoped that the more fortunate

Americans would freely rescue their neighbors. Public relief, he felt, might weaken the work ethic and create a class of loafers and subsidy seekers. The spread of government would destroy individual opportunity and initiative and ultimately character as well. Bureaucratic federal aid would be harmful to his Quaker vision of an American community in which neighbors took care of one another.[52]

Hoover also believed that a strong federal relief role might damage the economy and prevent a recovery. He felt this type of assistance had caused Europe's economy to collapse by weakening the work ethic. In addition, it would make impossible a balanced budget, which was necessary for confidence to be restored.[53] At a time of high unemployment, this theory was unpopular and seemingly incomprehensible. The public wondered how Hoover could justify federal aid to corporations and even animals but not to individuals. (An extreme case of his seemingly contradictory philosophy was Hoover's decision to make available money to save livestock but not to help the farmer.)[54] Hoover, who had gained an international reputation for his work in aiding the hungry people in Europe and Russia after World War I, was determined not to extend such federal aid to the needy in the United States.

As the Depression persisted into 1930, Hoover was forced to reconsider his reluctance to act. In December 1930, Congress appropriated $117 million for public improvements. In February 1931, it enacted the Wagner-Graham Stabilization Act, providing for additional public works. As the Depression continued into 1932, Hoover reluctantly authorized a much more ambitious federal public works program but under strict guidelines. In July of that year, he signed the Emergency Relief Construction Act, which appropriated $2 billion for public works and $300 million for direct loans to the states. The projects must be self-liquidating (pay for themselves) and the states had to agree to a kind of "pauper's oath."[55] His greatest concern was that these expenditures would threaten his goal for a balanced budget, which was crucial to the nation's financial soundness and vital to restoring business confidence. He preferred the increased spending needed to relieve the Depression to come mainly from private, not public, sources. He warned about the danger of the country being "plunged into socialism and collectivism; with its destruction of human liberty," which an expanded federal relief role might bring.[56]

One of Hoover's most famous initiatives, the Hawley-Smoot Tariff, also became one of his most criticized. Like the earlier Agricultural Marketing Act, the Hawley-Smoot Tariff emerged from the special session of Congress in

1929 with the goal of helping the farmer. Fulfilling a pledge made during the 1928 campaign, Hoover originally was interested in merely raising rates on agricultural products but, after the various special interests became involved, the rates were raised on many industrial products as well. Although initiated before the Great Depression began, the Hawley-Smoot Tariff in its final form emerged as one of Congress's major anti-Depression measures. Its rates were not the highest in history but were high enough to raise concern among many economists. Would the high tariff disturb trade relations and thus worsen the international economic situation? Putting aside his own reservations, Hoover signed the measure. Unfortunately, the fears of the more than one thousand noted economists who had hoped for a veto were borne out when Europe retaliated with its own high tariffs and international trade declined.[57]

Even as the economic crisis worsened, Hoover continued to stress a limited role for the federal government and a more active role for voluntary organizations and state and local governments. He looked back to the cooperative efforts he stimulated during World War I and the Mississippi flood crisis of 1927 as guidelines. Hoover defined the presidential mission as one of organizing voluntary forces within a community to encourage a spirit of competition. Federal legislation was the last resort in any problem and other remedies would probably have to be employed because the United States could not legislate itself out of a worldwide economic depression.[58] In spite of the seriousness of the crisis, his activism had definite limits.

When the federal government did act, Hoover believed that the president rather than Congress should take the lead. Unlike his successor, Franklin Roosevelt, he had an uneasy relationship with Congress. He believed that Congress had no substantive role to play in an economic crisis and was actually contemptuous of politicians (who felt the same way about him).[59] Congress should only act, Hoover stated, when all the interested parties met both at lower levels of government and in the private sector and actually prepared their own solutions.

For all his talk about presidential initiative, Hoover did not have the temperament or the personality to lead the nation in a crisis. He disliked the political process and public speaking. Described as a man of "extreme reason," he was also called a "first class intellect" and a "second class temperament." He was very serious, lacked a sense of humor, and could not uplift the nation with the dour expression that he conveyed. According to Secretary of State Stimson, there was "never a joke cracked in Cabinet meetings" and "the ever-present feeling of gloom pervaded the Administration."[60] Hoover's was not a reassuring personality to inspire and uplift the nation during the worst economic crisis in American history.

In early 1932, the beleaguered Hoover launched his boldest strike against the Great Depression, the creation of the Reconstruction Finance Corporation. The RFC made the Hoover administration the first in American history to use the power of the federal government to intervene directly in the economy in time of peace.[61] This program, which authorized vast loans to business and banks but no direct relief for unemployment, was a tacit admission that voluntarism alone would not solve the problem. The RFC initially was created mainly to help smaller banks and financial institutions but later was expanded to help industries, banks, and farmers. The RFC also provided public works loans, but such loans had to be self-liquidating. This leading tool to fight the Depression ultimately lasted nine years and cost $50 billion but was not able to end the economic crisis by itself. It did serve, however, as a transition to the more activist policies of the subsequent New Deal. Because of Hoover programs such as the RFC, Franklin Roosevelt's key advisor, Rexford Tugwell, later said, "We didn't admit it at the time but practically the whole New Deal was extrapolated from programs that Hoover started."[62]

By his last year in office, Hoover was moving in contradictory directions. He had temporarily suspended his reliance upon voluntarism and private sources of credit. By 1932, private charities accounted for only 1.4 percent of the money spent on relief. In spite of strong personal reservations, Hoover shifted his philosophy ever more toward using government as the principal remedy for the Depression. Yet he also called for a tax increase at the end of 1931 to balance the budget, fearing a further erosion of public confidence if efforts were not made to balance the federal budget. By this act, he became the first president in American history to ask for a tax increase in time of severe depression.[63]

The decade of the 1920s began with a depression and ended the same way. The 1929 Depression proved to be the most serious in American history, far worse in depth and longevity than the downturn of 1920. Unemployment climbed to at least 25 percent and many other people were working part time at low wages. Many farmers lost their farms and relief payments for the unemployed were barely above the starvation level. Unlike the earlier economic downturns in Hoover's adult life, the Depression of 1929 did not self-correct and his economic philosophy ultimately was rejected by the voters in the 1932 election.

Hoover's failure to deal with the Great Depression discredited the economic philosophy he had developed during his lifetime. Better suited for more normal times, he proved inadequate in coping with the Great Depression, which dominated nearly his entire presidency. His theories of voluntarism and associationalism and his belief in a relatively unregulated laissez-faire economic system were unable to resolve the economic crisis. Hoover was nevertheless reluctant to surrender his economic philosophy. He especially criticized the failure of the business community to act more selflessly, stating, "You know, the only trouble with capitalism is capitalists; they're too damn greedy." [64]

9

Legacies

THE 1920S WAS A DECADE enshrouded in myth, probably the most misunderstood decade in American history. Not merely a time of frivolous release
from the tensions of World War I, the decade was actually a period of profound social change and new directions in U.S. foreign relations. Virtually
every important American institution was tested during this period. So important were these changes that the 1920s can be considered the beginning of
modern America.

The decade of the 1920s traditionally has been described by historians as
a time in which little happened except the economic excesses that brought on
the Great Depression of 1929. This interpretation reflects the historians' preoccupation with politics, which was far less active in the postwar period than
during the progressive years that preceded the war or the New Deal period of
the 1930s.[1]

In the social and cultural arena, the period was one of amazing vitality, innovation, and change. These changes were fostered by outstanding technological development and a new type of industrial economy typified by mass
production and mass consumption, which accelerated the breakdown of old
habits and patterns of thought. The new society of the 1920s was characterized by vast changes in religion, political philosophy, folkways, moral pre-
cepts, and the uses of leisure time.

To many historians, the 1920s traditionally was the period of Frederick
Lewis Allen's *Only Yesterday*. Was this a time of never-ending drinking parties,
with revelers always one step ahead of the police? Was it an era of "wonderful
nonsense," symbolized by women in skimpy clothing and such public displays
as flagpole sittings? Many saw the period as one that abandoned meaningful

social reforms and a responsible foreign policy. Above all, was this a time of crass materialism and an endless pursuit of riches?

Having viewed society through such a negative prism, historians not surprisingly looked at America's political leaders in a similarly negative fashion. Were the presidents of the 1920s incompetent, narrow-minded, or too confined to the views of an outdated past? Presidents Harding, Coolidge, and Hoover are among the most criticized chief executives in our nation's history. Did they represent only selfish interests and neglect the true responsibilities of their office? Did President Woodrow Wilson, long a hero of American historians, fight a valiant struggle toward the end of his presidency only to be defeated by the forces of reaction, bigotry, and greed? With such interpretations of the decade, little wonder that many historians felt a sense of relief at America's "rescue" by the reform-minded and internationalist presidency of Franklin D. Roosevelt

But as with most stereotypes, simple explanations do not suffice to explain deep social changes for the decade. Rather than simply being an orgy of fun and irresponsibility, the 1920s reflected a period of profound social and institutional changes for the nation, one of the most important being its shift from a rural base to an urban one. More than just an economic change, the older rural values that had guided the nation for a long time were reexamined by a newer, less restricted urban culture that reflected crucial new scientific and technological breakthroughs. "It was during those years that the country first became urban, particularly in the cast of its mind, in its ideals and folkways."[2]

Rural America did not surrender its leadership role without a struggle and there was a determined counterattack throughout the decade. The United States did not give up its old ideals and attitudes easily and the conflicts between the representatives of the older elements of traditional American culture and those of the new day were often bitter. This was a period of massive cultural conflict focusing upon such matters as religion, marriage, and moral standards, as well as the issues of race, Prohibition, and immigration. America went through a period of intolerance toward minority groups, aliens, and radicals. Were these negative feelings caused by "a frightened determination of the old and essentially rural-minded majority to maintain its supremacy over rapidly increasing urban groups professing other social and religious faiths"?[3]

A principal target in this emerging cultural war was the immigrant. One of the most "American" of all traditions, open immigration was sharply curtailed in a series of landmark immigration laws during the 1920s. Behind the new nativism was the nature and volume of the immigration, which came mainly from southern and eastern Europe. Was anti-immigrant feeling a typical American response during periods of stress in the nation? Did the New Immigrant bring dangerous ideas into the nation? Could he ever be Americanized and turned into a loyal citizen? In the post-World War I era, the nation ultimately turned to restriction in an attempt to preserve its historic ethnicity and values.

In the area of religion as well, the old order attempted to block the forces of change. The rural Protestant old guard was losing its dominance to the more liberal Protestant ideas of the city, as well as being weakened by seemingly endless hordes of Catholic and Jewish immigrants. In the deep South and parts of the Middle West, fundamentalists mounted a campaign that expressed itself through the Ku Klux Klan, anti-evolution laws, and a new series of blue laws. The Protestant fundamentalists fought this battle in several arenas but were ultimately unsuccessful. In the Scopes trial of 1925, the battleground was the teaching of Darwin's theories in the public schools, a development that threatened to undermine traditional religious values. Although the legal system ruled in favor of the fundamentalists, the modernists administered a decisive defeat to the anti-evolutionists in the court of public opinion.

An even more famous manifestation of the rural counterattack was the rise of the Ku Klux Klan. This self-professed campaign for the old-fashioned Protestant rural values and Anglo-Saxon culture reached a peak membership in the mid-1920s of between four and five million. The Klan was a countermovement against the new urban civilization. More than merely a symbol of white supremacy, during the decade it targeted the New Immigrants and "immoral people" (such as those with new sexual values and opponents of Prohibition). While easy to dismiss today as an un-American terrorist organization, the Klan in the 1920s reflected the deep pain felt by millions of Americans who believed the older America was rapidly disappearing.

The debate over Prohibition also represented the deep divisions in American society. The old order had triumphed with the passage of the Eighteenth Amendment in 1919. Although it drew limited urban progressive backing, the core of Prohibitionist support was in older rural America. As with the Scopes trial, Prohibition proved to be a pyrrhic victory for the old order. In spite of passage of the Eighteenth Amendment and the Volstead Act, widespread opposition to the ban on alcohol made Prohibition ultimately un-enforceable. This attempt to impose old-fashioned morality on a rapidly changing society was a dismal failure.

Another social value that was under attack by the traditionalists was the new sexual freedom of women. Did the movies and the automobile corrupt the sexual values of the young? An attempt to police the movies by appointing a morals czar had only a limited effect. When the sexual battleground moved from the parlor to the automobile, anything short of a chaperone accompany-ing young people was a hopeless gesture. As the main practitioners of the new sexual freedom, the "new woman" sought more social freedom rather than political freedom. The new freedom of women in the 1920s was especially fo-cused on play.[4] With their political rights expanded by gaining the vote through the Nineteenth Amendment and with interest rising in expanded job opportunities, women also sought freer modes of dress, the right to drink and smoke in public, and more sexual freedom. Helpless to resist these new social trends, the traditionalists again fought a losing battle.

As the nation moved from the country to the city, more economic oppor-tunities opened up for the new urban majority. In contrast to the stagnant liv-ing standard of the farmer, urban wages rose during the decade as business became more efficient. During the 1920s, with the ever-increasing use of Frederick Taylor's "scientific management" theory and a greater reliance upon electricity as a source of power, American business expanded greatly. The volume of consumer goods on the market gave America a higher standard of living, which was known as "Coolidge prosperity." But while wages in-creased slower than business profits, higher salaries coupled with a shorter workweek gave Americans a significantly higher standard of living than any other nation in the world. Unlike the rural population, which faced both de-clining income and weakening cultural dominance, urban dwellers were living better and "freer" than ever before.

These changes in society were in sharp contrast to an apparent return to older political values. Domestically, government was less active during the decade and greater freedom was given to the business community. Each of the three Republican presidents of the decade professed his faith in American business and gave businessmen a freedom unseen since the late nineteenth century. As production, profits, and personal consumption standards rose dra-matically, faith in business as a way of life spread throughout the nation. There was lavish praise for business leaders as the pillars of society, a status that only changed after the 1929 stock market crash. The wide deference given to business by both politicians and the public rested upon the belief that the system had given Americans a better life. The new technology developed by business provided more free time and the tools to occupy the newly "leisured" masses. The automobile, the moving picture, and the radio all became commonplace during the 1920s. This technology, affording the masses both leisure time and money, was responsible for a major social revolution in the country, ushering the United States almost overnight into the "age of play."

Because of the diminished role of political leaders, it has been easy for historians to see everywhere plots, failed crusades, and dereliction of duty. In spite of the usual folklore spread by historians, there was no dramatic progressive-to-conservative shift in 1920. During his last two years, Woodrow Wilson was not a progressive. His crackdown on radicals—often at the expense of civil liberties—and his pro-business and antilabor approach to returning the nation's economy to peacetime conditions diminished the change that occurred with the victory of Harding. After the turmoil from labor disturbances, the Red Scare, and social problems that immediately followed the war, voters sought equilibrium rather than a radical change in political direction.

Entrusted with running the government during the 1920s, Republican leaders found greater acceptance with the public than with historians. These scholars generally have given short shrift to the three Republican presidents and defended Wilson as a martyr to a noble cause. A former history student reminisced, "We never paid any attention to what the books said about Harding and Coolidge because we knew the professors were in a hurry to get to Roosevelt."[5] Another scholar added ruefully, "We knew more about the Socialists and Communists in the 1920s than we did about the Republicans."[6] The scholarly Woodrow Wilson was usually depicted in marked contrast to Harding, Coolidge, and Hoover, with their limited imaginations and abilities. Yet each of these Republicans was amazingly popular while he served (until the outbreak of the Great Depression). The elections of 1920, 1924, and 1928 were landslide victories for the Republican Party, indicating that the country supported the pro-business policies that seemingly had led to the highest standard of living in the world.

In recent years, historians' judgments have become more aligned with public opinion of the 1920s. Harding was an experienced politician who was highly regarded until his reputation was brought down by scandals (in which he was not personally involved). In 1969, Robert K. Murray became one of the first historians to pronounce Harding's presidency a "success."[7] Calvin Coolidge was well educated and more scholarly than he wished the public to know. Coolidge "was far more skillful as a politician and more believable as a human being than the cracker barrel caricature who has appeared in lectures and textbooks for a long time."[8] Herbert Hoover was a self-made millionaire businessman who succeeded in a host of political projects before the Great Depression. While in office, these conservative leaders were seen as architects of prosperity at a time when the public would not have permitted a more activist type of government.

In foreign affairs as well, historians have eased their previous hostility toward the three Republicans who served during the decade. Wilson traditionally was depicted as the champion of international collective security who was eventually defeated by the forces of isolationism, usually symbolized by America's rejection of the League of Nations. Historians today argue that the terms *noncommittal* or *rejection of collective security* more accurately describe American diplomacy during the 1920s than *isolationism*. America's economic power and economic interests that intertwined with other nations made an isolationist foreign policy impossible. The United States actually took several important diplomatic initiatives during the decade. Although it rejected the League of Nations, it cooperated extensively with various League commissions. The first meaningful arms-limitation agreement in history was negotiated at the instigation of the United States. Agreements were reached to stabilize the diplomatic situation in Asia in an attempt to contain an expansionist Japan. The United States even reversed the long-standing interventionist policy in Latin America dating back to Theodore Roosevelt and began removing its occupation troops from several countries. The most famous American initiative of the decade, perhaps obscuring all others, was the ill-fated Kellogg-Brand Pact to outlaw offensive war. Because these agreements depended upon international goodwill and were not enforced by treaty obligation, they foundered when the Great Depression ended the global truce of the 1920s.

Other foreign policy matters also demonstrated an active American diplomatic policy in the 1920s. The United States was directly involved in the seemingly insoluble dispute with Europe after World War I concerning the payment of German reparations to the victorious Allies and their own repayment of war loans to the Americans. Political realities at home made it difficult for any president to urge cancellation of more than $10 billion in Allied loans.

When the Allies were reluctant to pay and tied repayment to collection of German reparations, the United States initiated a solution that seemed to satisfy the Allies, the American public, and Germany. The amount of reparations was scaled back substantially, American loans to Germany made it possible to begin reparations payments, and the Allies then began to "repay" their loans to the United States. This financial shell game ultimately was undone by the Great Depression, which ended the cycle of loans to obtain repayment of earlier loans.

By focusing so keenly on a foreign policy based on international goodwill and a domestic policy with a strong pro-business slant, were the Republican presidents guilty of irresponsible and unrealistic policies, as many historians have charged? There is no evidence that anyone during the 1920s predicted anything like the coming World War II or the cataclysmic economic depression of 1929. Before the Great Depression, nobody foresaw the rise of Nazi Germany. In spite of obvious problems in the economy, no major figure predicted such a deep and protracted economic downturn. When the economy became overspeculative by the late 1920s, there were limited, albeit unsuccessful, steps taken by the Federal Reserve System to curb speculation. President Hoover took a more cautious attitude than had his predecessor Coolidge regarding potential problems in the economy, but, politically speaking, it was nearly impossible to urge a major redirect of economic policies and the speculative bubble ultimately burst. After 1929, President Hoover was more involved than any previous president in responding to economic depression and his policies were greatly expanded by his successor, Franklin Roosevelt. Hoover was caught in a difficult situation; without knowing how deep the depression would become or how long it would continue, it was difficult to make long-range policies to fight it.

The decade of the 1920s offers several important legacies to both historians and the American people. U.S. institutions can be severely tested during times of social change, especially during a wartime emergency. World War I had major influences on America both during the war and in the decade that followed. Economically the war caused a major expansion in farm production to meet the new demand in Europe, which was followed by an agricultural depression when the market severely contracted. By the end of the decade, the United States was taking an active role in aiding the farmer for the first time in its history and a precedent was set for more active government intervention in the economy.

In race relations, both the war and changing demographic patterns led to the first major race riots in American history. Fear of a more "assertive" black veteran after the war and changing neighborhood patterns fostered by a massive emigration of black people to the North led to riots in several northern cities in 1919. As the racial conflict between whites and blacks mounted during the early 1920s, various radical black movements grew rapidly. The largest black nationalist movement, led by Marcus Garvey, numbered in the millions by the mid-1920s. More similar in sentiment to the Black Muslims than to the mainstream civil rights movement, Garvey's movement was a forerunner rather than a beginning of the modern black protest movement.

Another shock to the system was a widespread fear of Communism, which occurred for the first time in American history. The Russian Revolution, the founding of the American Communist Party, a wave of labor strikes in 1919, and the unsettled atmosphere immediately after the war led to massive hysteria in the United States and a diminution of civil liberties. The confusion after World War I—just as it would after World War II—proved to be fertile ground for enforcing conformity and attacking unpopular views. The United States also began a long tradition of extreme hostility and suspicion toward the Soviet Union, interrupted only by the World War II crisis. The end of the Cold War in the early 1990s finally ended a source of concern that had lasted seven decades.

The 1920s was also the last decade when the United States practiced traditional laissez-faire economic policy, unfettered by the welfare state. The economy had been subject to ever-increasing regulation since the progressive era began in 1901 during the Theodore Roosevelt administration. By 1921, an impressive array of governmental machinery was in place to oversee the economy. From 1921 through 1929, when the Great Depression began, the economy had reverted back to a less-regulated state, with many of the progressive innovations being ignored or circumvented. The economic expansion that began in 1923 seemed to vindicate this philosophy, and only after the outbreak of the Great Depression did the laissez-faire idea fall into disrepute.

More than any previous era, the post-World War I decade witnessed vast social changes brought about by the new technology. During the 1920s, the nation became more uniform in culture, reflecting the rise of radio and the motion picture industry. Now Americans could experience the same entertainment and hear the same news all around the country. The great expansion of the automobile industry gave Americans a greater freedom to see other parts of the nation and to become less provincial. At the same time that traditionalists were trying to preserve the older culture and values, Americans were exposed to a greater variety of new experiences than ever before.

The 1920s was a period of great change and served as a transition to the modern age. Perhaps government could have played a greater role in "cushioning" the fallout from these changes. Most of the drama was played out in the private sector, unlike the activist days of New Deal government. In this time of a rapidly changing economy, a new relationship with the outside world, and new morals and manners—all taking place within the context of an expanding economy—the government played a minor role. The progression toward change proved to be unstoppable. As in the case of Prohibition, the Scopes trial, and anti-immigrant policies, temporary victories by the old order were ultimately reversed. The abandonment of laissez-faire for the welfare state, already beginning in response to the worsening Depression, was one of the most important changes.

During the 1920s, many of the elements of modern America could already be seen. Urban America now outnumbered the rural population. The industrial revolution was giving the American people the highest standard of living in the world. The United States was playing an active role in international relations. Early stirrings of the "new Negro" and the "new woman" could be seen. The new media entertainment industries were already being formed. America's love affair with the automobile was in full swing. The fundamentalists, although weakened, remained defenders of the old order and later would be revived as the "Christian Right." Still to be defined, in this turbulent decade of momentous change in American society, was the proper role of government.

The decade of "wonderful nonsense" was actually one of the most important transition periods in American history. As the communications revolution continues and Americans become exposed ever more to their fellow countrymen and to people from around the world, what will be the impact on the nation's core values and institutions? If the 1920s serve as a guide, that impact will be substantial.

Notes

Selected Readings

Bibliography

Index

Notes

1. Prelude to the Twenties

1. Burl Noggle, *Into the Twenties* (Urbana: Univ. of Illinois Press, 1974), 4–5.

2. Robert K. Murray, *The Harding Era* (Minneapolis: Univ. of Minnesota Press, 1969), 71.

3. Ibid., 75.

4. "Wilson's Legacy to Harding," *Nation* 112 (23 Feb. 1921): 282–83.

5. Murray, *Harding Era,* 71.

6. Ibid., 74.

7. Noggle, *Into the Twenties,* viii.

8. Murray, *Harding Era,* 75.

9. Geoffrey Perrett, *America in the Twenties: A History* (New York: Simon and Shuster, 1982), 29.

10. David Shannon, *Between the Wars: America, 1919–1941* (Boston: Houghton Mifflin, 1965), 17.

11. Ibid., 22.

12. Murray, *Harding Era,* 73.

13. Ibid., 83.

14. Ibid., 84.

15. Ibid., 86.

16. Shannon, *Between the Wars,* 23.

17. Murray, *Harding Era,* 87.

18. Perrett, *America in the Twenties,* 34.

19. Ibid., 38.

20. Shannon, *Between the Wars,* 27.

21. Ibid., 24.

22. Ibid.

23. Ibid., 25.

24. Murray, *Harding Era,* 87.

25. Perrett, *America in the Twenties,* 50.

26. Shannon, *Between the Wars,* 21.

27. Noggle, *Into the Twenties,* 84.

28. Murray, *Harding Era,* 87.

29. Noggle, *Into the Twenties,* 105.

30. William Leuchtenberg, *The Perils of Prosperity, 1914–1932* (Chicago: Univ. of Chicago Press, 1958), 72–73.

31. Shannon, *Between the Wars,* 27.

32. George Mowry, ed. *The Twenties: Fords, Flappers, and Fanatics* (Englewood Cliffs, N.J.: Prentice-Hall, 1963), 121.

33. Ibid., 122.

34. Ibid., 123.

35. Perrett, *America in the Twenties,* 62.

36. Otis L. Graham Jr., *The Great Campaigns* (Englewood Cliffs, N.J.: R. E. Krieger, 1971), 113.

37. Noggle, *Into the Twenties,* 99.

38. Perrett, *America in the Twenties,* 53.

39. Noggle, *Into the Twenties,* 113.

40. Ibid., 113.

41. Perrett, *America in the Twenties,* 70–71.

42. Noggle, *Into the Twenties,* 101.

43. Ibid., 111.

44. John Higham, *Strangers in the Land* (New Brunswick, N.J.: Rutgers Univ. Press, 1955), 233.

45. Robert K. Murray, *Red Scare: A Study in National Hysteria, 1919–1920* (Minneapolis: Univ. of Minnesota Press, 1955), 233.

46. Perrett, *America in the Twenties,* 74.

47. Mowry, ed. *Fords, Flappers, and Fanatics,* 136.

48. Perrett, *America in the Twenties,* 21.

49. Murray, *Harding Era,* 78.

50. Ibid., 77.

51. Ibid., 78.

52. Thomas A. Bailey, *Woodrow Wilson and the Great Betrayal* (New York: Macmillan, 1947), 277.

53. Richard Hofstadter, *The American Political Tradition and the Men Who Made it* (New York: Alfred A. Knopf, 1959), 276.

54. Perrett, *America in the Twenties,* 78.

55. Ibid., 79.

56. Noggle, *Into the Twenties,* 156–57.

57. Perrett, *America in the Twenties,* 88.

58. Noggle, *Into the Twenties,* 160.

59. Ibid., 153–54.

60. Ibid., 154.

61. Ralph Andrist and the editors of American Heritage, *History of the 1920s and 1930s* (New York: American Heritage/Bonanza Books, 1987), 26.

62. Noggle, *Into the Twenties,* 166.

63. Ibid., 165.

64. Ibid., 174.

2. The Travails of Warren G. Harding

1. Arthur Schlesinger Jr., "Our Presidents: A Rating by 75 Historians," *New York Times Magazine,* 29 July 1962, 12–13, 40.

2. Morris Werner and John Starr, *Teapot Dome* (New York: Viking, 1959), 9–38.

3. Andrew Sinclair, *The Available Man* (New York: Macmillan, 1965), 67.

4. Ibid., 24.

5. Ibid., 91.

6. Ibid., 102.

7. Murray, *Harding Era,* 41–42.

8. Ibid., 36–37.

9. Wesley Bagby, "The Smoke-Filled Room and the Nomination of Warren G. Harding," *Mississippi Valley Historical Review,* 16 (Mar. 1955): 673–74.

10. Randolph C. Downes, *The Rise of Warren Gamaliel Harding, 1865–1920* (Columbus: Ohio State Univ. Press, 1970), 410.

11. Robert K. Murray, *The Politics of Normalcy* (New York: W. W. Norton, 1973), 15.

12. Herbert Margulies, "The Election in Wisconsin: The Return to Normalcy Appraised," *Wisconsin Magazine of History* 41 (autumn 1957): 22.

13. Sinclair, *Available Man,* 162.

14. Ibid., 162.

15. Murray, *Harding Era,* 69–70.

16. Margulies, "Election in Wisconsin," 22.

17. Murray, *Harding Era,* 180.

18. Robert K. Murray, "President Harding and His Cabinet," *Ohio History* 75 (spring-summer 1966): 124.

19. Sinclair, *Available Man,* 222–24; Murray, *Politics of Normalcy,* 21.

20. Sinclair, *Available Man,* 230.

21. Michael Parrish, *Anxious Decades: America in Prosperity and Depression, 1920–1941* (New York, W. W. Norton, 1992), 24.

22. Sinclair, *Available Man,* 219.

23. Robert Sobel, *Coolidge* (Washington, D.C.: Regnery, 1998), 213–14; Murray, *Harding Era,* 172.

24. Sinclair, *Available Man,* 203.

25. Murray, *Harding Era,* 172.

26. Ibid., 175.

27. Ibid., 177.

28. Ibid., 176.

29. John Braeman, "The American Policy in the Age of Polity: A Reappraisal," in *Calvin*

Coolidge and the Coolidge Era, ed. John Earl Haynes (Washington, D.C.: Library of Congress, 1998), 32.

　　30. Murray, *Harding Era,* 182–83.

　　31. Ibid., 183.

　　32. Ibid., 232.

　　33. Sinclair, *Available Man,* 202.

　　34. Ibid., 24.

　　35. Murray, *Harding Era,* 201.

　　36. Ibid., 205.

　　37. Ibid., 206.

　　38. Sinclair, *Available Man,* 249.

　　39. Ibid., 204.

　　40. Ibid., 253.

　　41. Parrish, *Anxious Decades,* 25.

　　42. Murray, *Harding Era,* 399.

　　43. Parrish, *Anxious Decades,* 26

　　44. Murray, *Harding Era,* 399.

　　45. Ibid., 401.

　　46. Sinclair, *Available Man,* 232–33.

　　47. Murray, *Harding Era,* 407.

　　48. Parrish, *Anxious Decades,* 55.

　　49. Murray, *Harding Era,* 230.

　　50. Ibid., 235.

　　51. Sinclair, *Available Man,* 254.

　　52. Murray, *Harding Era,* 262.

　　53. Ibid., 231.

　　54. Sinclair, *Available Man,* 219.

　　55. Perrett, *America in the Twenties,* 181.

　　56. Sinclair, *Available Man,* 212.

　　57. Murray, *Harding Era,* 384.

　　58. Parrish, *Anxious Decades,* 22–23.

　　59. Sinclair, *Available Man,* viii.

　　60. Gaston Means, *The Strange Death of President Harding* (New York: Guild, 1930), 247–53.

　　61. Murray, *Harding Era,* 512.

3. The Triumph of Calvin Coolidge

　　1. Donald McCoy, "A President Restrained," in *The 1920s: Problems and Paradoxes,* ed. Milton Plesur (Boston: Allyn and Bacon, 1969), 29.

　　2. Ibid., 34–35; William Allen White, *A Puritan in Babylon* (New York: Macmillan, 1938), 10.

　　3. White, *Puritan in Babylon,* 12.

4. Ibid., vii.

5. Ibid., viii.

6. Shannon, *Between the Wars,* 34.

7. White, *Puritan in Babylon,* 40.

8. Parrish, *Anxious Decades,* 49.

9. White, *Puritan in Babylon,* 46.

10. Donald McCoy, *Calvin Coolidge: The Quiet President* (New York: Macmillan, 1967), 293.

11. Ibid., 68.

12. Ibid., 78–79.

13. Ibid., 102.

14. Ibid., 121.

15. Ibid., 124.

16. Parrish, *Anxious Decades,* 7.

17. Ibid., 7.

18. Murray, *Harding Era,* 40.

19. White, *Puritan in Babylon,* 230, 236.

20. Robert Ferrell, *The Presidency of Calvin Coolidge* (Lawrence: Univ. of Kansas Press, 1998), 61.

21. George Mowry, *The Urban Nation, 1920–1960* (New York: Hill and Wang, 1965), 45.

22. McCoy, *Quiet President,* 255.

23. Perrett, *America in the Twenties,* 180.

24. Jules Abels, *In the Time of Silent Cal* (New York: G. P. Putnam's Sons, 1959), 229.

25. White, *Puritan in Babylon,* 221.

26. Mowry, *Urban Nation,* 45.

27. Ibid., 45–46.

28. Perrett, *America in the Twenties,* 194.

29. John Braeman, "The American Polity in the Age of Normalcy," in *Calvin Coolidge and the Coolidge Era,* ed. Haynes, 25.

30. McCoy, *Quiet President,* 314–15.

31. Ibid., 156.

32. Ibid.

33. White, *Puritan in Babylon,* 252.

34. McCoy, *Quiet President,* 200.

35. Parrish, *Anxious Decades,* 55.

36. Perrett, *America in the Twenties,* 181; Sobel, *Coolidge,* 279.

37. McCoy, *Quiet President,* 247.

38. Parrish, *Anxious Decades,* 67.

39. Ibid., 69; John D. Hicks, *Republican Ascendency, 1921–1933* (New York: Harper and Row, 1960), 98–99.

40. Mowry, *Urban Nation,* 54.

41. McCoy, *Quiet President,* 254.

42. Hicks, *Republican Ascendency,* 101.

43. McCoy, "A President Restrained," 28.

44. McCoy, *Quiet President,* 413.

45. McCoy, "A President Restrained," 29.

46. Ibid., 32.

47. White, *Puritan in Babylon,* 310.

48. Mowry, *Urban Nation,* 48.

49. Shannon, *Between the Wars,* 44.

50. Ferrell, *Presidency of Calvin Coolidge,* 31.

51. Hicks, *Republican Ascendency,* 108.

52. Parrish, *Anxious Decades,* 54–55.

53. Sobel, *Coolidge,* 311, 326.

54. Ferrell, *Presidency of Calvin Coolidge,* 171.

55. White, *Puritan in Babylon,* 344.

56. Ibid., 332.

57. Ibid., 336.

58. Parrish, *Anxious Decades,* 204.

59. White, *Puritan in Babylon,* 361.

60. Ibid., 362.

61. Ibid., 400.

62. Ibid., 411.

63. Parrish, *Anxious Decades,* 48.

64. Abels, *Silent Cal,* 222.

65. Perrett, *America in the Twenties,* 193.

66. Sobel, *Coolidge,* 328.

67. Ibid.

4. The Search for World Peace and Stability in the Twenties

1. L. Ethan Ellis, *Republican Foreign Policy, 1921–1933* (New Brunswick, N.J.: Rutgers Univ. Press, 1968), 33–34.

2. Ibid., 32.

3. Leuchtenberg, *Perils of Prosperity,* 108.

4. Shannon, *Between the Wars,* 49.

5. Murray, *Harding Era,* 375.

6. John Chalmers Vinson, "Charles Evans Hughes," in *An Uncertain Tradition: American Secretaries of State in the Twentieth Century,* ed. Norman Graebner (New York: McGraw-Hill, 1961), 129.

7. Ibid., 145.

8. Selig Adler, *The Uncertain Giant, 1921–1941* (New York: Macmillan, 1968), 15.

9. Shannon, *Between the Wars,* 15.

10. Adler, *Uncertain Giant,* 17.

11. Ibid.

12. Foster Rhea Dulles, *America's Rise to World Power, 1898–1954* (New York: Harper and Row, 1955), 126.

13. Adler, *Uncertain Giant,* 17.

14. Vinson, "Charles Evans Hughes," 135–36.

15. Ellis, *Republican Foreign Policy,* 67.

16. Shannon, *Between the Wars,* 52.

17. Murray, *Harding Era,* 372.

18. Shannon, *Between the Wars,* 53.

19. Vinson, "Charles Evans Hughes," 139

20. Adler, *Uncertain Giant,* 62.

21. Leuchtenberg, *Perils of Prosperity,* 113.

22. Ellis, *Republican Foreign Policy,* 105.

23. Ibid., 81.

24. Ibid., 133.

25. Vinson, "Charles Evans Hughes," 141.

26. Ibid.

27. Adler, *Uncertain Giant,* 66.

28. Dulles, *America's Rise to World Power,* 153.

29. Vinson, "Charles Evans Hughes," 141.

30. Ibid., 143.

31. Adler, *Uncertain Giant,* 53.

32. Ibid., 54.

33. Ibid., 55.

34. Ibid., 79.

35. Ellis, *Republican Foreign Policy,* 193.

36. Ibid., 203.

37. Ibid., 26.

38. Adler, *Uncertain Giant,* 90.

39. Ibid., 91.

40. Hicks, *Republican Ascendency,* 160.

41. Ibid.

42. Ibid., 161.

43. Adler, *Uncertain Giant,* 91.

44. L. Ethan Ellis, "Frank B. Kellogg," in *An Uncertain Tradition: American Secretaries of State in the Twentieth Century,* ed. Graebner, 166.

45. Ibid.

46. Ibid.

47. Ibid.

48. Ibid., 146–47.

49. Ellis, *Republican Foreign Policy,* 252.

50. Ibid., 259.

51. Adler, *Uncertain Giant,* 107–08.

5. A New Culture Emerges

1. Mowry, ed. *Fords, Flappers, and Fanatics,* 1.

2. Mowry, *Urban Nation,* 1–2.

3. Edward Earl Purinton, "Big Ideas from American Business," in *Fords, Flappers, and Fanatics,* ed. Mowry, 3–5.

4. Mowry, ed. *Fords, Flappers, and Fanatics,* 14.

5. Stuart Chase, "The Tragedy of Waste," in *Fords, Flappers, and Fanatics,* ed. Mowry, 16.

6. Frederick Lewis Allen, *Only Yesterday* (New York: Harper and Row, 1957), 186.

7. Ibid., 238.

8. Mowry, *Urban Nation,* 2.

9. Robert L. Duffus, "The Age of Play," in *Fords, Flappers, and Fanatics,* ed. Mowry, 44.

10. Perrett, *America in the Twenties,* 222.

11. Mowry, ed. *Fords, Flappers, and Fanatics,* 75.

12. Parrish, *Anxious Decades,* 159.

13. Ezra Bowen and the editors of Time-Life Books, *This Fabulous Century: 1920–1930* (New York: Time, 1969), 134.

14. Ibid., 139–42.

15. Allen, *Only Yesterday,* 220.

16. Mary B. Mullett, "The Biggest Thing that Lindbergh has Done," in *Fords, Flappers, and Fanatics,* ed. Mowry, 81.

17. Parrish, *Anxious Decades,* 179.

18. Allen, *Only Yesterday,* 218.

19. Parrish, *Anxious Decades,* 179–81.

20. Lloyd Lewis, "The Deluxe Picture Palace," in *Fords, Flappers, and Fanatics,* ed. Mowry, 58.

21. Robert Sklar, *The Plastic Age* (New York: George Braziller, 1970), 43.

22. Perrett, *America in the Twenties,* 228.

23. Mowry, *Urban Nation,* 28; Parrish, *Anxious Decades,* 167–68.

24. Sklar, *Plastic Age,* 56.

25. Shannon, *Between the Wars,* 88–89.

26. Keith Sward, *The Legend of Henry Ford* (New York: Atheneum, 1968), 37.

27. Mowry, ed. *Fords, Flappers, and Fanatics,* 51.

28. Andrist, *History of the 1920s and 1930s,* 28.

29. John A. Garrity, ed. *Dictionary of American Biography* (New York: Harper and Row, 1974), 371.

30. Shannon, *Between the Wars,* 94.

31. Mowry, *Urban Nation,* 18–20.

32. John Hope Franklin and Alfred A. Moss Jr., *From Slavery to Freedom* (New York: McGraw-Hill, 1994), 365–69.

33. Ibid., 374.

34. Bowen, *This Fabulous Century,* 91.

35. Mowry, ed. *Fords, Flappers, and Fanatics,* 173.

36. Parrish, *Anxious Decades,* 142.

37. Mowry, *Urban Nation,* 23; Allen, *Only Yesterday,* 115–16.

38. Mary Cable and the editors of American Heritage, *American Manners and Morals* (New York: American Heritage Publishing, 1969), 347.

39. Allen, *Only Yesterday,* 100.

40. Ibid., 108–12.

41. Ibid., 112.

42. Perrett, *America in the Twenties,* 152–57.

43. Allen, *Only Yesterday,* 90.

44. Gilman M. Ostrander, "The Revolution in Morals," in *Change and Continuity in Twentieth Century America: The 1920s,* ed. John Braeman, Robert H. Bremner, and David Brody (Columbus: Ohio State Univ. Press, 1968), 335.

45. Parrish, *Anxious Decades,* 155.

46. Andrist, *History of the 1920s and 1930s,* 81.

47. Perrett, *America in the Twenties,* 148.

48. Andrist, *History of the 1920s and 1930s,* 82; Shannon, *Between the Wars,* 99.

49. Parrish, *Anxious Decades,* 187.

50. Allen, *Only Yesterday,* 228.

51. Ibid., 235.

52. Ibid., 237.

53. Shannon, *Between the Wars,* 96.

54. Allen, *Only Yesterday,* 232.

55. Ibid., 238.

56. Parrish, *Anxious Decades,* 200.

57. Shannon, *Between the Wars,* 97.

58. Ibid., 98.

59. Mowry, *Urban Nation,* 28; Perrett, *America in the Twenties,* 204.

6. The Dark Side of the Twenties

1. Shannon, *Between the Wars,* 65.

2. Ibid., 80.

3. Higham, *Strangers in the Land,* 294.

4. Mowry, ed. *Fords, Flappers, and Fanatics,* 136–45.

5. Parrish, *Anxious Decades,* 117.

6. Ibid., 118.

7. David Chalmers, *Hooded Americanism: The First Century of the Ku Klux Klan* (Garden City, N.Y.: Doubleday, 1965), 4.

8. Parrish, *Anxious Decades,* 121–22.

9. Chalmers, *Hooded Americanism,* 4.

10. Ibid., 5.

11. Leuchtenberg, *Perils of Prosperity,* 213.

12. Ibid., 213.

13. James F. Timberlake, "The Political Argument," in *The 1920s: Problems and Paradoxes,* ed. Plesur, 217.

14. Ibid., 217.

15. Abels, *Silent Cal,* 89.

16. Parrish, *Anxious Decades,* 97.

17. Ibid., 97.

18. Ibid., 98.

19. Abels, *Silent Cal,* 81.

20. Joseph K. Willing, "Profession of Bootlegging," in *Fords, Flappers, and Fanatics,* ed. Mowry, 98–99.

21. Parrish, *Anxious Decades,* 99.

22. John Gunther, "The High Cost of Hoodlums," in *Fords, Flappers, and Fanatics,* ed. Mowry, 114.

23. Leuchtenberg, *Perils of Prosperity,* 215.

24. Mowry, ed. *Fords, Flappers, and Fanatics,* 93.

25. Parrish, *Anxious Decades,* 104.

26. Timberlake, "The Political Argument," 219.

27. Shannon, *Between the Wars,* 73.

28. Leuchtenberg, *Perils of Prosperity,* 204–05.

29. Shannon, *Between the Wars,* 73.

30. Leuchtenberg, *Perils of Prosperity,* 206.

31. Mowry, *Urban Nation,* 31.

32. Ibid.

33. Leuchtenberg, *Perils of Prosperity,* 207–08.

34. Higham, *Strangers in the Land,* 272.

35. Leuchtenberg, *Perils of Prosperity,* 206.

36. Higham, *Strangers in the Land,* 272.

37. Leuchtenberg, *Perils of Prosperity,* 207.

38. Higham, *Strangers in the Land,* 275.

39. Ibid., 277.

40. Ibid., 278.

41. Ibid., 282–84.

42. Ibid., 286–87.

43. Leuchtenberg, *Perils of Prosperity,* 207.

44. Shannon, *Between the Wars,* 74.

45. Ibid., 75; Parrish, *Anxious Decades,* 112.

46. Shannon, *Between the Wars,* 75.

47. Higham, *Strangers in the Land,* 329–30.

48. Leuchtenberg, *Perils of Prosperity,* 218.

49. Ibid., 221.

50. Mowry, *Urban Nation,* 27.

51. Leuchtenberg, *Perils of Prosperity,* 219.

52. Ray Ginger, *Six Days or Forever?: Tennessee v. John Thomas Scopes* (New York: Oxford Univ. Press, 1958), 155.

53. Leuchtenberg, *Perils of Prosperity*, 221.

54. Mowry, *Urban Nation*, 30.

55. Leuchtenberg, *Perils of Prosperity*, 222.

56. Parrish, *Anxious Decades*, 124.

57. Ibid., 125.

58. Ibid.

59. Abels, *Silent Cal*, 77.

60. Ibid., 78.

61. Francis Russell, "Sacco Guilty, Vanzetti Innocent?," *American Heritage* 13 (June 1962): 111.

7. The Rise and Fall of Business

1. George Soule, *Prosperity Decade: From War to Depression, 1917–1929* (New York: Harper and Row, 1947), 96.

2. Alex Groner and the editors of American Heritage and Business Week, *The History of American Business and Industry* (New York: American Heritage, 1972), 286.

3. Soule, *Prosperity Decade*, 230.

4. Ibid., 105.

5. Ibid., 106.

6. Ibid., 105.

7. Thomas Childs Cochran and William Miller, *The Age of Enterprise: A Social History of Industrial America* (New York: Harper and Row, 1961), 342.

8. Ibid., 344.

9. Ibid., 304–05.

10. Ibid., 307.

11. Sudhir Kakar, *Frederick Taylor: A Study in Personality and Innovation* (Cambridge: MIT Press, 1970), 55–56, 68–69.

12. Ibid., 70–71.

13. Parrish, *Anxious Decades*, 34.

14. Perrett, *America in the Twenties*, 338.

15. Ibid., 323.

16. Ibid., 354.

17. Ibid., 355.

18. Soule, *Prosperity Decade*, 164; Parrish, *Anxious Decades*, 38.

19. Parrish, *Anxious Decades*, 38.

20. Soule, *Prosperity Decade*, 170.

21. Perrett, *America in the Twenties*, 224; Groner, *American Business and Industry*, 279.

22. Groner, *American Business and Industry*, 280.

23. Soule, *Prosperity Decade*, 155.

24. Ibid., 187.

25. Cochran and Miller, *Age of Enterprise*, 337.

26. Perrett, *America in the Twenties*, 327.

27. Soule, *Prosperity Decade*, 205; Perrett, *America in the Twenties*, 324.

28. Perrett, *America in the Twenties*, 323.

29. Ibid., 325.

30. Soule, *Prosperity Decade*, 215.

31. Ferrell, *Presidency of Calvin Coolidge*, 73.

32. Perrett, *America in the Twenties*, 326.

33. Soule, *Prosperity Decade*, 326–27.

34. Shannon, *Between the Wars*, 124.

35. Soule, *Prosperity Decade*, 126.

36. Groner, *American Business and Industry*, 285.

37. Soule, *Prosperity Decade*, 280; Shannon, *Between the Wars*, 119–20.

38. Soule, *Prosperity Decade*, 295.

39. Ibid., 293.

40. Martin L. Fausold, *The Presidency of Herbert Hoover* (Lawrence: Univ. of Kansas Press, 1985), 77.

41. Shannon, *Between the Wars*, 125.

42. Ibid.

43. Soule, *Prosperity Decade*, 293.

44. Perrett, *America in the Twenties*, 379.

45. Soule, *Prosperity Decade*, 309.

46. Shannon, *Between the Wars*, 125.

47. Perrett, *America in the Twenties*, 384.

48. Ibid., 389.

49. Ibid.

8. The Tragedy of Herbert Hoover

1. David Burner, *Herbert Hoover: A Public Life* (New York: Alfred A. Knopf, 1978), x.

2. Ibid., 10.

3. Hofstadter, *American Political Tradition*, 283.

4. Burner, *Herbert Hoover: A Public Life*, 60.

5. Ibid., 96.

6. Ibid., 115.

7. Hofstadter, *American Political Tradition*, 280.

8. Burner, *Herbert Hoover: A Public Life*, 131.

9. Ibid., 131.

10. Fausold, *Presidency of Herbert Hoover*, 10.

11. Burner, *Herbert Hoover: A Public Life*, 138.

12. Fausold, *Presidency of Herbert Hoover*, 13.

13. Joan Hoff Wilson, *Herbert Hoover: Forgotten Progressive* (Boston: Little, Brown, 1975), 77.

14. Ibid., 57.

15. Ibid., 59.

16. Ibid., 92.

17. Burner, *Herbert Hoover: A Public Life*, 173–74.

18. Wilson, *Forgotten Progressive*, 99.

19. Ibid., 66.

20. Ibid., 68.

21. Ibid., 72.

22. Ibid., 105.

23. Ibid., 108.

24. Burner, *Herbert Hoover: A Public Life*, 192.

25. Wilson, *Forgotten Progressive*, 115.

26. Ibid., 117.

27. Ibid., 121.

28. Fausold, *Presidency of Herbert Hoover*, 21.

29. Wilson, *Forgotten Progressive*, 125.

30. Ibid., 132.

31. Burner, *Herbert Hoover: A Public Life*, 197.

32. Ibid., 211.

33. Ibid., 201.

34. Burner, *Herbert Hoover: A Public Life*, 212–13; Wilson, *Forgotten Progressive*, 135.

35. Fausold, *Presidency of Herbert Hoover*, 59.

36. Hicks, *Republican Ascendency*, 216–17.

37. Gilbert C. Fite, "The Farmer's Dilemma, 1919–1929," in *Change and Continuity in Twentieth Century America: The 1920s*, ed. Braeman, Bremner, and Brody, 98; Burner, *Herbert Hoover: A Public Life*, 237.

38. Burner, *Herbert Hoover: A Public Life*, 241.

39. Ibid., 245–46.

40. Wilson, *Forgotten Progressive*, 142.

41. Ibid., 143.

42. Burner, *Herbert Hoover: A Public Life*, 250–51.

43. For example, see Hicks, *Republican Ascendency*, 217.

44. Hofstadter, *American Political Tradition*, 295–96.

45. Ibid., 291.

46. Ibid., 290, 295.

47. Ibid., 293–94.

48. Ibid., 295–96.

49. Wilson, *Forgotten Progressive*, 146.

50. Hofstadter, *American Political Tradition*, 297–98.

51. Wilson, *Forgotten Progressive*, 150.

52. Burner, *Herbert Hoover: A Public Life*, 260–61.

53. Wilson, *Forgotten Progressive,* 157.

54. Hofstadter, *American Political Tradition,* 303.

55. Parrish, *Anxious Decades,* 256.

56. Wilson, *Forgotten Progressive,* 151.

57. Hicks, *Republican Ascendency,* 222.

58. Martin L. Fausold and George Mazusan, *The Hoover Presidency: A Reappraisal* (Albany: State Univ. of New York Press, 1974), 85–86.

59. Ibid., 92.

60. Ibid., 91.

61. Hofstadter, *American Political Tradition,* 299.

62. Wilson, *Forgotten Progressive,* 158.

63. Ibid., 157.

64. Ibid., 166.

9. Legacies

1. Mowry, ed. *Fords, Flappers, and Fanatics,* 1.

2. Ibid., 1.

3. Ibid., 121.

4. Paul Carter, *The Twenties in America* (Arlington Heights, Ill.: Harlan Davidson, 1975), 14.

5. Ibid., 38.

6. Ibid.

7. Murray, *Harding Era,* 534.

8. Carter, *The Twenties in America,* 38.

Selected Readings

IN PREPARING THIS BOOK, I have used many sources, from accounts written by contemporaries shortly after the period to more scholarly works written by historians many years later. I have also drawn on primary sources, written both by participants in the events of the 1920s and by observers. Using material from many perspectives affords the reader a more complete and balanced account of this dynamic period in United States history. Here I have listed some of the most important of these sources for any reader seeking further information.

Perrett, Geoffrey. *America in the Twenties: A History.*
New York: Simon and Schuster, 1982.

Perrett's goal in writing this book was to provide the first complete account of the period "that everyone seems to know." The true story of the decade is more complex than generally realized. Even historians have had difficulty explaining the 1920s. Perrett described the period as "the most derided decade in American history as well as the most glamorous."

Perrett sees the decade as a watershed in American history. Since much of America was still living in the manner of the nineteenth century, this led to cultural conflict. Perrett presents a very wide-ranging and thorough examination of the period, covering topics ranging from the story of architect Frank Lloyd Wright to the origins of jazz. No important aspect of the twenties is omitted from this scholarly account, and each is examined in an interesting manner.

To accomplish this, Perrett relies on an enormous number of sources. Published in 1982, the book is still perhaps the best account of the 1920s and appeals to readers at all levels. Those seeking biographical studies will find a fascinating cast of characters. Those interested in the economy will find skillful analyses of such important issues as the farm problem and labor's difficulties, and explanations of the complex factors precipitating the Great Depression. Perrett succeeds in pulling together these accounts of fascinating people, economic shifts, and cultural upheaval into a vivid picture of what he regards as "a much beloved and much maligned period in American history." No serious student of the twenties will ignore this book.

For additional information, see Faulkner, Harold U., *From Versailles to the New Deal* (New Haven, Conn.: Yale Univ. Press, 1951); Hicks, John D., *Republican Ascendency, 1921–1933* (New York: Harper and Row, 1960); Parrish, Michael, *Anxious Decades: America in Prosperity and Depression, 1920–1941* (New York: W. W. Norton, 1992); Plesur, Milton, *The 1920s: Problems and Paradoxes* (Boston: Allyn and Bacon, 1969); and Shannon, David, *Between the Wars: America, 1919–1941* (Boston: Houghton Mifflin, 1965).

Noggle, Burl. *Into the Twenties.*
Urbana: Univ. of Illinois Press, 1974.

This relatively short (only 213 pages) but extremely readable book deals with the intriguing question, "Did the conservative 1920s begin in 1918 or 1920?" Was Woodrow Wilson, the reformist Democratic president, the true father of "normalcy," rather than conservative Republican Warren G. Harding?

World War I had caused major changes in American society, and the transition from wartime to peacetime conditions was filled with problems. After the Armistice, the nation faced a postwar depression, labor disturbances, shifts in the racial balance that provoked race riots, fears of unlimited immigration by southern and eastern Europeans, fears of Communism, and the need to shape a new foreign policy while restoring conditions to "normal" at home. Noggle gives very low grades to the Wilson administration during this crucial transition period, arguing that because Wilson failed to resolve these problems to the satisfaction of the American people, he predisposed the nation toward conservatism and laid the groundwork for the Republican victory in the presidential election of 1920.

Perhaps too preoccupied with re-making the world order through the Treaty of Versailles and the League of Nations, Wilson failed to deal aggressively with the problems at home. He failed to address the race riots or to ease America's fears concerning immigration. Moreover, some of his policies after 1918 were surprising for a reformist president. He allowed a harsh crackdown on Leftist dissenters, and his administration took a more pro-business tilt in 1919, especially in returning the economy to peacetime conditions.

As the postwar turmoil continued into the Twenties, the public eventually turned to the Republicans. Noggle points out that when the Republicans actually took control in early 1921, the country was already predisposed toward a more conservative direction.

The transition period between the Armistice of November 1918 and the inauguration of Harding in March 1921 deserves further study, according to Noggle. Not intended to be a definitive work, *Into the Twenties* aims to inspire further research into the period. It is written in an interesting style and can be enjoyed by the general public as well as the scholar.

For additional information about this period, consult Bailey, Thomas, *Woodrow Wilson and the Great Betrayal* (New York: Macmillan, 1947); Coben, Stanley, *A. Mitchell Palmer* (New York: Columbia Univ. Press, 1963); Cronon, E. David, *Black Moses: The Story of Marcus Garvey and the Universal Negro Improvement Association* (Madison: Univ. of Wisconsin Press, 1970); Murray, Robert K., *Red Scare: A Case Study in National Hysteria, 1919–1920* (Minneapolis: Univ. of Minnesota Press, 1955); and Williams, William Appleman, *American-Russian Relations: 1781–1947* (New York: Rinehart, 1952).

Murray, Robert K. *The Harding Era.*
Minneapolis: Univ. of Minnesota Press, 1969.

This is one of the most important and thorough biographies of Harding, drawing on an enormous base of research into contemporary sources, including personal manuscript collections, government documents, newspapers, and biographies. Murray proclaims Harding " a success" as president. Noting that Harding entered office at a very difficult time, filled with crises and divisions, Murray contends that he led the country through the transition from war to an era of greater peace and prosperity, acting not merely as a "bystander" but as a healing and mediating force.

Harding set the agenda for the decade. His platform of 1920, which had a decided tilt in favor of business, was widely accepted by the public. It included immigration reduction, debt collection, economy in government, a high tariff, and reduction of the national debt. Harding's key achievements in office included debt reduction, business recovery, the Washington Conference, and the creation of the Budget Bureau. The election of 1924, in which Coolidge was elected, served as a referendum on Harding's policies. He left Coolidge a better legacy in 1923 than the divided and troubled nation he had inherited from Woodrow Wilson.

Murray laments that for all Harding's accomplishments, he is remembered most for the scandals of the early 1920s and the myths they engendered. Was he nominated in a "smoke-filled room" in 1920? Was he murdered by a vengeful wife in 1923? Was his administration dominated by the dishonest "Ohio gang"? Was he a hopelessly uninformed dupe of his subordinates? *The Harding Era* attempts to refute these persistent myths.

This book is the most scholarly of several that appeared shortly after the opening of the Harding papers in the early 1960s. *The Harding Era* carefully recounts the Harding administration, calling it one of the most important short presidencies in

American history. The myths that have sprung up around Harding do a disservice to the true story of his administration.

For further information about Harding, see Adams, Samuel Hopkins *Incredible Era* (Boston: Houghton Mifflin, 1939); Bagby, Wesley *The Road to Normalcy: The Presidential Campaign and Election of 1920* (Baltimore: Johns Hopkins Univ. Press, 1962); Downes, Randolph *The Rise of Warren Gamaliel Harding: 1865–1920* (Columbus: Ohio State Univ. Press, 1970); Murray, Robert K., *The Politics of Normalcy* (New York: W. W. Norton, 1973); and Sinclair, Andrew, *The Available Man* (New York: Macmillan, 1965).

McCoy, Donald. *Calvin Coolidge: The Quiet President.* New York: Macmillan, 1967.

McCoy gives a good political and personal account of a president he regards as successful for his times. He depicts Calvin Coolidge as an able president who fitted in with his era, noting that while he was not a daring risk-taker, the times did not require these qualities. Nor would they have welcomed them.

Coolidge entered the presidency with a late-nineteenth-century, laissez-faire outlook. Unlike Woodrow Wilson or Theodore Roosevelt, Coolidge would not seek vast reforms, preferred a limited role for the federal government that let private individuals seek their owns rewards in society. Identifying the national welfare with the success of the business community, he did nothing to harass business while he was president. In line with his conservative economic views, he stressed tax-cutting and lowering the national debt.

In foreign affairs as well, he was not an innovator. He followed a cautious approach that avoided national commitments that might lead to war. He supported naval limitation and even the ill-fated Kellogg-Briand pact in his attempt to preserve the peace.

Coolidge was quiet and shy, close to his family but not a good social mixer. Influenced by his Puritan New England upbringing, he was "thrifty with his words and his money." His honesty and idealism were unusual qualities in such a cynical profession, and his tenure was not marred by political or personal scandal. Coolidge was amazingly popular while president. But though he maintained the confidence of the public while the "Coolidge prosperity" continued, the outbreak of the Great Depression after his departure from office later tarnished his long-term reputation.

McCoy's book goes far beyond merely describing the politics of the administration. It is a thorough account, filled with anecdotes of Coolidge as he grew up and rose politically. It may be too detailed for readers interested only in the main points of Coolidge's life.

For other perspectives on President Coolidge, see Abels, Jules, *In the Time of*

Silent Cal (New York: G. P. Putnam's Sons, 1959); Ferrell, Robert, *The Presidency of Calvin Coolidge* (Lawrence: Univ. Press of Kansas, 1998); Haynes, John Earl, ed., *Calvin Coolidge and the Coolidge Era* (Washington, D. C.: Library of Congress, 1998); Sobel, Robert, *Coolidge* (Washington, D.C.: Regnery, 1998); and White, William Allen, *Puritan in Babylon* (New York: Macmillan, 1938).

Graebner, Norman, ed. *An Uncertain Tradition:*
**   *American Secretaries of State in the Twentieth Century.***
**   New York: McGraw-Hill, 1961.**

This excellent collection of essays concerns the secretaries of state of the twentieth century, focusing not only on their own goals and work but on their interplay with the presidents under whom they served, the Senate, and the public. By examining the patterns of foreign policy from this vantage point, it gives the reader more insight into its formulation. The section on the 1920s deals with secretaries Charles Evans Hughes, Frank B. Kellogg, and Henry L. Stimson. Even though they served under different presidents, there are several patterns of foreign policy common to all three.

During the 1920s, American foreign policy returned to "normalcy"—the traditional policy of avoiding foreign commitments that might lead to war. This explains the reluctance of the United States to join the League of Nations and its acceptance of several treaties that involved no actual obligations. The strategy for peace focused on naval limitation agreements and the Kellogg-Briand Pact to outlaw offensive war. The Senate and the public could accept these agreements since they did not involve any plan for sanctions or force. The United States preferred to rely on "moral force" or the honor system instead. After the disappointing aftermath to World War I involving such controversies as debt repayment and fights over colonies, the United States was determined not to be dragged into any further wars.

The essays make clear the overall context in which foreign policy operated during this decade. The United States focused on domestic matters, especially as business kept expanding. Moreover, the public did not want a more ambitious foreign policy, especially in the absence of any obvious crisis. The three presidents in office during the 1920s, who were not expert in foreign affairs, also wished to avoid foreign ventures.

The format of the book is original, looking at foreign policy through the eyes of the secretary of state. The authors look at the personality of each secretary as he set foreign policy. Hughes was politically astute in formulating foreign policy, always careful not to ignore the Senate and public opinion. Kellogg was very cautious on foreign commitment; ultimately he became best known for the Kellogg-Briand Pact to outlaw offensive war. (This agreement required no binding obligations by any of the parties.) Stimson did not have as fine-tuned a political sense as the other two and was overruled by Hoover when he wanted to take a more aggressive position in foreign policy.

The essays are well-written and very comprehensive. The reader will gain a clear sense of foreign policy during the decade, as well as the political parameters within which it operated.

To further study this topic, see Adler, Selig, *The Uncertain Giant, 1921–1941* (New York: Macmillan, 1968); Dulles, Foster Rhea, *America's Rise to World Power, 1898–1954* (New York: Harper and Row, 1955); Ellis, L. Ethan, *Republican Foreign Policy, 1921–1933* (New Brunswick, N. J.: Rutgers Univ. Press, 1968); and Sprout, Harold and Margaret Sprout, *Toward a New Order of Sea Power: American Naval Policy and the World Scene, 1918–1922* (Princeton: Princeton Univ. Press, 1940).

Allen, Frederick Lewis. *Only Yesterday.*
New York: Harper and Row, 1957.

This book was written in 1931, soon after the twenties ended, and some of its themes have been reinterpreted by later historians. Yet it remains a fascinating tale of one aspect of the period; its frivolity and let-loose attitude. It set the standard for books on the twenties for many years. Based on limited sources, it is not the most scholarly work of the period, yet it became one of the most interesting and successful.

The main purpose of the book is to describe the frenzied, almost irresponsible atmosphere of the decade, particularly the party mood of people determined to escape from problems by enjoying the present. It does mention the serious side of the decade, but this is not the author's main focus.

Allen believed that America was searching for something better after the sacrifices of war, the responsibilities of reform, and Woodrow Wilson's attempt to change the world. The changes brought by the end of war, an expanding economy, and several important breakthroughs in science and technology brought about corresponding shifts in manners and morals, replacing the previous age of reform with an age of play.

Allen's work is based largely on the secondary sources of the period, along with the newspapers and magazines of the day. It gives the reader an excellent "feel" for the decade, when many Americans tried to escape from previous concerns by improving life at home and abroad. This book, now somewhat dated by later research, was seen as a classic when it appeared in the 1930s.

Those interested in a closer examination of this topic should also consult the following books: Cable, Mary, and the editors of American Heritage, *American Manners and Morals* (New York: American Heritage Publishing, 1969); Andrist, Ralph K., and Edmund O. Stillman, eds., *The American Heritage History of the 1920s and 1930s* (New York: American Heritage/Bonanza Books, 1987); Edey, Maitland A., ed., *This Fabulous Century: 1920–1930* (New York: Time, 1969); Leuchtenberg, William, *The Perils of Prosperity* (Chicago: Univ. of Chicago Press, 1958); and Carter, Paul, *The Twenties in America* (Arlington Heights, Ill.: Harlan Davidson, 1975).

Mowry, George Erwin, ed. *The Twenties: Fords, Flappers, and Fanatics.*
Englewood Cliffs, N.J.: Prentice-Hall, 1963.

This excellent book is a relatively short edited collection of essays, all dealing with the theme of changing cultural values. Beyond his introductions to each section, Mowry relies on well-written articles that give a "sense" of the period. They cover a wide variety of topics, ranging from reactions to Charles Lindbergh's flight in 1927 to descriptions of bootlegging. Mowry's book will satisfy readers with vastly divergent interests.

The essays examine changes that brought happiness to Americans and others that badly divided society. Several cultural changes were strongly opposed by more conservative Americans. Mowry includes a selection in which the Imperial Wizard justifies the need for the Ku Klux Klan. Another essay focuses on the Chicago race riot of 1919, the most serious in a number of tragic racial conflicts that helped to usher in an ugly racial climate during the decade. The book also deals with former Attorney General A. Mitchell Palmer's crusade against the Left during the Red Scare of 1919–20.

Some of the cultural issues raised by Mowry are still debated by society. He examines the conflict between fundamentalist Protestants and modernist Protestants that ultimately led to a debate about the proper role of public schools in dealing with topics relating to religion. Mowry also describes the rise of the black nationalist leader Marcus Garvey, who attracted a vast following in the racially charged atmosphere of the 1920s. Garvey proved to be a forerunner of other black nationalist groups, such as the Black Muslims. The role in society of the "new woman" of the 1920s has become a debate about the place of modern women in society.

All of the readings are contemporary (written during the 1920s). Many were written by the subjects of the essays and can be considered original sources. Each is very readable and informative. Most important, they lend insight into both sides of a decade generally known only for its frivolity.

For further information on this aspect of the decade, see Chalmers, David, *Hooded Americanism: The First Century of the Ku Klux Klan* (Garden City, N. Y.: Doubleday, 1965); Franklin, John Hope, and Alfred A. Moss, Jr., *From Slavery to Freedom* (New York: McGraw-Hill, 1994); Ginger, Ray, *Six Days or Forever? Tennessee v. John Thomas Scopes* (New York: Oxford Univ. Press, 1958); and Higham, John, *Strangers in the Land* (New Brunswick, N. J.: Rutgers Univ. Press, 1955).

Soule, George. *The Prosperity Decade: From War to Depression, 1917–1929.*
New York: Harper and Row, 1947.

Soule has written a very thorough economic history of the period from the United States' entry into World War I to the outbreak of the Great Depression. He does not focus on individuals; rather, his attention is on economic trends and changing economic institutions.

During World War I the American economy was very prosperous. The farmer was better off than ever, factories were at full production, unemployment was low, and workers earned high wages. Labor unions also made important gains during this time.

The end of the war, however, brought some serious dislocations. The economy went into a short depression, agriculture began a sharp decline that continued through the 1920s, and labor suffered through high unemployment and, in many cases, a loss of union recognition. Although business cut back on production, it was in good shape; companies generally used their huge war-time profits as a cushion during this period.

When the economy rebounded by 1923, the big winner clearly was business. Farmers still suffered, and the wages of workers grew only slowly (in contrast to a rapid growth of profits by business). This pattern continued until 1929, when the stock market crash helped trigger the Great Depression.

Soule attempts to explain the causes of the Great Depression in this very readable and highly detailed study. One of the biggest problems leading to the crisis was the imbalance between production and the purchasing power of consumers. The economy had undergone a "production revolution," leading to an over-abundance of consumers goods just as workers' wages declined and farm prices dropped, making it difficult for most people to purchase these goods. The problem was "resolved" by an enormous extension of credit during the decade. When a limit on consumer debt was reached, demand for consumer goods dropped and the economy went into a serious decline.

Soule argues that no single, simple preventive measure could have prevented the Great Depression. A small wage increase would not have been sufficient, and a sharp cut in prices would not have been realistic. Only a drastic rise in income or a substantial cutback in production might have corrected the imbalances that led to the greatest economic collapse in United States history. Soule clearly indicates that such a shift in the economy would not have been brought about easily.

For additional information on this topic, see Cochran, Thomas Childs, and William Miller, *The Age of Enterprise: A Social History of Industrial America* (New York: Harper and Row, 1961); Galbraith, John Kenneth, *The Great Crash: 1929* (Boston: Houghton Mifflin, 1955); Groner, Alex, et al., *The History of American Business and Industry* (New York: American Heritage Publishing, 1972); Kakar, Sudhir, *Frederick Taylor: A Study in Personality and Innovation* (Cambridge: MIT Press, 1970); and Sward, Keith, *The Legend of Henry Ford* (New York: Atheneum, 1968).

Wilson, Joan Hoff. *Herbert Hoover: Forgotten Progressive.*
Boston: Little, Brown, 1975.

This is a very informative, yet readable biography of President Herbert Hoover. Wilson explains the origins of Hoover's political philosophy and its apparently successful application through Hoover's political career until the Great Depression demonstrated its shortcomings.

The Quaker religion was a defining influence on Hoover's political and personal altitudes; it stressed hard work, public service, ambition, and a desire for wealth. He applied these views while serving both as commerce secretary and as president. Hoover believed in individual achievement but without ruthless competition. He favored a co-operative economic system in which participants are not only personally ambitious but also community-minded. He called for "ordered liberty," a compromise between personal interest and the interests of society. During the 1920s, he tried to restructure the American political and economic system along these lines.

Wilson identifies Hoover as a "forgotten progressive." Although Hoover was favorably disposed toward business (being a successful businessman himself), he also wanted to help workers, farmers, and youths, to conserve natural resources, and to support civil rights measures. Overshadowing all these beliefs were his views on the economy, which ultimately defined his place in history.

The Great Depression of 1929 tested these economic views. Hoover did not favor aggressive relief or welfare policies, even during the depression. He hoped that a cooperative spirit among all elements in society—business, labor, the unemployed, and farmers—would somehow pull the nation through the crisis. Unfortunately, the measures he suggested to implement this philosophy were unsuccessful. His theories were better suited to prosperous times, and his reputation suffered from his failure to take more forceful action to address the depression. This rather shy president, who did not enjoy the "give and take" of politics, preferring instead a "harmony of interests," was ultimately overwhelmed by the economic crisis.

Wilson has thoroughly researched her book, relying heavily on the Hoover papers at the Hoover Library as well as on a substantial collection of secondary sources, both published and unpublished.

For additional information about President Hoover, consult: Burner, David, *Herbert Hoover: A Public Life* (New York: Alfred A. Knopf, 1978); Eble, Kenneth, *Herbert Hoover* (Boston: G. H. Hall, 1980); Fausold, Martin L., *The Presidency of Herbert Hoover* (Lawrence: Univ. Press of Kansas, 1985); Fausold, Martin L., and George Mazusan *The Hoover Presidency: A Reappraisal* (Albany: State Univ. of New York Press, 1974); and Hofstadter, Richard, *The American Political Tradition and the Men Who Made It* (New York: Alfred A. Knopf, 1959).

Bibliography

Abels, Jules. *In the Time of Silent Cal*. New York: G. P. Putnam's Sons, 1959.

Adler, Selig. *The Uncertain Giant, 1921–1941*. New York: Macmillan, 1968.

Allen, Frederick Lewis. *Only Yesterday*. New York: Harper and Row, 1957.

Andrist, Ralph, and the editors of American Heritage. *History of the 1920s and 1930s*. New York: American Heritage/Bonanza Books, 1987.

Bagby, Wesley. "The Smoke-Filled Room and the Nomination of Warren G. Harding." *Mississippi Valley Historical Review* 16 (Mar. 1955): 657–74.

Bailey, Thomas A. *Woodrow Wilson and the Great Betrayal*. New York: Macmillan, 1947.

Bowen, Ezra, and the editors of Time-Life Books. *This Fabulous Century: 1920–1930*. New York: Time, 1969.

Burner, David. *Herbert Hoover: A Public Life*. New York: Alfred A. Knopf, 1978.

Cable, Mary, and the editors of American Heritage. *American Manners and Morals*. New York: American Heritage Publishing, 1969.

Carter, Paul. *The Twenties in America*. Arlington Heights, Ill.: Harlan Davidson, 1975.

Chalmers, David. *Hooded Americanism: The First Century of the Ku Klux Klan*. Garden City, N.Y.: Doubleday, 1965.

Cochran, Thomas Childs, and William Miller. *The Age of Enterprise: A Social History of Industrial America*. New York: Harper and Row, 1961.

Downes, Randolph C. *The Rise of Warren Gamaliel Harding: 1865–1920*. Columbus: Ohio State Univ. Press, 1970.

Dulles, Foster Rhea. *America's Rise to World Power, 1898–1954*. New York: Harper and Row, 1955.

Eble, Kenneth. *Herbert Hoover*. Boston: G. H. Hall, 1980.

Ellis, L. Ethan. *Republican Foreign Policy, 1921–1933*. New Brunswick, N.J.: Rutgers Univ. Press, 1968.

Fausold, Martin L. *The Presidency of Herbert Hoover.* Lawrence: Univ. Press of Kansas, 1985.

Fausold, Martin L., and George Mazusan. *The Hoover Presidency: A Reappraisal.* Albany: State Univ. of New York Press, 1974.

Ferrell, Robert. *The Presidency of Calvin Coolidge.* Lawrence: Univ. Press of Kansas, 1998.

Franklin, John Hope, and Alfred A. Moss Jr. *From Slavery to Freedom.* New York: McGraw-Hill, 1994.

Garrity, John A., ed. *Dictionary of American Biography.* New York: Harper and Row, 1974.

Ginger, Ray. *Six Days or Forever?: Tennessee v. John Thomas Scopes.* New York: Oxford Univ. Press, 1958.

Graebner, Norman, ed. *An Uncertain Tradition: American Secretaries of State in the Twentieth Century.* New York: McGraw-Hill, 1961.

Graham, Otis L., Jr. *The Great Campaigns.* Englewood Cliffs, N.J.: R. E. Krieger, 1971.

Groner, Alex, and the editors of American Heritage and Business Week. *The History of American Business and Industry.* New York: American Heritage, 1972.

Haynes, John Earl, ed. *Calvin Coolidge and the Coolidge Era.* Washington, D.C.: Library of Congress, 1998.

Hicks, John D. *Republican Ascendency, 1921–1933.* New York: Harper and Row, 1960.

Higham, John. *Strangers in the Land.* New Brunswick, N.J.: Rutgers Univ. Press, 1955.

Hofstadter, Richard. *The American Political Tradition and the Men Who Made it.* New York: Alfred A. Knopf, 1959.

Kakar, Sudhir. *Frederick Taylor: A Study in Personality and Innovation.* Cambridge: MIT Press, 1970.

Leuchtenberg, William. *The Perils of Prosperity, 1914–1932.* Chicago: Univ. of Chicago Press, 1958.

Margulies, Herbert. "The Election in Wisconsin: The Return to Normalcy Appraised." *Wisconsin Magazine of History* 41 (autumn 1957): 15–22.

McCoy, Donald. *Calvin Coolidge: The Quiet President.* New York: Macmillan, 1967.

Means, Gaston. *The Strange Death of President Harding.* New York: Guild, 1930.

Mowry, George. *The Urban Nation, 1920–1960.* New York: Hill and Wang, 1965.

———, ed. *The Twenties: Fords, Flappers, and Fanatics.* Englewood Cliffs, N.J.: Prentice-Hall, 1963.

Murray, Robert K. *The Harding Era.* Minneapolis: Univ. of Minnesota Press, 1969.

———. *The Politics of Normalcy.* New York: W. W. Norton, 1973.

————. *Red Scare: A Study in National Hysteria, 1919–1920.* Minneapolis: Univ. of Minnesota Press, 1955.

————. "President Harding and His Cabinet." *Ohio History* 75 (spring-summer 1966): 108–25.

Noggle, Burl. *Into the Twenties.* Urbana: Univ. of Illinois Press, 1974.

Parrish, Michael. *Anxious Decades: America in Prosperity and Depression, 1920–1941.* New York: W. W. Norton, 1992.

Perrett, Geoffrey. *America in the Twenties: A History.* New York: Simon and Shuster, 1982.

Plesur, Milton, ed. *The 1920s: Problems and Paradoxes.* Boston: Allyn and Bacon, 1969.

Russell, Francis. "Sacco Guilty, Vanzetti Innocent?" *American Heritage* 13 (June 1962): 4–9, 107–11.

Schlesinger, Arthur, Jr. "Our Presidents: A Rating by 75 Historians." *New York Times Magazine,* 29 July 1962, 12–13, 40.

Shannon, David. *Between the Wars: America, 1919–1941.* Boston: Houghton Mifflin, 1965.

Sinclair, Andrew. *The Available Man.* New York: Macmillan, 1965.

Sklar, Robert. *The Plastic Age.* New York: George Braziller, 1970.

Sobel, Robert. *Coolidge.* Washington, D.C.: Regnery, 1998.

Soule, George. *Prosperity Decade: From War to Depression, 1917–1929.* New York: Harper and Row, 1947.

Sward, Keith. *The Legend of Henry Ford.* New York: Atheneum, 1968.

Werner, Morris, and John Starr. *Teapot Dome.* New York: Viking, 1959.

White, William Allen. *Masks in a Pageant.* New York: Macmillan, 1928.

————. *A Puritan in Babylon.* New York: Macmillan, 1938.

Wilson, Joan Hoff. *Herbert Hoover: Forgotten Progressive.* Boston: Little, Brown, 1975.

"Wilson's Legacy to Harding." *Nation* 112, 23 Feb. 1921, 282–83.

Index